The Path to Enlightenment

In memory of Bakshi Geshe Wangyal,
a most skilled teacher,
founder of the Buddhist Monastery of America,
Washington, New Jersey.

The Path to Enlightenment

H.H. the Dalai Lama

Edited and Translated by
Glenn H. Mullin

Snow Lion Publications
Ithaca, New York

Snow Lion Publications, Inc.
P.O. Box 6483
Ithaca, New York 14851 USA
607-273-8519

ISBN 1-55939-032-8

Library of Congress Cataloging-in-Publication Data

Bstan-'dzin-rgya-mtsho, Dalai Lama XIV, 1935-
    The path to enlightenment /H.H. Dalai Lama; compiled, edited, and
translated by Glenn H. Mullin; translated with Tse-pak Rig-zin and
Lob-Zang Da-wa.
       p. cm.
    Includes the text of Bsod-nams-rgya-mtsho, Dalai Lama III's Byan
chub lam gyi rim pa'i khrid yig gser źun ma in English.
    ISBN 1-55939-032-8
    1. Bsod-nams-rgya-mtsho, Dalai Lama III, 1543-1588. Byań chub lam
gyi rim pa'i khrid yig gser źun ma. 2. Tsoń-kha-pa Blo-bzań-grags-pa,
1357-1419. Lam rim bsdus don. 3. Lam-rim. I. Mullin, Glenn H. II.
Rigzin, Tsepak, 1957-. III. Dawa, Lobzang. IV. Bsod lam gyi rim pa'i
khrid yig gser źun ma. English. V. Title.
BQ7645.L35B7633 1994
294.3'923—dc20   94-39647
                                       CIP

Contents

Preface

The Third Dalai Lama, Gyalwa Sonam Gyatso, a supremely high one with power over the three worlds, was invited by Altan Khan to visit the Mongol nation. He accepted, and the marvelous deeds that he performed there in order to propagate the Buddhadharma in general and the doctrines of the Second Buddha Tsongkhapa in particular left a lasting impression on the land.

One of the Third Dalai Lama's most popular written works is his *Essence of Refined Gold,* which extracts the heart of Lama Tsongkhapa's *Great Exposition of the Stages on the Spiritual Path.* Although brief, it summarizes the meaning of all Buddha's teachings and is easily put into practice.

A few years ago His Holiness the Fourteenth Dalai Lama, a master of all doctrines, gave a discourse upon the Third Dalai Lama's *Essence of Refined Gold* to a number of fortunate trainees. I offer my prayers that Glenn's translation of the root text and his compilation of a commentary based upon His Holiness' discourse may be of lasting spiritual benefit to those in the great Western Lands with a sincere interest in the Buddhist path to enlightenment.

Yongzin Trijang Rinpoche
Junior Tutor to H.H. the Dalai Lama
Fifteenth Day of the Fourth Tibetan Month,
Iron Bird Year

Foreword

I am very happy and honored to write a brief foreword to this excellent work presenting His Holiness the present Dalai Lama's commentary on *The Essence of Refined Gold* by Sonam Gyatso, the Third Dalai Lama of Tibet. I feel it is especially auspicious in that Glenn Mullin has dedicated the volume to my original teacher, the late Venerable Geshe Wangyal, whose tireless efforts have been instrumental in helping His Holiness the Fourteenth Dalai Lama spread the Buddhadharma in America. The taming of America is similar in many ways to His Holiness the Third Dalai Lama's taming of Mongolia.

The Dalai Lamas of Tibet are one the wonders of our planetary history, and their contribution has not at all come to an end. They are the political and spiritual reincarnation of the Bodhisattva, or Buddhist Messiah, Avalokiteshvara, who comes into our violent history to "tame" our emotional wildness and enlighten our intellectual confusion.

The deeds of Sonam Gyatso, such as the taming of the fiery Mongol nations, bear striking witness to the power of the spirit of enlightenment, with its detachment, love, and wisdom triumphant over egotism, greed, and violence. Glenn Mullin is a skilled translator of Tibetan, whose devotion to His Holiness the present Dalai Lama and religious commitment to realizing the Dharma shine through his well-chosen words. His useful work proves that academic linguistic qualification is only a first step in the process of translation. After it must come a commitment to the spirit of the original writings, a selfless determination to submerge the ego formed in a mother culture into the culture of the original text, and then a single-minded discipline to reconstruct the vitality and integrity of the original in the mother tongue.

The great translators of Tibet, who brought the Buddhist civilization to their people, were never concerned with their personal fame or profit. Yet they were honored as "eyes of the nation" (Tib., *Lo-tsva-ba;* Skt., *Lokacakshu*), national treasures who became living eyes for their contemporaries to see the wisdom and beauty of the worlds beyond their borders. Glenn Mullin has joined this ancient fraternity of Lotsawas by giving us a wonderful series of works revealing the inner life and outer deeds of all the Dalai Lamas. May all enjoy them and be inspired by the gentle triumphs of this prince of peace. And may His Holiness the living Dalai Lama long continue creating yet another such wonderful biography on the planetary scale of modern times!

Prof. Robert Alexander Farrar Thurman
March 14, 1985
Amherst College, Massachusetts

Translator's Introduction

Whenever he taught, the Third Dalai Lama Gyalwa Sonam Gyatso set aside magic and mystery, and spoke only on the basic foundations of Buddhist practice, the simple everyday methods for cultivating spiritual awareness. His teachings had a profound influence on the people who came to hear him, and wherever he went he left behind monasteries and spiritual centers that over the centuries to follow would reshape the civilizations he had contacted. Due to his work the gentle doctrines of the Buddha spread like the rising sun over a land that previously had known only conflict and war.

Because of his dedication to an intensive schedule of teaching, the Third Dalai Lama was unable to write as extensively as had his predecessors. Nonetheless, several dozen titles did issue from his pen. Included in this book is perhaps his most famous work, *Essence of Refined Gold*. It is hoped that this will reveal the clarity and direct simplicity of the Third Dalai Lama as an author and teacher. I have included Tsechokling Yeshey Gyaltsen's *Biography of the Third Dalai Lama* at the end of the volume as an appendix to give a sketch of the training and magnificent deeds of this Lord of Yogis, a master of masters who contributed so greatly to the spiritual and cultural development of Asia.

The brevity of the Third Dalai Lama's composition suits the Central Asian approach to spiritual literature, wherein people rarely just read a book by themselves, but rather prefer to have it read to them by a lineage master, either at large public gatherings or in smaller, more private groups. The tradition is that the master doing the reading should have received the text in an unbroken oral transmission going back over the generations to the lifetime of the original author. The reading usually incorporates commentary, anecdotes and personal reflections on the meaning of the text, thus bringing it to life and contextualizing its import to the needs of the specific audience. An ancient and somewhat obscure scripture is thus brought into a more modern age with a transformed edge to it. During the twelve years that I resided in India (between the years 1972-1984) I had the pleasure of attending several dozen such public "readings" given by His Holiness the present Dalai Lama, as well as many by his two principal gurus; some were centered on ancient Indian texts, including several by Nagarjuna (second century C.E.); others were centered on more recent Tibetan works. In each case His Holiness would take the classical scripture and, blending reading and commentary, would speak for five or six hours a day over a period lasting from a week to a month, thus churning the milk of an ancient classic in order to extract the fresh butter of a contemporary understanding.

I first received the transmission of *Essence of Refined Gold* from the Dalai Lama in 1976, when he led an extensive reading of it in the main temple at Dharamsala, India. The audience included several hundred high lamas and scholars, dozens of accomplished yogis, and several thousand lay people. To address the varied backgrounds in the audience, His Holiness combined profundity and simplicity in his explanation of the text, leaving all who attended with a sense of magic and awe.

Most educated Westerners are now somewhat aware of the tradition of the Dalai Lamas and what it represents. Many are also aware of the central details of the present Dalai Lama's life. His autobiography *Freedom in Exile* achieved a considerable readership around the world, and numerous books such as *The Dalai Lama: A Policy of Kindness* which present his quintessential message for working toward individual and world peace are now in print. When he won the Nobel Peace Prize in 1989 he was thrust dramatically onto the center of the international stage.

It has been personally wonderful for me to witness not only the growth of interest in this most amazing personage, but also the increased receptivity to his message by peoples the world over. And of course even though His Holiness is a Buddhist monk and spends much of his time teaching to traditional Buddhist societies in Asia, he dedicates an equal amount of his schedule to travelling the world in order to meet with spiritual and secular leaders, speak in universities, lead interfaith services, and so forth. On these travels he makes no attempt to "convert" Western people to Buddhism, but rather attempts to inspire within them a commitment to the universal spiritual values of love, compassion, wisdom and so forth, that are commonly valued within all great spiritual traditions. As he once put it, "My religion is love and compassion, because these are qualities that all living beings require. Regardless of whether or not one follows any religious tradition, love and compassion are valued by all."

Several times during my residence in Dharamsala Christian monks came to him and requested him to give them Buddhist ordination; he refused, stating that for them to be good Christian monks was sufficient, and that if they were interested in Buddhism they should just study and practice whatever aspects of Buddhist doctrine they felt were useful to them, and to incorporate these into their usual Christian training as complementary elements. Once when I spoke to him before embarking upon a teaching tour of my own he said to me, "Remember, our purpose is not to make more Buddhists, it is to make more enlightened beings. When you teach Buddhism, don't encourage people to become Buddhists; just encourage them to cultivate the qualities of love, compassion, universal responsibility and wisdom within themselves. If some special people with strong karmic connections want to formally become Buddhist then that is acceptable; but in general the emphasis should be on a commitment to inner spiritual values, not to any specific religious tradition."

Without a doubt the most precious phase of my own life was the twelve-year period I spent in Dharamsala on the mountain where His Holiness has resided during much of his life as a refugee in India. During those years I had the great honor and pleasure of annually attending half a dozen discourses and tantric initiations that he gave in various places around India, as well as several dozen private meetings and interviews with him. I never ceased to be amazed by his delightful combination of personal power and humility, his intensity yet simplicity and playfulness.

One of the most memorable public meetings was at a morning talk he gave one year at Delhi University. He was passing through the city en route to Europe, and had a luncheon appointment with the President of India. After his talk he invited questions from the audience, and these generated considerable excitement. Then a young student at the back stood up and asked an almost painfully silly question. The audience giggled. Someone in his entourage jumped up and announced that it was time for His Holiness to leave for his luncheon date, adding that the President could not be kept waiting. His Holiness did not move from his chair, but rather simply looked at the audience and replied, "First I should answer this question." Again the member of his entourage mentioned the President's name. His Holiness sat quite still and then said in a very quiet voice, "My problem is that if I were to make a difference between the president of a country and a junior student in a college, I could no longer call myself the Dalai Lama." He then proceeded to speak in great depth to the question that had been put to him, bringing into his answer a sense of profundity which nobody had imagined lay dormant in the original inquiry, yet somehow transferring the beauty of his words from his own person to that of the young student. He received a standing ovation.

The Chinese Communist takeover of Tibet in 1959, and the Dalai Lama's subsequent flight to India as a refugee, together with his long years in exile, would perhaps have broken a lesser man's spirit. Somehow His Holiness has endured the experiences in such a manner as only to grow from them. He often quotes the Mahayana precept, "See those who harm you as manifestations of the guru, come to teach you strength and courage." Certainly he has practiced this instruction in his own life, and has reaped the according rewards.

Perhaps the Dalai Lama's greatest charm is his ability to make every individual who comes to him feel like the most loved and respected person on earth. After a Kalachakra initiation in Bodh Gaya in 1973 I stood in line with a hundred and fifty thousand others to receive his personal blessings. After three days in line in the hot sun I finally found myself in the temple in front of him. I expected him to look tired, or perhaps even bored, after such an ordeal. He looked at me as though I were his closest friend returning from a long absence, stroked my beard, and whispered laughingly into my ear, "Chokyi trogpo nyingpo, tashi delek," which translates as "Long-time spiritual friend, welcome."

The Dalai Lama often says of himself, "I am nobody special, just a simple Buddhist monk." And in fact he is just that. It is a type of simplicity that touches to the heart of humanity, and inspires the most profound sense of hope in the innate goodness and joy of simply being human.

I have attempted to capture that sense of humility punctuated with innate joy and goodness, which I regard as the qualities most precious to his heart.

The subject of *Essence of Refined Gold* is the *Lam Rim*, a term that refers to both a lineage of spiritual methodology and also a genre of literature aimed at elucidating that methodology. *Lam Rim* literally means "stages on the (spiritual) path." The lineage was brought to Tibet in 1042 by the illustrious master Atisha Dipamkara Shrijnana. The prototype for the literature is Atisha's *Bodhidpathapradipa*, or *A Lamp for the Path to Enlightenment*,[1] which Atisha wrote for the Tibetans a few years after his arrival in Tibet. The work enjoyed immediate popularity, and over the centuries that followed, hundreds of commentaries to its central themes, or the *Lam Rim*, sprang forth from the pens of Tibetan authors.

Atisha's *Lam Rim* tradition was in fact a synthesis of numerous Indian Buddhist lineages. However, its two principal components were the wisdom teachings that had come from Buddha to Manjushri and Nagarjuna; and the method/energy teachings from Buddha to Maitreya and Asanga.[2] Both of these lines were transmitted from generation to generation, and in the eleventh century they were united by Atisha. He acquired the former from his Indian master Vidyakokila the Younger. As for the latter lineage, to receive this he had to travel to Indonesia. The tradition had been passed to an Indonesian master by the name of Dharmakirti,[3] and when Dharmakirti returned to his homeland the lineage went with him. Atisha had heard of this transmission and of how it had become lost to India. Therefore he booked passage on a boat and set out on the long journey. Thirteen months later he arrived in Indonesia, or Suvarnadvipa,[4] "The Golden Islands." There he met with the great guru Dharmakirti and was accepted as a disciple. He remained studying and practicing under this master for the next twelve years, until he himself had accomplished the teachings of which he had come in search. Only then did he return to India.

It is said that during his life Atisha studied with more than fifty gurus, but of all his teachers he felt most deeply indebted to the Indonesian master Dharmakirti. When Atisha came to Tibet he taught with special vigor the lineages that he had received from this guru.

Atisha's visit to Tibet itself is a poignant story.[5] King Yeshey Od had been trying for years to get Atisha to come and teach in his Himalayan kingdom, but due to Atisha's importance in the Indian monasteries the monastic abbots would not grant their permission. Then an event occurred that caused them to change their minds. King Yeshey Od fell into the hands of the Garloks and was put up for ransom, the amount demanded being the weight of his body in gold. His nephew Jangchub Od managed to raise almost the required quantity, but when he brought it to the Garloks it was found to be a few pounds short. However, King Yeshey Od had in mind a different purpose for the gold. He instructed his nephew to send it to India as an offering to the monasteries with a request that they send Atisha to teach in Tibet, stating that in addition to the gold he was offering the life of a king. Yeshey Od thus died at the hands of the Garloks and his gold went to India.

The Indian abbots consented to allow Atisha to go to Tibet for a period of three years. The three became six, and in the end Atisha remained until his death thirteen years later.

Atisha had hundreds of disciples in Tibet, but of them all the foremost was Lama Drom Tonpa, who is often said to have been an early incarnation of the Dalai Lamas. It was to Lama Drom that Atisha left most of his lineages, including the *Lam Rim* lineage that is the subject of *Essence of Refined Gold*. Lama Drom divided the tradition into three lines of transmission, and these were not to be reunited for three hundred years. Then in the fourteenth century Jey Rinpochey Lama Tsongkhapa, root guru of the First Dalai Lama, collected together the fragmented lineages. Since then the complete tradition has always been passed on intact.

There are different ways of speaking about Tibetan religious history and of dividing the Tibetan traditions into sects. The most common is to do so by the periods of translation of the Indian scriptures. Those sects which had formed prior to the eleventh century and which follow the translation terminology of the eighth-century master Padma Sambhava are generally referred to as the Nyingma, or Old Ones. In earlier times numerous sects were included in this category, but today they are more or less amalgamated and are generally considered to be one sect.

In the middle of the eleventh century Tibet experienced something of a renaissance, and again there was a move to examine the Indian scriptures. At this time, the translation terminology was revised and standardized. Three principal sects, together known as the Sarma, or New Orders, formed at this time: the Kagyu, the Sakya and the Kadam. This latter was the tradition produced by Atisha's work in Tibet.

Each of these orders of Tibetan Buddhism had direct roots in a specific Indian master: the Nyingma in Padma

Sambhava, the Kagyu in Naropa, the Sakya in Virupa and the Kadam in Atisha. The work of synthesizing and fusing these lineages was not to occur for another three hundred years, when Lama Tsongkhapa studied under forty-five Tibetan masters representing all the major traditions. In the early 1400s Tsongkhapa established Ganden Monastery to house and preserve his fusion lineage.

In combining the various Tibetan traditions Lama Tsongkhapa needed a common denominator, a common base upon which all could stand. He found the key to this in Atisha's *Lam Rim* tradition, which had already found its way into most Tibetan sects. It became the basis of the Kagyu Order when Milarepa's chief disciple, Gampopa, composed his *Jewel Ornament of Liberation*[6]; and its influence upon the Sakya was so profound that the Sakya Lama Jamyang Khyentse Rinpochey referred to the Sakya as being Kadam-based.[7] Furthermore, a glance at the works of the Nyingma formulator Longchen Rabjampa reveals the extent of the impact that Kadam *Lam Rim* had upon the tradition of the Old Ones.

To emphasize the importance he wished to place on the *Lam Rim* tradition, Lama Tsongkhapa composed three works on the subject, often called the *Lam Rim Che Dring Chung* or *Great, Medium and Concise Treatises on the Lam Rim Tradition.* The first of these is extremely detailed, being over one thousands pages (or five hundred folios) in length. The second is just under half as long, providing a less formal guide. The third is a brief verse work expressed in terms of Lama Tsongkhapa's personal meditational experiences. This latter text is also known as the *Lam Rim Nyam Gur,* or *Song of the Lam Rim Tradition,* or *Song of the Stages on the Spiritual Path.*

Of the hundreds of Tibetan commentaries that have been written on the *Lam Rim* methods, eight have been singled out by the Tibetan masters as being especially noteworthy. These are simply called the *Lam Rim Chenpo Gye* or *Eight Great Lam Rims.* The first three of these are the above works of Lama Tsongkhapa. Then follows the Third Dalai Lama's *Essence of Refined Gold.* Next is the First Panchen Lama's *Easy*

Path to Enlightenment[8] and, after that, the Fifth Dalai Lama's *Sacred Word of Manjushri*.[9] Seventh in the list is the Second Panchen Lama's *A Guide to the Quick Path*.[10] Finally we have Dvakpo Ngawang Drakpa's *Path of the Excellent Scriptures*.[11] The list as here arranged is in order of the dates of composition of the texts and not of importance or length.

For our purposes the two most important of these *Lam Rim* scriptures are Lama Tsongkhapa's *Song of the Stages on the Spiritual Path* and the Third Dalai Lama's *Essence of Refined Gold*. This latter work is a "word commentary" (Tib., *tshig-'grel*) to the former, and quotes much of it.

Thus the Third Dalai Lama's text is a commentary to the contemplative and highly mystical *Lam Rim* poem of Lama Tsongkhapa. Its rather brief length of twenty-three folios has over the centuries maintained its status among the dozens of *Lam Rim* treatises as a favorite for public discourses. As the present Dalai Lama puts it later in his own commentary to *Essence*, the text incorporates all the central doctrines and practices of the classical Indian Buddhist tradition, from the initial method of cultivating a working relationship with a spiritual master, up to the highest tantric yogas of illusory body and clear light mind that induce the final experience of enlightenment.

I originally translated and published the Third Dalai Lama's *Essence* in 1978 in a small volume of early Dalai Lama works I brought out with Tushita Books of India. Curiously enough, the following year His Holiness visited Mongolia for the first time (in this incarnation), and as a gift to the Mongolians took them a number of Tibetan copies of *Essence of Refined Gold* printed with gold ink, since the Third Dalai Lama four centuries earlier had taught this text extensively in Mongolia. Later I discovered that His Holiness also took along thirty copies of my English translation to give to the Russian and Mongolian officials he met who could not read Tibetan but who had access to the English language.

However, from the point of view of a Western reading audience there were a number of problems with this straightforward translation of *Essence of Refined Gold.* The Tibetan text is brilliant and powerful; but it contains such a wide range of ideas in so concise a form (only twenty-three folios, or forty-six pages) that it is not easily understood by the uninitiated. The oral commentary to the text given by His Holiness in 1976 makes an excellent guide to the basic text. Moreover, the discourse was a "meaning commentary" (Tib., *don-'grel*), and thus covered the material of the Third Dalai Lama's text in a general and direct manner, dealing with the central themes of the work rather than the specific technicalities. Therefore I approached His Holiness in 1981, asking him for permission not only to translate his teaching on *Essence* but also for his blessings to edit it for a Western audience. In addition, I requested and received his permission to intersperse relevant comments he had made in private interviews I had attended over the years when these threw light on the topics being discussed by the Third Dalai Lama in *Essence.*

Also included in this book is a prayer by the Third Dalai Lama to be read in conjunction with *Lam Rim* meditation. The text begins with the usual Mahayana procedures of taking refuge; generating the four immeasurable thoughts of love, compassion, joy and equanimity; making symbolic offerings to the visualized assembly; and so forth. It then goes on to call upon the various gurus in the lineage of transmission of the *Lam Rim* method, beginning with Buddha and the early Indian masters, then the Kadam gurus who followed from Atisha's work in Tibet, and finally Lama Tsongkhapa and the Gelukpa masters who came after him. The prayer concludes with Tsongkhapa's *Foundation of All Perfections,* which provides the meditator with a reminder of the principal *Lam Rim* topics. Ideally, after reading the prayer the practitioner would sit in silent meditation for at least half-an-hour.

Originally this text was included by the Third Dalai Lama in *Essence of Refined Gold.* However, with the permission of the late Kyabje Ling Rinpochey, Senior Tutor of the present

Dalai Lama, I have here placed it on its own. It does not sit well in the middle of *Essence* from the perspective of a Western reader, for whom it breaks the flow and upsets the tone of an otherwise clear prose work. By itself, however, it works well as an independent text. In fact it is more common to find a lineage prayer such as this at the end of a treatise rather than in the middle. For example, the First Dalai Lama does just that with his short commentary to the Atisha *Lojong* tradition.[12]

I have also provided as an appendix a translation of a traditional biography of the Third Dalai Lama taken from a collection of biographical materials entitled *Lam Rim Lagyugi Namtar* (Tib., *Lam-rim-bla-rgyud-gi-rnam-thar*), or "Lives of the Gurus in the Lam Rim Transmission," the *magnum opus* of Tsechokling Kachen Yeshey Gyaltsen, the guru of the Eighth Dalai Lama. This work is a wonderful source of historical knowledge, outlining the biographies of the principal Indian and Tibetan masters in the *Lam Rim* transmission lineage, from Buddha until the late eighteenth century. Accounts of all the names listed by the Third Dalai Lama in *A Lam Rim Preliminary Rite* are to be found in Tsechokling's excellent history. His biography of the Third Dalai Lama provides an excellent portrait of the master's life, times and principal accomplishments.

The teachings of the Third Dalai Lama had a profound effect upon the development of Asia. It is my sincere wish that his teachings may also prove useful to the West. He did not say anything Buddha or Tsongkhapa had not said; but he restated their words in a way that brought new meaning to them. For this reason his *Essence of Refined Gold* is as popular in Tibetan and Mongolian circles today as it was four hundred years ago.

In closing I should say something about my system of romanization of Tibetan and Sanskrit names and terms. In general, I have tried to simplify the presentation of Tibetan names and terms. Tibetan formal spelling abounds in silent letters—prefixes, superscripts, subscripts and suffixes—that are either totally unsounded in speech or else completely alter the pronunciation of the root letter of the syllable. For instance, *mKhas-grub* is simply pronounced *Khe-drub*; and *bsTan-pa* pronounced *ten-pa,* etc. It seems more sensible to write these as they sound, not as they are transliterated, except in cases where I feel the formal spelling is relevant. In this latter instance the word is set in parenthesis, e.g., (Tib., *grags-pa*). However, in the notes and bibliography, all Tibetan is presented in full transliteration.

Acknowledgments

I would like to acknowledge the generous assistance of the following individuals in the development and preparation of this volume: H.H. the Dalai Lama, Kyabjey Ling Rinpochey, Ven. Denma Locho Rinpochey and his translator Tubten Tardo, Geshe Tsering of Ganden Monastery, Ms. Diane Short, Kevin Garreth, Tsepak Rigzin, Lozang Dawa, Ms. Roberta Mandell, Vivienne Stewart, Hilary Shearman, Wayne Schlepp, Geshe Lobzang Tenpa, Geshe Tashi Wangyal, Gyatso Tsering and the staff at the Library of Tibetan Works and Archives, and Ven. Zasep Tulku.

If this rendition arouses a spark of the universal spirit of enlightenment within even one reader, that alone will send out a wave of positive energy that will endure until the end of time. But then that too is but a blink of the cosmic eye.

Glenn H. Mullin
Ottawa, Canada 1994

The Path to Enlightenment

Tsongkhapa

ONE

The Nature of the Instruction

HIS HOLINESS:

Buddha Shakyamuni made great efforts to arouse and accomplish the mind of enlightenment in order to benefit the countless sentient beings. Accounts of his training can be read in the *Jataka Stories* as well as in various sutras and later works. After attaining enlightenment he turned the Wheel of Dharma for beings of good fortune, revealing what must be overcome and what must be accomplished in order to transcend the stages and levels leading to higher rebirth, liberation and omniscient perfection. Indeed, his teachings are like an eye through which can be seen all levels of reality, a fabulous medicine able to open the doors of conventional and ultimate wisdom. These diamond methods were transmitted through, and clarified by, an unbroken chain of Indian masters such as Nagarjuna and Asanga. Eventually they spread throughout India, Southeast Asia, China, Japan, Korea, Nepal, Tibet and the entirety of Central Asia. In all of these countries the pure Dharma was molded and shaped in accordance with the experiences of the lineage masters, who expressed the teachings in ways most suited to the time, culture and dispositions of those training under them. Thus Buddhism came to have many faces; but the essence of all valid transmissions remains the same: to overcome negativity, to increase goodness and to cultivate and liberate the mind.

Buddhism was transmitted through a number of lineages in Tibet. Although each of these manifests slightly different ways of presenting the teachings in accordance with the needs of the disciples and the times and areas of Tibet where the lineages were introduced, in that all accept the four seals of Buddhist doctrine, all practice a path combining the Sutrayana and Vajrayana, and all possess methods whereby enlightenment can be accomplished in one lifetime, the differences are not that important. Again, there are differences in details of practice within Theravadin, Chinese, Japanese and Tibetan Buddhism, yet the essential thread from which they are woven is the fundamental substance of Buddha's golden speech. The differences are more in the way of ornaments placed on top of the thread in order to further delight trainees with specific needs. We do not need one form of Buddhism, just as the world does not require one religion. Although all humans are equal, each of us has our individual background, our unique way of seeing and appreciating things, our own spiritual and philosophical tastes. Just as the world has developed a variety of foods to fulfill the individual fancies of different peoples, the variety of religions and subjects within religions is something positive, providing paths for a wider spectrum of trainees. In Tibet we encouraged this type of personal religious freedom to the point that there emerged the saying, "Every lama is his own sect." Diversity is both beautiful and necessary.

Although the last century has seen a great decline in religious interest throughout the world, the hope that the materialistic approach devoid of spiritual foundation can bring lasting happiness has been rapidly evaporating over the last decade. People are once again beginning to appreciate the need for inner development as opposed to the usual hand-to-mouth animal existence. Technology and materialistic endeavor are not negative forces in themselves, but when not coupled with spiritual training they do not bring any deeper knowledge and happiness to the mind, and are very dangerous to the world. The bomb, chemical pollution and police state societies controlled by ultramodern spying and killing devices are a few such examples. There is great hope for our world if technology and spiritual development can go hand-in-hand, but if we continue in our present direction of using our technological and scientific knowledge for little more than exploitation of people and resources, for power politics and international business intrigue, then it becomes very difficult to say how pleasant the outcome will be.

Many spiritual traditions still thrive throughout the world. The great lack is not in the teachings but in our not having the inclination to study and practice them. There are many masters alive today who can show us the paths and practices, but we do not take up training under them. Who can we blame but ourselves if in this way we generate no spiritual experience?

THE THIRD DALAI LAMA:

> To the feet of the accomplished masters,
> Embodiment of the Three Jewels,
> Profoundly I turn for spiritual inspiration;
> Bestow upon me your transforming powers.

Here, for spiritually inclined beings who wish to take advantage of the opportunities afforded by human life, is a treatise on the *Lam Rim* tradition of meditation, a tradition known as *Stages on the Spiritual Path Leading to Enlightenment.*

What is the *Lam Rim* tradition? It is the essence of all teachings of Buddha, the one path traveled by high beings of the past, present and future, the legacy of the masters Nagarjuna and Asanga, the religion of supreme people traveling to the earth of omniscience, the unabridged synthesis of all practices included within the three levels of spiritual application. This is the *Lam Rim* tradition.

Lam Rim is an especially profound aspect of Dharma, for it is a tradition of practice sound in origin. It has neither fault nor shortcoming, for it is a complete training perfectly uniting both method and wisdom aspects of the path. It provides all levels and grades of the techniques passed through Nagarjuna and Asanga, from the practices meant for beginners up to and including the final technique before full buddhahood, the stage of non-practice.

This structured Dharma of taintless origin is like the wish-fulfilling gem, for through it, infinite beings can easily and quickly accomplish their purposes. Combining the rivers of the excellent teachings of both the Hinayana and Mahayana scriptures, it is like a mighty ocean. Revealing the principal points of both the Sutrayana and Vajrayana, it is a complete tradition with complete teachings. Outlining the main techniques for taming the mind, it is easily integrated into any practice, and, being a teaching combining the lineages of Guru Vidyakokila, a sage of the Nagarjuna School, and Lama Serlingpa [Dharmakirti], a sage of the Asanga School, it is a precious ornament. Therefore, to hear, contemplate or meditate upon a *Lam Rim* discourse is fortunate indeed.

To quote Jey Rinpochey's *Song of the Stages on the Spiritual Path,*

From Nagarjuna and Asanga,
Banners unto all mankind,
Ornaments amongst the world's sages,
Comes the sublime *Lam Rim* lineage
Fulfilling all hopes of practitioners.
It is a wish-fulfilling gem,
Combining the streams of a thousand teachings;
It is an ocean of excellent guidance.

HIS HOLINESS:

The two Indian formulators of the *Lam Rim* lineage are Nagarjuna and Asanga, both of whom were prophesied by Buddha Shakyamuni in many sutras and tantras. The ultimate source of the lineage, however, is Buddha Shakyamuni[1] himself who, in terms of his personal kindness to the beings of the present age, is a white lotus amongst the thousand Buddhas of this fortunate aeon. Buddha Shakyamuni turned the wheel of 84,000 teachings, which were passed to his successors principally through two lineages: the profound wisdom lineage that eventually came down to Nagarjuna; and the method lineage of vast activities, that eventually came down to Asanga. Both of these masters studied extensively, made intensive retreats and attained great realizations. They wrote numerous texts elucidating the doctrine and structuring it for effective study and practice. Eventually these two lineages came to Dipamkara Atisha, who unified them and brought them to Tibet. When asked to teach an oral tradition method that would best suit the disposition of the Tibetan people, he transmitted the *Lam Rim* teachings. The tradition has been passed on in an unbroken lineage from that time to the present day.

The *Lam Rim* is a most excellent teaching, for it incorporates all the instructions given by Buddha, including those of both the Sutrayana and Vajrayana. Containing basic as well as high teachings, it can be practiced by people of all levels of intelligence and development. Thus it is a vast ocean containing the jewels of every Dharma method, jewels producing benefits that extend not only to the limits of this life but reach far into future existences, even to the goals of liberation and omniscient enlightenment. Should we be able to complete the fundamental *Lam Rim* practices and engage in the extraordinary trainings of Highest Tantra, even full enlightenment in one lifetime becomes possible.

The aim in the beginning of *Lam Rim* practice is to gain an appreciation of the human potential and to become aware of the unsatisfactory nature of lower existences. We then become mindful of the karmic laws of evolution and seek inspiration from the Enlightened Ones, the Teachings and the Spiritual Community. The aim in the middle stage of practice is to transcend the hope of high rebirth and to inspire the mind to seek nirvana, or liberation from the most subtle forms of samsaric suffering. As nirvana is accomplished through the higher trainings in discipline, meditation and wisdom, these practices are introduced here. Finally, once stability in these two levels has been accomplished, one contemplates how not only oneself but all beings are immersed in samsaric suffering. One thus generates the bodhimind, the Mahayana attitude of universal responsibility that aims at the attainment of omniscient enlightenment as the supreme method of benefiting the world. One then enters into the practice of the six perfections, four ways of amassing trainees, and two stages of tantra, as expedient methods of accomplishing enlightenment and benefiting both oneself and all others without exception in a final and ultimate way.

This is the vast and profound spectrum of practices of the *Lam Rim* as embodied in Atisha's short treatise, *A Lamp for the Path to Enlightenment*. Atisha passed the transmission to Lama Drom Tonpa, who split it into three lineages which he eventually passed to the three Kadampa Brothers. These three masters of the Kadampa Order widely propagated the *Lam Rim* teachings. The lineage coming from them—the

Shungpawa or Scriptural Tradition, *Man-ngapa* or Oral Tradition, and *Lam Rimpa* or Experiential Tradition— became
known as the "Three Kadam Streams." Lama Tsongkhapa
received all three of these lines and unified them once again.
In accordance with the nature of the "Three Streams," he
composed three commentaries to Atisha's *A Lamp for the Path
to Enlightenment.*

In the first of his three commentaries, the *Great Exposition
of the Stages on the Spiritual Path,* Tsongkhapa puts aside the
branches and leaves of the teachings and goes directly to
the essential practices, placing special emphasis upon meditative concentration and profound insight. This section of
the work is presented from his personal reflections and provides a unique approach based upon his own meditations.
The text abounds in quotations from early Indian scriptures,
thus indicating the sources of the various *Lam Rim* practices.

Tsongkhapa's second commentary, *An Intermediate Exposition of the Stages on the Spiritual Path,* embodies the oral
tradition *Lam Rim* teachings. Much shorter than the *Great
Exposition,* it is less encyclopedic and is structured for a more
streamlined practice.

Finally, his third commentary, *A Concise Exposition,* which
is also known as *Song of the Stages on the Spiritual Path,* is a
poem expressing his own experiences in *Lam Rim* training.
The Third Dalai Lama's *Essence of Refined Gold* is largely a
commentary to the meaning of this short work.

Over the centuries many *Lam Rim* scriptures have been
written by the great practitioners and lineage gurus. One of
the most important of these writings is the Third Dalai
Lama's *Essence of Refined Gold.* It has remained one of the
most popular *Lam Rim* manuals since its composition some
four hundred years ago.

In the *Lam Rim* view, the deepest impulse of all sentient
beings is to experience happiness and to avoid suffering.
Different cultures throughout the world have made many
systematic investigations into how these two goals may be
achieved. Many philosophies of human happiness have
emerged and many methods whereby happiness may be

gained have been developed. Most of these methods, however, aim at producing a type of happiness that reaches only within the limits of this lifetime. Their basis and scope is fundamentally materialistic. They demonstrate an amazing lack of knowledge of death and its significance, and of the spiritual processes that give peace to the mind in this life as well as a knowledge that enables one to enter the stage after death with fearlessness and competence. In this context Buddha Shakyamuni said, "He who fears when there is no cause to fear is a fool. He who does not fear when there is a cause to fear is a fool. Both fall from the way." To ignore death and its implications will not prevent us from dying nor will it help us to enter the after-death state with any degree of spiritual maturity.

The difficulty with a purely materialistic interpretation of life is that, in addition to ignoring an entire dimension of the mind, it does not deal effectively with the problems of this life. A materialistic mind is an unstable mind, for its happiness is built on transient, physical circumstances. Mental disease is as high among the affluent as it is among the poor, which is a clear indication of the limitations of the approach. Although it is essential to maintain a reasonable material basis on which to live, the emphasis in one's life should be on cultivating the mental and spiritual causes of happiness. The human mind is very powerful and our worldly needs are not so great that they must demand all of our attention, especially in light of the fact that materialistic success solves so few of the many challenges and problems that confront men and women throughout their lives, and it does nothing for them at death. On the other hand, if one cultivates spiritual qualities such as mental harmony, humility, non-attachment, patience, love, compassion, wisdom and so forth, then one becomes equipped with a strength and intelligence able to deal effectively with the problems of this life; and because the wealth one is amassing is mental rather than material, it will not have to be left behind at death. There is no need to enter the after-death state empty-handed.

It is definite that all of us must die. Although what occurs to the mind after the body dies cannot be held up and demonstrated to the eye as can a material phenomenon, from accounts given to us by sages, philosophers and people with clairvoyance, there can be little doubt that the mind continues to evolve. Moreover, the types of living beings in existence are not limited to those having gross physical bodies, such as the people, animals, insects, etc., that we witness around us. Not only Buddhism, but many independent spiritual cultures throughout the world have perceived the existence of other realms, such as hell beings, ghosts, various celestial beings, and so forth.

The nature of samsaric evolution is not such that death is followed by nothingness, nor that humans are always reborn as humans and insects as insects. On the contrary, we all carry within us the karmic potencies of all realms of cyclic existence. Many beings transmigrate from higher to lower realms, others from lower to higher. The selection of a place of rebirth is not directly in our own hands but is conditioned by our karma and delusions. They who possess spiritual understanding can control their destiny at the time of death, but for ordinary beings the process is very much an automatic chain reaction of karmic seeds and habitual psychic response patterns. Totally unprepared for the spiritual situations that confront them after death, untrained persons are thrown into a fit of confusion and terror. Unable to recognize or relate to the states of consciousness that arise, eventually they seek a womb in which to escape their sorrow, and wander until they find the realm and conditions most suited to their spiritual level and to the karmic forces of previous actions that are propelling them.

Death holds very little hope for ordinary worldly persons with no spiritual experience. Having passed their entire lives ignoring death and sheltering themselves from thoughts of it, when it strikes they become utterly shocked and lose all courage and confidence. Everything that confronts them is unknown, for they never took the time to apply the methods that reveal the nature of mind, birth, life and death. Control over one's future evolution is to be won during one's life, not at the time of death. The yogi Milarepa said, "Fearing death I took to the mountains. Now I have realized the ultimate nature of the mind and no longer need to fear." The root cause of one's spiritual development is oneself. Buddha said, "We are our own savior or we are our own enemy." Until now we have lived largely under the power of delusions and, as a result, although we instinctively desire happiness we create only the causes of frustration and sorrow. We wish to avoid suffering, but because our minds are not cultivated in wisdom we run directly towards suffering like a moth caught in the light of a flame.

Our repeated experience of frustration, dissatisfaction and misery does not have external conditions as its root cause. The problem is mainly our lack of spiritual development. As a result of this handicap, the mind is controlled principally by afflicted emotions and illusions. Attachment, aversion and ignorance rather than a free spirit, love and wisdom are the guiding forces. Recognizing this simple truth is the beginning of the spiritual path.

Our present condition is not something causeless nor is it something caused by chance. It is something we ourselves have steadily constructed through our series of past decisions and the actions of body, speech and mind that arose from them. To place the blame upon an external person or thing is just a source of further confusion and negativity, increasing rather than solving the difficulty.

How can one break the cycle of compulsive, uncontrolled evolution? Only by going to its root cause, the deluded mind that binds and controls us and that causes us to engage in the endless string of meaningless and negative ways that do little but fatigue the spirit. Buddha said, "Mind is the forerunner of all events." A sage with a mind of wisdom, compassion and power dwells in joy and creates only causes of joy. Conversely, the more deluded one is, the more miserable is one's present condition and the fewer are the causes of joy created by one's activities throughout life. Spiritually developed persons benefit both themselves and others as a spontaneous expression of their exalted state of being, whereas undeveloped persons just bring suffering and confusion to themselves and others. The presence of a delusion within the mind in itself creates tension, and its effects upon one's stream of activities creates infinite seeds of future problems. A mind of serenity brings peace and calm into its environment wherever it goes, whereas a negative mind spreads only negativity. If we want happiness for ourselves and if we want to give happiness to others in our communications with them, there is no alternative to cultivating a state of spiritual harmony within our mindstream. When one's state of consciousness has been purified of distorting elements and emotional afflictions, when ignorance is replaced by wisdom and weakness by strength, then the stream of activities that spontaneously arises gives birth to countless seeds of happiness and joy.

Spiritual happiness is not like that gained through materialistic, political or social success, which can be robbed from us by a change in circumstances at any moment and which anyway will definitely be left behind at death. As spiritual happiness does not depend solely upon deceptive conditions such as material supports, a particular environment, or a specific situation, then even if these are withdrawn it has further supports.

To purify the mind means to counteract and uproot all sources of emotional disturbance and delusion—both those inborn and those conceptually formed—together with the seeds of the previous karmic instincts that we have accumulated upon our mindstream over our lives since beginningless time. When the delusions are totally removed, one no longer has the mental conditions that cause one to create further negative karma; and when the seeds of negative karma are purified, one no longer carries within oneself the causes of frustration and misery. This is why persons who seek happiness and wish to overcome suffering are wise to exert themselves in spiritual methods.

Nagarjuna writes in his *Letter to a Friend*, "We wish happiness but we chase sorrow. We wish to avoid sorrow but we run directly to it." The meaning here is that we waste our time in superficial and negative ways instead of cultivating spiritually wholesome disciplines. If we hope to eliminate the control that karma and delusion exert over our mindstream, we must apply an effective method. All beings seek happiness; but most of them, lacking knowledge of how to gain it, find themselves continually immersed in frustration and pain. What we need is an effective approach.

There is no realm in samsara where we have not taken birth, no samsaric pleasure we have not enjoyed and no form of life we have not known over our countless stream of previous lives. Yet even now as humans most of us are like blind animals, unable to discern the patterns of life unfolding within us, leaving spiritual aims behind and chasing only the biological and emotional needs of the senses. Totally unaware of the spiritual methods that produce everlasting joy, we admire the ignoble and have distaste for the noble. Rather than giving ourselves to vain and negative pursuits, we should take note of the words of the Kuntang Rinpochey: "Having found a rare and precious human rebirth, guard it with the stick of mindfulness. Stretch to the realm of liberation."

At this time when we have a human body and mind and have met with the profound teachings of the Great Way, we should take advantage of the opportunity and engage in spiritual methods. If we do not practice now while we have an incarnation most suitable to the attainment of enlightenment, what hope do we have for progress in the future? Many types of sentient beings, such as dogs and insects that live near a temple, meet with the teachings but, not having an appropriate physical or mental basis, they are unable to comprehend them or put them to use. No matter how much we love an animal, we are not able to teach it how to meditate and cultivate spiritual qualities. Whenever Atisha would meet a dog he would stroke it lovingly and whisper into its ear, "Because of your previous negative karmic actions you are now unable to practice the holy teachings." Atisha did not do this out of a lack of compassion but because the dog lacked a basis capable of practice and he wished to lay an instinct of the teachings upon its mindstream.

Unlike animals, we human beings are capable of engaging in the highest meditations and of attaining enlightenment in one lifetime. Moreover, if we engage in negative ways and wrong views instead of applying ourselves to spiritual methods, or if we are born in remote areas where a lineage of instruction does not exist, then our human life does not give us the same opportunities for growth. For example, although for centuries Tibet was a country rich in the study and practice of the Great Way, the Chinese have prohibited spiritual activities there for several decades now. To lack this basic freedom is a great obstacle to the attainment of enlightenment. Those of us who have the opportunity to study and meditate are indeed fortunate. As Shantideva said, "Now when we have ability and have met with the teachings, we should engage in spiritual practice."

Human life is something rare and precious, but it is also quite impermanent. Even as we sit here it is undergoing continual change. If we look around us and ask ourselves how many of our friends and acquaintances have died over the last year, the ever-present reality of our impermanent nature becomes obvious. When someone dies there is great sorrow and lamenting on the part of friends and relatives, but before long this feeling is gone. The corpse is burned or buried, all possessions are disposed of, and soon even the name of the deceased is forgotten. We all intellectually realize that we ourselves are going to die, but the mind always tries to insulate itself from this fact. Somehow we feel very solid and we imagine the reality of our death to be somewhere very far away in the future. But every moment it creeps closer to us, and not one of us can guarantee that we will remain alive even until this evening.

An aspect of death that most terrifies many beings is that suddenly one is totally alone and unsupported by anything but one's spiritual knowledge. When this is strong one is able to deal effectively with every circumstance that death brings; but when it is weak, one must enter the dangerous path of the bardo empty-handed. Then one's heart will fill with regret and one will realize the error of not having pursued deeper goals.

Buddhism speaks of the Three Jewels of Refuge—the Enlightened Ones, the Teachings and the Spiritual Community. In a sense, the Enlightened Ones are the ultimate refuge because they are the ones who give the teachings. But actually the ultimate refuge is the Dharma that they teach, for it is through the study and practice of the teachings that we gain enlightenment and protection from suffering. Dharma here has two meanings: the transmission of the teachings, which are to be studied and mastered; and the transmission of realization, which is gained through practice. It is through applying the Dharma methods that remove faults, increase strengths and give birth to insight and knowledge that we benefit from the existence of the Enlightened Ones. Thus Dharma is the immediate object of refuge, and the Enlightened Ones and Spiritual Community are the teachers and friends on the way.

From amongst the three spiritual goals discussed in the *Lam Rim* literature—high rebirth, liberation and complete enlightenment—most world religions expound relatively uniform methods for producing high rebirth as a human or in a heaven. All Buddhist schools expound the first two paths—those leading to high rebirth and nirvana, or liberation from cyclic existence. A unique quality of the Mahayana is that it emphasizes paths leading to omniscience. Within the Mahayana, only those schools that contain tantric methods have the ability to produce complete enlightenment in a human being in one lifetime; schools relying solely upon Sutrayana methods must work on the principle of establishing a spiritual direction in this life that will culminate in enlightenment only after a string of future lives. Nonetheless, although there are many levels and forms of Dharma practice, they all share the fundamental aim of leading sentient beings from darkness to light, evil to goodness, ignorance to clarity.

From the beginning of our practice we should cultivate the discipline of abandoning harmful, destructive ways and cultivating simple virtues such as kindness, patience, non-violence and so forth. Instead of meaningless literature we should try to read from the biographies and writings of past masters. Being mindful of all activities of body, speech and mind, we should continue our life with our practice kept as an inner treasure, not as an ornament to be flaunted before others. There is a Tibetan saying: "Change your mind; leave the rest as it is." This is particularly good advice for beginners.

As human beings we have a very special opportunity, an opportunity not found in lower forms of life. The human mind is something very unique and precious. Possessing an unusual elasticity and capacity for wisdom, it can evolve at a rate found in no other life-form. Human beings can fall into the most profound spiritual darkness or attain to the exalted state of perfect illumination. What happens to us lies in our own hands. If we cultivate our minds with spiritual methods and generate positive, creative lifestyles and directions, no doubt we will be benefited. Alternatively, if we merely chase superficial goals and pay no attention to the deeper needs of the mind, we are bound to fall into frustration and confusion.

When we look for the sources of all the problems that confront human life we usually blame everything but the root cause: our lack of spiritual discipline and realization. Particularly in this degenerate age, the world atmosphere is so very negative and the conditions around us conducive to little but evil karma and meaningless distractions, that not to have the protection of spiritual knowledge is to leave ourselves totally defenseless against the negative mind. When delusions overpower the mind, destructive actions and suffering are certain to follow. Thus the vicious circle of samsaric existence catches us in its current and before long we are unable to exert even a semblance of control. Our life passes us in darkness, and death leaves us standing naked with only the memories of fruitless pursuits to accompany us into future existences.

Now is the time to extract life's essence. We should look to the Enlightened Ones, the lineages of spiritual transmission and the community of accomplished practitioners, and should apply ourselves to the teachings. This does not mean that today we are ordinary and tomorrow we apply all instructions, but rather that slowly and carefully we study and contemplate the teachings and then gradually work through the various levels of meditation. Our minds have been familiarized with samsaric ways for countless lifetimes, so we should not expect the path to be either quick or easy. Steady, persistent effort and a clear, inquisitive mind are the prerequisites to success. Different trainees generate spiritual progress at different rates depending on their karmic background and the strength and correctness of their practice, so we should apply ourselves without expectations. A Western monk once came to me and told me that even though he had been practicing for five years he had gained no results. I replied that because his mind had known nothing but samsara for millions of lifetimes, he should be more exact and persistent in his efforts. If we practice well, there is no doubt that progress will one day open within us.

Is spiritual practice really worthwhile? Is it really possible to eliminate from within ourselves the forces that give rise to suffering? As is said, "The ultimate nature of mind is clear light." Consciousness has many levels, and although the coarser levels are affected by the defiling forces, the most subtle level remains free of gross negativities. In the Vajrayana this subtle level of consciousness is called the mind of clear light. The delusions and emotional afflictions as well as the dualistic mind of right and wrong, love and hatred, etc., are associated only with the coarse levels of consciousness. At the moment we are totally absorbed in the interplay of these coarse states, so we must begin our practice by working within them. This means consciously encouraging love over hate, patience in place of anger, emotional freedom rather than attachment, kindness over violence, and so forth. Doing this brings an immediate peace and calm to the mind, thus making higher meditation possible. Then, because grasping at a self and at phenomena as being truly existent is the cause of all the vast range of distorted states of mind, one cultivates the wisdom that eliminates this ego-grasping. To overcome ego-grasping is to overcome the entire host of mental distortions.

The delusions are not something solid, not something founded on reality. They simply disappear when we apply the meditative antidotes to them. As they are based on deeply rooted beliefs in a reality that does not exist, they are quickly uprooted by wisdom and other spiritual qualities. This is how the mind is separated from the negative forces within it and how suffering is forever overcome.

To attain liberation from samsara one must perfect the three higher trainings: self-discipline, meditative concentration, and the wisdom of emptiness. In a sense, the most important of these is the wisdom of emptiness; for when we understand the empty, non-inherent nature of the self and phenomena, the endless forms of delusion that arise from grasping at true existence are directly eliminated. However, in order for the training in wisdom to mature and become strong, one must first develop meditative concentration; and in order to develop and support concentration one should cultivate the training in self-discipline, which calms the mind and provides an atmosphere conducive to meditation. When one practices all three of these higher trainings and takes them to perfection, liberation from samsara is definite.

The three higher trainings are basically contained within the Hinayana Vehicle, which in the *Lam Rim* system of practice does not refer to a school of Buddhism but to a set of disciplines and meditations that are to be mastered. However, the substance of *Lam Rim* training is contained within the Mahayana. As one would in a democracy, one looks to the requirements of all beings. One thinks, "The majority is more important than just me, who is but one person. Moreover, in this and many previous lives others have shown great kindness to me. How can I neglect them by working for mere nirvana for myself alone? Even my ability to practice the teachings is due to their kindness. To repay them may I always manifest only as benefits them. However, because the only ultimate gift is the gift of wisdom, in order to be able to help them I myself must first develop insight into the deeper levels of truth. And as only omniscient Buddhas have complete power and knowledge enabling them to communicate with other beings in full accordance with their dispositions and needs, I should strive to attain perfect buddhahood." This aspiration to gain enlightenment in order to be of maximum benefit to the world is to be cultivated and sustained until it spontaneously pervades our every activity, from sleeping to meditating. The basis and essence of the Great Way, it opens the door to the practice of the six perfections, four ways of amassing trainees, and two stages of tantra, and transforms our every thought, word and deed into potential causes of complete enlightenment.

Thus although the Third Dalai Lama's *Essence of Refined Gold* is a brief text, it contains a guide to the entire corpus of Buddhist thought and practice, including the Hinayana, Mahayana and Vajrayana methods. A discourse upon it can be given in a few hours, or can be extended over many months or even years.

The principal source of the *Lam Rim* tradition is the collection of Mother Sutras, or the *Sutras on the Perfection of Wisdom*, that were spoken by Buddha Shakyamuni. Nagarjuna studied these with the Bodhisattva Manjushri and, after gaining a final understanding of Buddha's meaning in the doctrine of emptiness, wrote important abridgements that came to be regarded as the basis of the Madhyamaka School's middle view free from philosophical extremes. Nagarjuna's presentation is ultimately profound in that it transcends the logical inconsistencies of the lower Buddhist schools and arrives more directly at Buddha's intent.

Another source of the *Lam Rim* approach to the path is *The Ornament of Clear Comprehension*[2] by Maitreya. It is said that Asanga, dissatisfied with his understanding of the *Sutras on the Perfection of Wisdom*, entered into an intensive meditation retreat that continued for twelve years. The retreat, however, was without success and, frustrated with disappointment, he gave up and left. On the wayside he encountered a half-dead bitch ridden with worms. Great compassion arose within him and he decided to remove the worms. To avoid harming the worms, he cut a strip of flesh from his body in which to put them. Suddenly the bitch transformed into the Bodhisattva Maitreya, and the purposes of Asanga's retreat were fulfilled. Based on his vision of Maitreya, Asanga later wrote down *The Ornament of Clear Comprehension*, an elucidation and abridgement of all the vast doctrines concerning the paths, practices and stages found in the *Sutras on the Perfection of Wisdom*. It is often said that the *Lam Rim* is fundamentally the quintessential oral instruction of *The Ornament of Clear Comprehension*.

Atisha, who brought the *Lam Rim* tradition to Tibet, studied for twelve years under Serlingpa, a recipient of Asanga's lineage, and often stated that, of his fifty-five teachers, Serlingpa had been most kind to him. Also very important in Atisha's life were Vidyakokila the Younger, from whom he received Nagarjuna's wisdom lineage, and Rahulagupta of Black Mountain, from whom he received many tantric doctrines.

The *Lam Rim* was then passed through a series of Kadampa masters and over the centuries that followed greatly influenced all sects of Tibetan Buddhism. In the New Kadam, or the Geluk Order, the *Lam Rim* was accepted as the fundamental approach to the practice of Dharma. In the beginning of his *Great Exposition*, Tsongkhapa clearly states that the essential inspiration in his composition can be attributed directly to Atisha and his *Lamp for the Path to Enlightenment*.

The author of *Essence of Refined Gold* was born in the Tolung area of Tibet. Shortly after his birth a clairvoyant yogi living in the area prophesied that he was the incarnation of the recently deceased Gyalwa Gendun Gyatso [the Second Dalai Lama]. Word of the prophecy spread, and a delegation came, examined the boy and placed him on a list of candidates. Later the Nechung Oracle certified that the boy was the true reincarnation of Gendun Gyatso, and also was an emanation of Guru Padma Sambhava. While still a youth Sonam

Gyatso himself experienced a vision of Tsongkhapa. Many such marvels occurred in his childhood. He was placed in Drepung for education, where he studied and practiced for many years.

A rather humorous anecdote: Because the First Dalai Lama's name was Gendun Drub and the Second's was Gendun Gyatso, in accordance with prophecy the Third Dalai Lama was originally named Gendun Drakpa, "He famed as Gendun." When he later took ordination under Panchen Sonam Drakpa, the aged Lama changed his name to Sonam Gyatso. The monks of Drepung complained about this but nonetheless he retained the name. Thus he seems to have lived his entire life under a name contradicting prophecy. In his writings the Fifth Dalai Lama criticized Panchen Sonam Drakpa for his unusual decision in changing Gendun Drakpa's name.

Gyalwa Sonam Gyatso was particularly kind to the peoples of what were then the more remote and primitive areas of Central Asia, spending the end of his life teaching, building monasteries and disseminating the *Lam Rim* teachings throughout Mongolia and many parts of eastern Tibet. Kumbum, the monastery that he built in Amdo, became one of Tibet's largest monastic institutions.

TWO

Three Perspectives on Practice

HIS HOLINESS:

The Third Dalai Lama's *Essence of Refined Gold* opens with a verse of homage to the Jetsun Lama,[3] the accomplished master. Here *Je* refers to the spiritual freedom wherein there is no attraction to gross activities, and instead the mind delights in the pursuit of higher goodness. Attainment of this state is the qualification of the first of the three levels of *Lam Rim* practice. *Tsun* refers to the freedom of spirit in which the mind is not attracted to even the highest samsaric perfection nor to the ecstasy of nirvana's serenity. These states are the qualifications of the second and third of the three *Lam Rim* levels of practice, respectively. The syllables *je* and *tsun* also indicate the accomplishment of the two yogic stages of Highest Tantra and consequently to the attainment of the form and wisdom of full illumination. In terms of the past, this line of homage is directed at the lineage of transmission gurus; in terms of the present, it means one's own teacher or teachers, and in terms of the future, it is made to oneself as the resultant refuge, a being who shall accomplish enlightenment. We reflect upon this Jetsun Lama in the beginning of the text in order to gather inspiration and to bring our study into a framework conducive to spiritual assimilation.

The *Lam Rim* is called the essence of all Buddha's teaching because its principal source is the *Sutras on the Perfection of Wisdom* and upon this foundation it presents a range of paths and practices incorporating all Hinayana, general Mahayana, and secret Vajrayana teachings originating from Buddha. As its main foundation is the *Sutras on the Perfection of Wisdom,* the subject of which is the deeper nature of existence, it is the one path traveled by superior beings of the past, present and future for it is nothing other than an understanding of this deeper truth that makes a person superior in the sense of being above the forces of delusion, afflicted emotions and negative karmic instincts. The *Lam Rim* incorporates the practices of all three levels of practice, yet as its aim is to lead the practitioner to the highest level— that of accomplishing omniscient illumination in order to benefit the world—it is called "a Dharma for supreme practitioners."

The *Lam Rim* is like a wish-fulfilling gem, for it contains all the various practices by which one can gain every joy, strength and level of realization, including nirvana and buddhahood. It is an ocean into which were poured the streams of countless Indian lineages of Buddhism and from which may be drawn forth the gems of every practice. These are presented within a structure designed for methodical, interpenetrating application. For example, the first meditational subject discussed in *Essence of Refined Gold*— how to cultivate correct attitudes toward the spiritual master— is not taught solely in accordance with the lower methods but is tempered with influences from Highest Tantra philosophy. This interwoven approach to practice is maximally effective, for the mind is ripened toward the higher techniques even when one is engaged solely in basic methods; and conversely, even when absorbed in the highest tantric practice we keep an eye open to see that the more conventional disciplines are not being violated. In this way we can fulfill the saying, "An external practice of the Hinayana, an internal practice of the general Mahayana, and secret practice of the esoteric Vajrayana." In the *Lam Rim* this range of subjects is not designed for intellectual consumption but purely for ease and effectiveness of practice.

A study of the *Lam Rim* provides the practitioner with four great benefits: the various doctrines of Buddha will be seen as non-contradictory; the various teachings will be taken as personal advice; the thought of Buddha will easily be found; and one will be held back from the great mistake of abandoning any aspect of the holy Dharma.

THE THIRD DALAI LAMA:

The *Lam Rim* teaching has four especially great facets:

(i) It reveals how all the various doctrines of Buddha are non-contradictory.

If one relies upon the *Lam Rim* teaching, all the words of Buddha will be effectively comprehensible. One will see that there are root practices and branch practices, and that there are direct and indirect teachings, all of which aim at creating helpful circumstances along the stages of spiritual development for a practitioner like oneself.

HIS HOLINESS:

Buddha wandered in India for almost fifty years teaching people in accordance with their individual dispositions. Sometimes he taught great yogis, scholars and meditators, sometimes kings and queens, sometimes ordinary people. Consequently his recorded words have many levels and purposes, some of these being at least ostensibly contradictory. For example, in certain of the [Hinayana] *Sutras on Discipline,* we see passages describing which forms of meat may be eaten and which are prohibited, whereas in the *Descent to Lanka Sutra,* a Mahayana treatise, meat is totally prohibited; and in certain Vajrayana scriptures we are admonished to eat meat. When we study and practice the *Lam Rim,* we see how at different stages in training, or for trainees of varying dispositions, the classification of what are root methods and what branch methods continually evolves. We gain the background with which to understand why Buddha taught certain methods for particular stages of training and types of trainees, and quite different methods for trainees of different stages and dispositions. Having this understanding provides us with the ability to read any spiritual treatise with comprehension, or to study any lineage of teachings without becoming confused or disturbed by ostensible contradictions. One will be enabled to appreciate every teaching for its own unique value to specific situations, levels of practice and types of trainees.

THE THIRD DALAI LAMA:

(ii) All the various teachings will be taken as personal advice.

The profound teachings of the sutras and tantras, as well as the treatises and dissertations written by later masters, and all the levels and branches of practice, will be seen as methods to be used to overcome negative aspects of the mind. The significance of all the teachings of Buddha and his successors—from the teaching on how to follow a spiritual master up to those on how to perceive the most profound aspects of reality—will come into one's own hand. One will learn how to practice contemplative meditation upon the words of the teachings and then settled meditation upon the central themes of those words. Thus all the teachings will be seen in perspective to one's own life and progress.

HIS HOLINESS:

Once one gains an overall perspective on the various paths and practices, one is able to understand not only how all spiritual instructions are non-contradictory, but also how all are to be adopted by oneself and integrated into one's own training. As Tsongkhapa writes in his *Great Exposition,* "We will be enabled to appreciate what practices are to be stressed and applied as root methods at the various stages of our training, and how all other teachings then temporarily become secondary, branch instructions to these." One is given an ability to safely and beneficially explore the full range of teachings in such a way that all precepts are seen as personal instructions from Buddha to be applied by oneself for the taming and cultivation of the mind. As in the example of eating animal products mentioned above, when we engage in certain Hinayana practices we can only eat specific types of meat and must exclude others; in certain general Mahayana practices and also in Kriya Tantra and so forth, meat must be altogether avoided; and when we engage in Highest Tantra we eat meat in accordance with the prescribed rites and meditations. In this way all levels of practice are seen not only as non-contradictory but also as methods to be adopted by just such a practitioner as oneself for the generation and attainment of various spiritual qualities.

In addition to presenting all practices as techniques to be used in the training of an individual such as oneself, the

Lam Rim provides us with both a practical and an intellectually satisfying path. For instance, in the *Lam Rim* training in guru yoga, one is not merely given a visualization or simple contemplation to pursue but is encouraged to explore the reasons for finding a guru and cultivating an effective relationship with him or her. This combination of meditative application and intellectual investigation is maintained throughout the *Lam Rim*, providing the spiritual aspirant with a well-rounded and solid understanding of all stages in training. This encourages one's individual confidence and sense of personal responsibility, two important qualities on the Buddhist path.

THE THIRD DALAI LAMA:

(*iii*) The thought of Buddha will easily be found.

Of course, the original words of Buddha and those of the later commentators are pure teachings, but for a beginner they are overwhelmingly numerous and, consequently, their meaning is difficult to fathom. Hence, although one may study and contemplate them, one probably will not gain experience of their actual essence; or, even if one should gain it, a tremendous effort and extent of time would be required. However, because the *Lam Rim* tradition has its source in Atisha's *Lamp for the Path to Enlightenment*, which incorporates all the various oral teachings of the supreme Indian masters, even someone like oneself could easily and quickly arrive at the thought of Buddha through it.

HIS HOLINESS:

The original words of Buddha are vast and extensive. The *Kangyur* [collection of translated words of Buddha] alone contains more than a hundred thick volumes of scriptures, and the *Tengyur* [collection of works of later Indian masters] more than two hundred volumes. A beginner would find it very difficult to wade through this amount of material, and even if one were able to read all of these works, there is little chance that one would be able to assimilate them intellectually or to integrate them all into one's personal practice. As most of these are on specific aspects of Dharma, it would be difficult and tedious to structure them into an effective practice. However, by relying upon an oral tradition such as

Atisha's *Lamp for the Path to Enlightenment,* one can very easily get the gist of the Buddha's teachings and can quickly develop a complete and comprehensive practice of all teachings within one's own stream of being.

THE THIRD DALAI LAMA:

> *(iv)* The great mistake of abandoning a lineage of Dharma will spontaneously be arrested.
>
> When one realizes the intent of Buddha, all his direct and indirect teachings will be seen as wise and skillful means for satisfying the diverse spiritual needs of the variety of beings. To say that some lineages of Dharma are perfect methods and should be practiced, whereas other lineages are imperfect and should be ignored, is the karma called "abandoning Dharma," a great negativity indeed. However, if one studies the *Lam Rim* one will see how all doctrines of Buddha and lineages coming from him are non-contradictory. Then the great mistake of abandoning an aspect of Dharma will never occur.

HIS HOLINESS:

Through gaining an overall view of the paths and practices and then contemplating why, for whom, and for what nature of training the Buddha expounded these, one comes to appreciate all teachings on their own grounds. Thus one is saved from falling into the greatest sin—that of saying, "This teaching is excellent and that useless, this sect is good and that bad," etc.

In the sutras it is said that sectarianism is a more severe evil than killing a thousand Buddhas. Why is this so?

The essential purpose of the Buddhas in giving teachings is to eliminate both mistaken states of mind and the experience of suffering. To achieve this aim is also the reason that they have worked to attain enlightenment. The Buddhas' only motivation is to benefit others, and they fulfill this by teaching. Therefore, despising any of their teachings is worse than despising the Buddhas. This is the implication of following one Dharma tradition while disparaging others.

Furthermore, the Buddhas themselves respect all the traditions of the teachings, so for us not to do so is to dishonor all the Buddhas. There are many ways to look at this sutra quotation. What is the duty, so to speak, of a Buddha? Only to teach Dharma. And it is Dharma that has brought that Buddha to the enlightened state. Now, in Buddhadharma we do not accept the theory of a creator; everything depends on oneself. The Buddhas cannot directly fulfill their wish to help beings. They can only do so through the media of their teachings. We might say that they are handicapped. Therefore, the teachings that they give are more precious and important than are they themselves. Because of the varying capacities and inclinations of beings, the Buddhas have taught various philosophies and methods of practice. If we follow one of these and yet belittle others, we abandon the Dharma and consequently the Buddhas as well.

THE THIRD DALAI LAMA:

These are the four great facets of the *Lam Rim* tradition. Who with any common sense would not be benefited by hearing a discourse on it, a thing the fortunate of India and Tibet have long relied upon, a genuinely high teaching to delight the heart, the tradition known as the *Stages on the Spiritual Path* for the three levels of spiritual application.

To quote Jey Rinpochey on these four effects arising from hearing, contemplating and meditating upon a *Lam Rim* discourse,

[Through it] one perceives all doctrines as non-
  contradictory,
All teachings arise as personal advice,
The intent of Buddha is easily found
And one is protected from the cliff of the greatest mistake.

Therefore the wise and fortunate of India and Tibet
Have thoroughly relied upon this excellent legacy
[Known as] the stages in the practices of
  the three spiritual beings;
Who of strong mind would not be intrigued by it?

HIS HOLINESS:

By studying and practicing an oral tradition teaching that takes the essence of all the scriptures, we gain the benefit of studying and practicing all the teachings. However, in order to touch upon this essential doctrine in a manner that will cause these beneficial effects to ripen upon us, we must approach our study and practice correctly. This means that we must clear our mind of preconceptions and superstition, must make an attentive effort, and must attempt to maintain consistency and regularity in our practice. To study and practice Dharma on the basis of preconceptions is like pouring pure food into a contaminated pot; to be inattentive is like trying to pour food into an overturned pot; and to be irregular and inconsistent in study and practice is like pouring food into a pot with a hole in its base. If we wish to gain full benefits from our efforts, we must replace these three wrong attitudes with openness, clarity, and consistency in application.

We should be constantly mindful of the six recognitions: that we are spiritually ill; that the Enlightened Ones are doctors; that the Dharma is the medicine we need; that the practice of the Dharma is like following a medical treatment; and that Buddha Shakyamuni was a most kind and wise being; and that his lineage of teachings is a most precious and valuable treasure for humanity.

THE THIRD DALAI LAMA:

This tradition, possessing such strength and impact, takes the heart of all the teachings of Buddha and structures it into steps for gradual evolution through the successive experiences of the path, running through the three levels of spiritual application. What an approach to Dharma! How can its greatness ever be described?

Consider the beneficial effects of hearing or teaching the *Lam Rim* even once: an understanding of Buddha and his teachings arises and, by means of pure attitudes and application, the person who is a vessel suitable for Dharma collects benefits equivalent to those gained by having heard all the words of Buddha. Therefore, abandon the three wrong attitudes—likened to a dirty pot, a pot with a hole in its bottom, and an upturned pot—and generate the six recognitions. In this way you will be able to gather the wealth of having approached the subject properly. Whether you are studying or teaching a *Lam Rim* text, do so purely and with intensity.

To quote Jey Rinpochey:

One session of hearing or teaching
This tradition embodying the essence of all Buddha's words,
Collects waves of merit equivalent
To hearing or teaching all Buddhadharma.

THREE

Where the Guru and Disciple Meet

THE THIRD DALAI LAMA:

>However, although merely hearing the *Lam Rim* teaching with the proper attitude is in itself an extremely dynamic experience, something should be said about the qualities of a *Lam Rim* teacher.

HIS HOLINESS:

In order to safely traverse the paths and stages that untie the knots of emotional and karmic bondage, one must correctly apply an effective method. The most certain way to ensure this correct application is to rely upon a fully qualified spiritual friend, someone who has personally realized the fruits of spiritual training and who has gained the ability to communicate his or her experiences to trainees.

The Vinaya [Hinayana], general Mahayana, and Vajrayana scriptures each give their own definitions of the qualifications that a valid teacher should possess. Within the Vajrayana, the lower and higher tantras each again demand their own specific qualifications from a teacher.

The reason behind the necessity for different qualities in the master that accord with the different types of study and practice is, simply, that the nature of any specific level of training demands a specific guru-disciple relationship. In general, the more powerful the method being applied, the more qualified the teacher must be. For instance, one must rely upon a guru who is a fully enlightened Buddha in order to engage successfully in the final yogas of Highest Tantra, whereas a disciple requiring guidance through the lower instructions basically only needs to search for someone well grounded in scriptural learning and insight into the relevant practices. However, the *Essence of Refined Gold* suggests that we search for a teacher having the six basic and four altruistic qualifications given in *The Ornament of Mahayana Sutras.*

The first three of the six basic qualities demanded of a *Lam Rim* teacher are the three higher trainings. Although these have their roots in the Hinayana Vehicle, all six can be given Hinayana, general Mahayana or Vajrayana interpretations.

The first of these is the higher training in discipline. Discipline is the foundation of the path, and a guru who does not have it will not be able to inspire it in his or her students. In such a case the result would be that, even if the students engage in the most potent yogas of Highest Tantra, they will remain like children playing a game of tin soldiers. The ice upon which their yogic palace is built will melt before the hot summer winds of the challenges that life brings.

Secondly, a *Lam Rim* teacher should have a mind that dwells in the serenity of meditative concentration, wherein the gross levels of emotional and psychic disturbances have been quelled. Without this, he or she will not have gained much personal experience in the meditational processes to be taught, and will not have been able to generate the third quality—the higher training in wisdom. Gurus without insight into the deeper levels of truth will be of little value as spiritual guides, for their minds will not be pacified of delusions and, in consequence, their teachings will not resonate with the pure Dharma. Gurus without wisdom are dangerous to both themselves and others, for the entire foundation of their experience will be distorted. They can easily manifest qualities such as sectarianism and materialistic grasping that are symptomatic of unqualified teachers. Should they lead students upon such paths the situation is precarious indeed.

The fourth and fifth qualities refer to the guru as a holder of scriptural and experiential transmissions of Dharma. A teacher who holds both of these transmissions will be able to set forth the vast and extensive practices without distortion or error, and will be able to lead students through the stages of learning balanced by inner experience. A path that combines these two will always be strong and stable. At the very least, a teacher should have more learning and insight into the subject concerned than the student, and should also have the four altruistic qualities mentioned in *Essence of Refined Gold.*

As all positive qualities beneficial to this and future existences are to be gained from developing a friendship with a spiritual master, one should do so wisely and carefully. There is little purpose in devoting oneself to a teacher who will only waste one's time and lead one through distorted experiences of the teachings. It is better to learn what to look for in a guru and to examine any prospective teacher very well before committing oneself to practicing under him or her.

Our relationship with our practice must be based on reason and common sense. The principal subject to be learned is the nature of the two levels of reality, the stages of which can be approached through a combination of hearing, contemplation and meditation. It is very important always to remember contemplation, which is the analysis and investigation of the teachings through the use of reason. The two truths are speaking about reality, not some intellectual fabrication. To investigate the teaching critically is fully encouraged in the same way that medical students are encouraged to apply their theories to real life and thus to witness their validity. Buddhism is speaking about life and the human situation, and is not merely a cultural relic from the past. Time may flow on, but the essential nature of the deeper problems and mysteries that human beings encounter in the course of their lives remains the same. Contemplation of the teachings of Buddha Shakyamuni is merely contemplation of certain facets of reality, and it will cause to unfold within us a deeper understanding of ourselves, our minds, and the nature of our sense of being. As the teachings are merely pointing out key facts of life, facts that, if realized, cause one to evolve in wholesome directions, a critical investigation of them will only inspire trainees with confidence. Reason well from the beginning and then there will never be any need to look back with confusion and doubt. It is important not to get too far ahead of ourselves in our application.

The essential nature of the two truths is something that is present at all times, yet we are not aware of it. Thus the vision of our mind does not attune to the actual nature of the reality within which we live. The purpose of the spiritual path is to bring about this attunement. When we follow a spiritual master who has realized the conventional and ultimate natures of existence, we place ourselves in a position of tremendous opportunity. As the scriptures have gone to such lengths to describe the characteristics of a qualified spiritual friend, we ourselves should do our part and exercise full reason in our choice. The lineages of Buddhist transmissions are quite clear, and it is not difficult to ascertain whether or not a particular teacher has received proper training. Then we have to decide whether or not the guru in question has a personality and manner of teaching that appeals to our own dispositions and sensitivities. It is difficult to train under someone if upon coming close to that person we discover that their way of doing just about everything annoys us. Think well about what a spiritual teacher means, and then approach the issue with the full force of critical reason.

THE THIRD DALAI LAMA:

In general, the qualities of the various masters of the Hinayana, Mahayana and Vajrayana methods are manifold, and any Buddhist master is a worthy teacher; yet the specific qualities required of those who would give a discourse upon the jewel-like *Lam Rim* tradition are as described in *The Ornament of Mahayana Sutras*: they should have realization, i.e., their mindstreams should be (*i*) tamed with realization of the higher training in ethical discipline, (*ii*) stilled with realization of the higher training in meditative concentration, and (*iii*) completely tempered with realization of the higher training in wisdom; (*iv*) they should have authoritative scriptural learning, i.e., they should have heard many teachings on the Three Baskets of Scriptures and so forth from competent masters; (*v*) they should be in possession of an awareness that can perceive emptiness; and (*vi*) they should have more learning and realization than do the disciples. These are the six necessary qualifications of *Lam Rim* teachers.

As well, they should have four altruistic attitudes: (*i*) skill and spontaneous creativity in applying the methods for generating progress within disciples, whom they teach out of a pure motivation free from grasping for wealth, fame or power; (*ii*) enthusiasm and joy in giving time and energy to teaching; (*iii*) diligence and perseverance in teaching; and (*iv*) they should beyond losing patience with disciples who practice poorly.

If you can find a guru possessing these six personal and four altruistic qualities, beg for the teachings. And then follow them well.

HIS HOLINESS:

Essence of Refined Gold now describes the qualities that a student of *Lam Rim* should possess. The first of these is a spirit of sincere inquiry. If we just read through the instructions unthinkingly, or read them thinking, "I am this or that sect, and this is just Tibetan Buddhism," or, "I am Kagyu and this is just Geluk doctrine," then we will close ourselves off from gaining any significant benefit in our study.

To read the *Essence of Refined Gold* with prejudiced attitudes is like putting a golden earring on a donkey, who is too stupid to distinguish between iron and a precious metal. Atisha wrote his *Lamp for the Path to Enlightenment* when requested by the people of Western Tibet to give them a quintessential oral teaching especially suited to Tibetans; perhaps in a sense the *Lam Rim* could be called "Lamaism." But, in that its source is none other than the doctrines of Buddha as gathered and clarified by prophesied Indian masters such as Nagarjuna and Asanga, every Buddhist tradition should be able to see reflections of their own practices throughout the *Lam Rim*. As the *Lam Rim* combines all essential practices of Hinayana, general Mahayana, and Vajrayana as taught and practiced in unbroken lineages since Buddha Shakyamuni, a study of it should enhance one's own training, regardless of sect or tradition.

As I said earlier, within Tibetan Buddhism, the *Lam Rim* teachings pervade all sects either directly or indirectly. Marpa himself met Atisha in Nepal, where he exchanged many teachings with him. Milarepa's chief disciple, Gampopa, was renowned for combining the streams of Atisha's *Lam Rim* tradition with Milarepa's lineage of mahamudra. When Atisha came to Tibet and traveled northward on his way to Toling, he passed the mountain later to become known as Sakya, where the Sakyapa sect was to establish their principal seat some years later. Atisha dismounted, prostrated towards the mountain and prophesied the establishment of the Sakya Monastery and the succession of early patriarchs of the sect. Atisha's own lineages, including the *Lam Rim*, were later to become an integral cornerstone of Sakyapa doctrine.

Sometimes we hear it said that the Gelukpa are too intellectual and that their use of analysis and reason are obstructive to meditation and the spiritual path. Personally, I feel that this is foolish talk by people of limited knowledge. The First, Second, Third, Fifth and Thirteenth Dalai Lamas all practiced widely within all sects of Tibetan Buddhism, particularly within the Nyingma order. These Dalai Lamas were all called "Drepung Lamas" and "Holders of the Yellow Hat," but they nonetheless respected all sects equally and studied with masters holding lineages that interested them, regardless of sect. To be close-minded towards a scripture or lineage of Dharma out of sectarian bigotry is to turn wholesome medicine into poison. This religious superiority complex just makes one into a fool. I have Gelukpa ordination and training, but Tibetan lineages are very interrelated, and one of the main Gelukpa meditations is a lineage brought to Tibet by the Kagyu founder, Marpa Lotsawa. Thirty percent of the remainder of my practice centers upon a Nyingma lineage. I have also met and exchanged ideas with many Japanese, Theravadin, and other masters. Most Tibetan lamas practice this way. When one understands the nature of the spiritual path there is never a need to see a contradiction in the types of Buddhist trainings. Buddha did not impart his vast array of teachings merely in order to confuse people as to what is pure Buddhism and what is not, what is high and what is low. Anyone who has gained a fundamental understanding of the intent of the Enlightened Ones can see the pure Dharma reflected in every word of every master, regardless of tradition or lineage. Just as a traveler will adopt different clothing in order to adjust to the climate of different countries, every lineage of the Dharma takes on a slightly unique character in accordance with the times and culture of its development. Yet when we check on the source of the lineage we will find it comes in an unbroken line from Buddha Shakyamuni. Perhaps it traces back to the First Turning of the Wheel and as such is in the Hinayana category of practices that take the Four Noble Truths, renunciation and the three higher trainings as their main points. Maybe it comes from the Second Turning and emphasizes the Mahayana middle view. Or perhaps it belongs to the Third Turning and is based upon the doctrine of mind-only. The lineage could also be a Vajrayana method which was transmitted secretly, or an oral tradition that unites a number of lineages. A trainee who has gained an appreciation for the breadth and depth of Buddhist doctrines collected and expounded by early Indian Buddhist masters such as Nagarjuna, Asanga, Vasubandhu, Dharmakirti, and so forth, will immediately be able to respect every lineage of Dharma on its own ground. We ourselves should attempt to follow this eclectic approach that so many of the past masters have taken. This does not mean we should mix our practices and make a big soup out of them. Rather, we should be open to all teachings as valid transmissions of the thought of the Enlightened Ones and as sources of knowledge that can support and strengthen whatever specific lineage we may be pursuing.

The second prerequisite quality of a *Lam Rim* trainee is critical intelligence. Teaching a student who lacks this sense of curiosity is like leading a monkey around on a chain. No matter how much faith we have, if we do not constantly maintain an inquisitive and critical attitude our practice will always remain somewhat foolish. Even the four initiations into Highest Tantra will be of no value to us if we do not cultivate the correct mental framework.

The aim of every teaching of the Enlightened One is to calm the negative mind and to give birth to spiritual qualities. But when we lack inquisitiveness, we are not able to determine how to apply the specific instructions to our own stream of being. To spend one's entire life at Dharma study and practice while still maintaining a barbaric mind is to permit a divine being to become a devil. When reading dozens of scriptures does not reduce our attachment, aversion, pride and so forth, it is time to reconsider our methods for bringing the teachings into our hearts and understanding them as living experiences.

This is especially true for beginners. It is very important to have a balanced approach to study and practice, and although use of the intellect is important and mandatory, we must be sure that our training goes beyond mere intellectualization and is taken home to the purpose of cultivating the mind and eliminating inner weaknesses. We should be like Atisha's disciple Lama Drom Tonpa, who said, "Whenever I study I also contemplate and meditate; whenever I contemplate, I also study and meditate; and whenever I meditate, I always study and contemplate. This is the Kadampa way." This interpenetrating threefold approach protects one from ever entering wrong paths or being misguided by erroneous instructions.

These are the two most important qualities of a spiritual aspirant. One should try to cultivate these, as well as the other prerequisites listed in the *Essence of Refined Gold*. Even the best guru and the highest teaching are unable to help us if we do not make the necessary efforts to cultivate effective attitudes and qualities within ourselves.

As Maitreya[4] has said, "The Buddha-essence pervades all that lives." The nature of the most subtle level of consciousness, which is pure and free from stains, is something possessed by all sentient beings. In this sense all living beings are equal. We all share the same situation: when the correct conditions come together, our buddha nature will evolve into omniscient buddhahood. Nonetheless, in terms of the path to enlightenment, we humans are in somewhat of a superior position to the lower forms of life, due to certain special features of our body and mind. The sophistication of our physical nervous system and our superior capacity for discriminating awareness provide us with far greater opportunities for spiritual development. Even worms will one day attain enlightenment, so why should we feel that spiritual progress is something beyond our reach? We may now have many faults and weaknesses, but if we apply ourselves to the teachings by means of study, critical analysis, and meditation, there is no reason for us not to experience the inner qualities that eliminate negativities from within the mind. These inner qualities are like antidotes that counteract the poisonous influence of the negative mind. Through prolonged familiarity with the meditative antidotes, the force of mental distortion and emotional affliction eventually subsides and the mind arises in its pure, undistorted state.

The Tibetan word for Buddha is *Sang-gyey.*[5] *Sang* indicates a state purified of all faults and weaknesses; and *gyey* refers to the expansion of wisdom to the limits of existence. In that we all have a certain degree of purity and knowledge, one might say that we are all Buddhas of varying sizes. Although the Buddha in us is still quite small compared to a fully enlightened one, full buddhahood is not something we cannot attain. Imperfection can be systematically eliminated from within the mind, and every quality of realization can be generated through correct training. All that is required is the cultivation of certain conditions. Our mind is now flavored with imperfection, but should we make intense efforts to develop competence in the various meditations that counteract these imperfect traits, no doubt they will be overcome. At the moment there still exist many lineages of valid teachings able to guide us to the states of immaculate knowledge wherein all inner faults have been overcome and the mind joyously abides in total freedom from distortion, emotional afflictions and the endless host of sufferings that these negative elements produce. There are also many spiritual masters alive on the face of this earth at this moment. But unless we make a personal effort to take advantage of these facts, our precious human rebirth will not prove that meaningful in the end.

THE THIRD DALAI LAMA:

The disciple should have three fundamental qualities: (*i*) sincerity, (*ii*) intelligence able to discriminate between beneficial and misleading forces on the path, and (*iii*) an intense longing to gain spiritual understanding and experience. As well, the disciple should have a fourth quality— appreciation for the Dharma and the Dharma teacher.

Sometimes six qualities are mentioned. A disciple fit to be led along the sublime path of *Lam Rim* practice must (*i*) have great interest in the Dharma; (*ii*) during the actual teaching be able to keep the mind alert and well focused; (*iii*) have confidence in and respect for the teacher and the teaching; (*iv*) abandon wrong attitudes toward the teaching and maintain receptive ones; (*v*) maintain conditions conducive to learning; and (*vi*) eliminate any unconducive conditions.

If you would give a discourse on the *Lam Rim*, try to maintain the qualities of a teacher as described above; and if you would listen to a discourse cultivate the above qualities of an ideal disciple within yourself.

HIS HOLINESS:

We humans are actually not that far from enlightenment. Our five senses are like the Emanation Body of a Buddha; our dream body, which is similar to the after-death form, is like a Buddha's Beatific Form; and the basis of both of these is the subtle mind of clear light which shares the nature of a Buddha's Wisdom Body. All we have to do is learn to transform these ordinary elements into their pure natures. Then buddhahood naturally comes into our hands.

THE THIRD DALAI LAMA:

While training in the *Lam Rim* tradition under the guidance of a fully qualified spiritual teacher, one should try to live in a quiet place pleasing to the mind. Arrange an altar having images of your teachers, Lord Buddha, a stupa and a scripture, as well as fresh, pure offerings. In front of this altar prepare a comfortable meditation seat, and either four or six times each day sit there in the seven-point meditation posture, perform the *Lam Rim Preliminary Rite* and meditate as instructed.

HIS HOLINESS:

In Tibet there was a tradition to study the *Lam Rim* while living either in retreat or semi-retreat. The student would be taught one subject of meditation at a time and would continue to practice it for weeks or months, until stability and signs of progress arose. Here it is important to choose a quiet, pleasant site as the place of practice, where the natural beauties of the environment imbue our mind with serenity and joy. One makes either two, four or six sittings daily, beginning these with a *Lam Rim Preliminary Rite*[6] and then engaging in whatever is the principal subject of meditation. One begins with contemplative meditation upon the range of topics and then absorbs in settled meditation upon one specific subject. In semi-retreat usually only one, two or three sittings are performed daily.

THE THIRD DALAI LAMA:

How to Rely Upon a Spiritual Master

The best way to rely upon a spiritual master is to practice contemplative meditation upon the master's mystical qualities and his or her beneficial function in your spiritual life.

Consider the countless ways in which the teacher is kind to you: the spiritual master is the root of all mystical attainment, the source of all goodness in this and in future lives, and the doctor who eradicates the disease of mental and psychophysical disturbances with the pill of Dharma. However, although you have wandered in samsara throughout the infinite past, never before have you met a guru; or even if you met one you did not correctly follow his or her teachings, for you are not yet a Buddha. Think, "I have now met with a spiritual master and so should try to practice as pleases him."

It is more kind to give a bowl of simple food to someone dying of hunger than to give a handful of golden coins to someone who has every luxury. For this reason it is said that one's personal guru is kinder than even Buddha himself. The scripture *Five Stages* states,

> The self-born Buddha
> Is a being gone to perfection;

But kinder than Buddha is one's own teacher,
Who personally gives one the oral teachings.

Contemplate how your guru is kinder than all the Buddhas of the past, present and future.

HIS HOLINESS:

The actual method of cultivating the correct attitudes towards the spiritual master is to practice contemplative meditation upon the guru's good qualities and the beneficial effects that he or she introduces into one's life. By reflecting again and again on the great kindness the guru performs, a confidence suitable for spiritual training under him or her is born. This process of reflecting on the role of the guru is important in the beginning as well as in the higher practices, for as we sit in contemplation we become faced with a stream of reactions, which if understood at an early stage can clear the mind of much doubt, confusion and superstition.

The spiritual master is the source of all spiritual progress. In this context, Geshe Potowa once said, "If even those who want to learn a common worldly trade must study under a qualified teacher, how much more so must we who seek enlightenment? Most of us have come from the lower realms and have no background or experience in the paths and stages to enlightenment; and, if we wish to gain this experience, why should we not study with someone qualified to teach us the methods that develop it?"

In the beginning of his *Great Exposition,* Lama Tsongkhapa writes, "The root of spiritual development is to cultivate an effective relationship with a master." This means that we must cultivate the correct attitudes and then demonstrate them correctly in action. This is the root that, if made strong, supports the trunk, branches, leaves and flowers of practice. When the roots of a tree are strong, the entire tree becomes strong, whereas when the roots are weak, the entire tree will remain weak.

The two principal attitudes to be cultivated are respect for the guru and appreciation for the beneficial effects he or she brings into our life. We should engender respect such that we see the guru as a Buddha. If we can do this, then we experience the guru as we would a Buddha and consequently are sufficiently inspired to practice what he or she teaches. The closer we are to someone, the more likely it is that we will be influenced by their advice. The spiritual master can show us the path to enlightenment, yet in order for his or her advice to be of benefit to us we must personally accomplish the practices. When we see the guru as a Buddha it becomes very easy to integrate our activities of body, speech and mind with what he or she teaches.

The instruction to see the guru as a Buddha is not unreasonable, for in many ways the spiritual master is Buddha himself. The Buddha who is regarded as the founder of Buddhism and who taught the various paths to enlightenment died some twenty-five centuries ago. The work of introducing us to and guiding us in our experience of the teachings today is performed by none other than our guru, the spiritual master. Thus, if we regard him or her as an ordinary person and fail to cultivate an effective relationship, there remains a wide gap between the Buddha and the being performing his work. Buddha is supreme of the Three Jewels of Refuge, the source of every excellence, and if we respect the Three Jewels, how can we not respect the person who performs their work specifically for us?

The teaching to see the guru as a Buddha actually comes from Highest Tantra. Both Hinayana and general Mahayana scriptures speak of the types of gurus, the necessity of having a qualified guru, the prerequisites needed by a guru, the attitudes to be held by the disciple, and so forth. These topics are also discussed in the tantric scriptures, with the exception that, in addition to the qualities mentioned in the above sutra categories, a tantric guru must be a Buddha. He or she must be able to impart the teachings on the two stages of practice in accordance with his or her own personal experience. Especially, the tantric guru must be able to give the "fourth initiation" from his or her own experience, which means introducing the disciple to the "great unions of training and beyond." Only a Buddha Vajradhara can do this. A master actually bestowing the four levels of initiation must have realized both semblant and actual clear lights as well as the illusory body which is the vehicle of the mind of clear light; he or she must also have realized the state of great union to which the disciple is being introduced.

From our side, even if the guru does not really have this attainment and is giving the initiation mainly to lay auspicious instincts on the mindstreams of trainees, in that the strength of the instinct is determined by the state of the mind in which it is planted, one gains the strongest instinct by regarding the initiating master as being a Buddha. This in fact is what the guru should be were he or she really to give the four initiations.

The relationship between a guru and a student is very important. The first step one must take in regards to establishing such a relationship is to learn the qualities of an ideal master. Before accepting any person as a guru, check carefully to be certain that he or she is qualified to act as a spiritual guide. Analyze your own feeling toward that person at great length, and ascertain whether or not you have the ability to train in accordance with their manner of teaching and to see them as a Buddha. Once you are convinced that you will be able to retain faith and correct attitudes towards that person, there is much to be gained by cultivating a relationship. On the other hand, no matter how qualified a master may be, if you are unable to feel any confidence and trust in his or her capabilities, there is little inspiration to be gained from studying a spiritual subject with that teacher. It is therefore our right and responsibility to be very selective when accepting anyone as our guru.

The reason why the qualities of a teacher are described at such length in the scriptures is because we should know what to look for when seeking a guru capable of opening up the Buddhist paths within us. To take up training under an unqualified teacher can be disastrous. It is said in the tantric scriptures that one is not unwise to examine a guru for twelve years before accepting that person as one's teacher. The choice of teachers is an important one and must be made carefully.

Not only does the guru perform the work of the Buddhas and thus equal them in activity, in terms of kindness the guru surpasses them. Of all Buddhas of the past who have manifested as universal teachers, it is said that Buddha Shakyamuni is kindest to us; for it is with his teachings that we have come into contact. The teachings of Buddha Kashyapa, who lived before him, have not come down to us. Moreover, even though Buddha Shakyamuni is most kind of the past Buddhas, still we are unable to receive teachings from him or witness his inspiring presence. Thus, neither of these two past Buddhas are able to help us directly.

Were all the Buddhas and lineage masters of the past to manifest before us at this very moment, we would not be able to recognize them as enlightened beings. Due to our not having a sufficiently strong karmic connection with them, they would be unable to affect us. The guru performs the great kindness of coming to us in an ordinary form which we can perceive and to which we can relate, and carries out the work of the Buddhas in our lives. The fact that a donkey like us is brought into the family of spiritual beings is purely due to the kindness of the guru. The Buddhas can only come to us through him or her. Thus if we do not respect the guru and heed his or her teachings, what hope do we have? We should meditate upon the guru's unexcelled kindness and give birth to profound appreciation.

The reason why we have been wandering unceasingly in cyclic existence since time immemorial is because we have not met a spiritual master before; or even if we have met one we did not cultivate an effective relationship with him or her. We should determine to take the opportunities afforded by our present human situation and cultivate a spiritual practice under the guidance of a master.

THE THIRD DALAI LAMA:

Approaching the Spiritual Master

In order to gain spiritual instruction, Buddha himself made offerings of material things, service and practice. For example, in one previous life he offered a hundred thousand pieces of gold to a master in order to receive the half-verse, "If there is birth there is death; stopping this process is bliss itself." In another life, this time as a king, he abandoned his wife and his only son for a single verse of the Dharma. On still another occasion he made his body into a lamp and burned it as an offering to his guru. In these and other ways he sacrificed wealth, possessions and other objects of attachment, and since one is a follower of Buddha one should do likewise. If you have heard many teachings from your guru, is his kindness not immeasurable?

Some people think that a teacher should be revered only if he or she has many obvious qualities. They say, "I go to him to hear his words on Dharma, not to see him," and "I can see no great traits in her, so there is no need for reverence." What fools! For instance, even if one's parents have no good qualities one should appreciate their kindness; for, by so doing, great benefits arise, whereas by not appreciating them only pain and confusion result. The same holds true of one's attitude towards the guru.

One feels that someone who gives one a little wealth is very kind, but the guru can give one every goodness of this and future lives. If you contemplate deeply, it becomes obvious that all stages of development— from that of a simple lay practitioner up to the states of bodhisattva and Buddha— depend completely upon pleasing the guru. There are many examples of people who have attained full enlightenment in one short lifetime by correctly devoting themselves to a master, and if you please your teacher with the offerings of material things, devotion and intensive practice, there is no reason why you could not do the same. Thus the importance of correctly approaching an all-kind guru cannot be over-stressed. Meeting with and being cared for in this and in future lives by a guru with whom one has a Dharmic relationship is purely one's own responsibility, so serve your guru well.

Without following a qualified teacher, there is absolutely no method which brings enlightenment. This point is stressed in all the sutras and commentaries. "Please practice as will please the guru," is said again and again. This should not be regarded as an undesirable task such as a prison sentence or the like; for who doesn't want good fortune? And as is stated in many sutras, tantras and shastras, there is no faster or more powerful way to increase your store of good fortune than by correctly following a guru.

However, when training under a spiritual master, be sure to maintain a correct attitude towards him or her. Whatever happens, do not permit the thought to arise that the guru may have faults or shortcomings. Meditate in this way not with words alone but from the depths of your heart, until the mere sound of the guru's name or a thought of the guru makes the hair on your body tingle and your eyes fill with tears.

In general, all the Buddhas and bodhisattvas have said that one should never see the ordinary failings of a human being in the guru. If you think that you see something low or base in your teacher, consider that it is just a reflection of your own impure attitudes. How are you able to really know what is and isn't base? Once when Arya Asanga did a retreat on Maitreya Buddha, he perceived Maitreya as a worm-ridden bitch. Naropa first saw his teacher Tilopa as a lunatic catching fish and eating them alive. And in the sutra called *A Meeting Between Father and Son*, Buddha manifested as a devil in order to work for the good of the world. In view of these incidents, how can you believe that the faults that you seem to see in your guru are real? Generate conviction that he or she is a manifestation of the Buddha.

It is taught in the *Root Text of the Guhyasamaja Tantra* and also in Ashvagosha's *Fifty Verses on Guru Yoga* that there is no graver error than saying or believing that one's guru has faults. Therefore, practice guru yoga as related in the biography of Lama Drom Tonpa—without doubts or wavering. Once you have accepted a guru, meditate so as not to give rise to any disrespectful or unworthy thoughts, even if your life is at stake.

As Jey Rinpochey wrote,

> The root of all causes producing
> Happiness here and hereafter, is the practice
> Of relying in thought and action
> Upon the sacred friends who reveal the path.
> Seeing this, follow them at any cost
> And please them with the offering of practice.
> I, a yogi, did that myself;
> You, O liberation seeker, should do likewise.

Jey Rinpochey gave this advice purely out of great compassion, and not because he wanted his disciples to honor or to glorify him.

HIS HOLINESS:

Because having a spiritual master would bring great kindness into our life, we should attempt to find one and establish a connection with him or her by making three types of offerings: material objects, service, and correct practice. In this context Milarepa said, "I do not have enough wealth to make a material offering, but instead I will please my guru by offering him correct practice." The result was that he attained enlightenment in one lifetime. The offering of practicing the teachings that one receives can sometimes be difficult to make, but, due to its fruits, it is the most precious. Teachers should not cherish material offerings over the offering of practice, and students should put forth every effort themselves to make this offering.

The offering of practice means always to live by the teachings of one's guru. But what happens when the guru gives us advice that we do not wish to follow or that contradicts Dharma and reason? The yardstick must always be logical reasoning and Dharma reason. Any advice that contradicts these is to be rejected. This was said by Buddha himself. If one doubts the validity of what is being said, one should gently push the point and clear all doubts. This task becomes somewhat more sensitive in Highest Tantra, where total surrender to the guru is a prerequisite; but even here this surrender must be made only in a particular sense. If the guru points to the east and tells you to go west, there is little alternative for the student but to make a complaint. This should be done with respect and humility, however, for to show any negativity towards a teacher is not a noble way of repaying his or her kindness.

The practice of guru yoga means that one ignores any negative traits that the guru may seem to have, and that one meditates upon his or her positive qualities. If we can develop the habit of always seeing the guru through his or her good qualities, our confidence naturally grows, and eventually we become able to take our preconceptions about faults he or she seems to display and transform them into spiritually useful tools. Perception of faults in the guru should not cause us to feel disrespect, for by demonstrating faults to us the guru is actually showing us what we should abandon. At least, this is the most useful attitude for us to take. An important point here is that the disciple must have a spirit of sincere inquiry and must have clear, rather than blind, devotion.

It is frequently said that the essence of the training in guru yoga is to cultivate the art of seeing everything the guru does as perfect. Personally I myself do not like this to be taken too far. Often we see written in the scriptures, "Every action seen as perfect." However, this phrase must be seen in the light of Buddha Shakyamuni's own words: "Accept my teachings only after examining them as an analyst buys gold. Accept nothing out of mere faith in me." The problem with the practice of seeing everything the guru does as perfect is that it very easily turns to poison for both the guru and the disciple. Therefore, whenever I teach this practice, I always advocate that the tradition of "every action seen as perfect" not be stressed. Should the guru manifest un-Dharmic qualities or give teachings contradicting Dharma, the instruction on seeing the spiritual master as perfect must give way to reason and Dharma wisdom.

Take myself, for example. Because many of the previous Dalai Lamas were great sages and I am said to be their reincarnation, and also because in this lifetime I give frequent religious discourses, many people place much faith in me, and in their guru yoga practice they visualize me as being a buddha. I am also regarded by these people as their secular leader. Therefore, this teaching of "every action seen as perfect" can easily become poison for me in my relationship with my people and in my effective administration. I could think to myself, "They all see me as a buddha, and therefore will accept anything I tell them." Too much faith and imputed purity of perception can quite easily turn things rotten. I always recommend that the teaching on seeing the guru's actions as perfect should not be stressed in the lives of ordinary practitioners. It would be an unfortunate affair if the Buddhadharma, which is established by profound reasoning, were to have to take second place to it.

Perhaps you will think: "The Dalai Lama has not read the *Lam Rim* scriptures. He does not know that there is no practice of Dharma without the guru." I am not being disrespectful of the *Lam Rim* teachings. A student of the spiritual path should rely upon a teacher and should meditate on that teacher's kindness and good qualities; but the teaching on seeing his or her actions as perfect can only be applied within the context of the Dharma as a whole and the rational approach to knowledge that it advocates. As the teachings on seeing the guru's actions as perfect is borrowed from Highest Tantra and appears in the *Lam Rim* mainly to prepare the trainee for tantric practice, beginners must treat it with caution. As for spiritual teachers, if they misrepresent this precept of guru yoga in order to take advantage of naive disciples, their actions are like pouring the liquid fires of hell directly into their stomachs.

The disciple must always keep reason and knowledge of Dharma as principal guidelines. Without this approach it is difficult to digest one's Dharma experiences. Make a thorough examination before accepting someone as a guru, and even then follow that teacher within the conventions of reason as presented by Buddha. The teachings on seeing the guru's actions as perfect should largely be left for the practice of Highest Tantra, wherein they take on a new meaning. One of the principal yogas in the tantric vehicle is to see the world as a mandala of great bliss and to see oneself and all others as Buddhas. Under these circumstances it becomes absurd to think that you and everyone else are Buddhas, but your guru is not!

In Tibet, due to the Dharma being so widespread, and due to the kindness of many past masters, the people were inspired by a great deal of faith. Even a small patch of red cloth was regarded as true Sangha. They had no difficulty in practicing "every action seen as perfect." Therefore, responsibility for the purity of the tradition rested in the hands of the lamas, and, unfortunately, it is very easy for a lama to become spoiled by the teaching, "every action seen as perfect."

Actually, the more respect one is given the more humble one should become, but sometimes this principle becomes reversed. A spiritual teacher must guard himself or herself carefully and should remember the words of Lama Drom Tonpa, "Use respect shown to you as a cause for humility." This is the teacher's responsibility. The student has the responsibility of using wisdom in his or her demonstration of faith and respect.

Faith generated is a virtue, but if it is not guided by wisdom it can get us into trouble. We Tibetans generally have so much faith that we take Dharma practices for granted. A monk who lives from the offerings of patrons, but does not abide within the practices, creates a negative karma equal to stealing from a temple. Someone who has spiritual qualities or who is engaged in intensive study or practice fulfills the qualification of receiving offerings and their acceptance is meaningful. But a bad monk would be better off to swallow a hot iron ball. A problem is that we usually only observe those teachings that feed our delusions and ignore those that would overcome them. This leniency can easily lead to one's downfall. This is why I say that the teaching on seeing all the guru's actions as perfect can be a poison. Many sectarian problems in Tibet were born and nourished by it.

The First Dalai Lama wrote, "The true spiritual master looks upon all living beings with thoughts of love and shows respect to teachers of all traditions alike. Such a one only harms delusion, the enemy within." The different traditions have arisen principally as branches of skillful methods for trainees of varying capacities. If we take an aspect of their teachings, such as the precept of "all actions seen as perfect," and use it for sectarian purposes, how have we repaid the past masters for their kindness in giving and transmitting Dharma? Have we not disgraced them? If we misunderstand and mispractice their teachings, it will hardly please them. Similarly, it is meritorious for a lama to perform rituals or give initations to benefit people, but if his or her motivation is only material benefit, that person would be better off going into business instead. Using the mask of Dharma to exploit people is a great harm. What the Chinese did to us was bad, but not as bad as the effects we would create by taking Dharma and using it for sectarian purposes or to exploit people. This rots the foundation.

In this context the great yogi Milarepa said, "When Dharma practitioners do not abide within their practices, all they do is harm the teachings." Just as intestinal worms can kill a lion, using the teachings for sectarianism and ex-ploitation can easily destroy the Dharma.

We erect elaborate altars and make extensive pilgrimages, but better than these is to remember Buddha's teachings: "Never create any negative action; always create goodness; aim all practices at cultivating the mind." When our prac-tice increases delusion, negativity and disturbed states of mind, we know that something is wrong.

It is sometimes said that a major cause of the decline of Buddhism in India eight hundred years ago was the prac-tice of Vajrayana by unqualified people, and sectarianism caused by corruption within the Sangha. Anyone teaching Tibetan Buddhism should keep this in mind when they re-fer to the precept, "every action of the guru is to be seen as perfect." This is an extremely dangerous teaching, particu-larly for beginners.

FOUR

The Human Situation

THE THIRD DALAI LAMA:

At this point the question may arise: "If one should try to rely upon a spiritual master who points out the path to enlightenment and should try to please the master by making the offering of practicing his or her teachings, what exactly is meant by 'offering of practice?'"

Practice means taking upon yourself the responsibility of continually living in accordance with the holy Dharma, the teachings given to you by your spiritual master. Through working with the guru and with the laws of cause and effect, you can take advantage of your extremely valuable human life, a life-form hard to find and, once found, very meaningful; a treasure more precious than a wish-fulfilling gem. Other than doing this, there is no offering of practice. Brace your teeth, and do not let the once-attained opportunity afforded by human life slip away. If you do not utilize this tremendous potentiality, is your heart not vain?

HIS HOLINESS:

At the moment, we have attained a human form having the eight freedoms and ten endowments conducive to spiritual practice. Even though in a sense all humans are equal, from the viewpoint of Dharma practice someone having all eighteen is special among the equals.

Several of the eighteen qualities are shared by all humans in all ages, but the rest are exclusive to beings of strong merit.

The first four of the eight freedoms are common to all humans: being free from rebirth in 1) the hells, 2) the ghost realms, 3) the animal world, and 4) the heavens of the long-lived gods. The remaining four refer to freedom from four unfavorable human states: 1) and 2) being free from a birth in either a remote or a barbaric place where an enlightened being has never lived and taught; 3) not possessing all the faculties of body and mind; and 4) living under the blinding influence of grossly distorted attitudes and beliefs.

The first five of the ten endowments are called personal: 1) having a complete human body; 2) being born in a land with a strong spiritual culture; 3) having all the normal faculties; 4) being free from having committed any of the five inexpiable karmic deeds; and 5) having interest in the spiritual path. The remaining five endowments are environmental: being born in an era 1) when an enlightened being has manifested; 2) when that being has taught the way; 3) when the teachings are still flourishing; 4) when followers of the lineage still exist; and 5) having the compassionate assistance of others in one's Dharma study and practice.

The first thing one must do is to recognize these qualities and identify which of them we have and which we lack. Having all eighteen is the ideal condition for Dharma practice.

We are all very fortunate to have been born in this present age. A human life in this era is extremely meaningful and powerful, being capable of achieving any goal including the exalted state of omniscient enlightenment. When we consider this fact, we realize that we have a most precious opportunity before us, and that if we waste it we will suffer a great loss. The value of recognizing the freedoms and endowments is that one will spontaneously experience the wish to use one's life in the pursuit of a meaningful existence.

To appreciate the significance of a human rebirth one only needs to contemplate the life of a hell being or ghost, or even an animal or insect. For example, a dog walking around the temple during a discourse can do little more than wag its tail and fall asleep in the sun. If we compare what it understands of the discourse and what a human understands, the contrast is obvious. This ability of humans to perceive and communicate deeper truths is spiritually very significant, because it gives us the power to look to achievements that transcend the limitations of this life alone.

It is by a stroke of good karma that we have not been reborn in the lower realms or in a time or place where the teachings of an enlightened being cannot be found, or in a black aeon when the practice of Dharma is not possible. It is also good fortune that we have not been reborn in a remote or barbaric place where the spiritual teachings have not reached. When we reflect upon these eighteen qualities from this point of view, we experience thoughts of appreciation for our auspicious situation and its rarity. What should one do when one has such a valuable opportunity? Practice Dharma and take the essence of life, the attainment of enlightenment. After the eighteen qualities have been identified, one should contemplate the meaningfulness of a precious human life. With a human body and mind one can meditate; gain an understanding of the karmic laws of cause and effect; generate a sense of the significance of the Three Jewels; cultivate the three higher trainings of discipline, meditative concentration, and the wisdom of emptiness; develop Mahayana qualities such as great compassion, love, and the bodhimind; engage in the six perfections and four ways of benefiting trainees; and practice the yogas of Highest Tantra, including the yogas of the coarse and subtle generation stage and the five steps of the completion stage. In brief, any man or woman of this southern continent who has a complete human form with the six elements and the energy channels in normal working order can engage in the practice of Highest Tantra and attain full and perfect enlightenment in this very lifetime. Of course one must also have the karmic causes that encourage successful spiritual practice, but this is another matter.

If by relying on this rare and precious human basis we can produce the highest achievement, we should take advantage of our situation and cultivate the range of spiritual practices, which are the causes of higher attainments. Through meditation upon the eighteen qualities and their meaningful nature, the confidence that one can practice Dharma and personally attain higher states of being is born. Persistence in this meditation causes this confidence to gain in strength, thus creating a solid mental basis able to support a Dharma practice.

The precious human rebirth is not only noble, but also very powerful, being able to effectively accomplish both material and spiritual goals. As this is the case, it is worthwhile to lift our vision above the lower forms of life such as the animals who know only how to satisfy material needs, and to cultivate the achievement of higher aims—the spiritual goals of higher rebirth, liberation from samsara, and omniscient illumination. However, if we do not use this human birth for meaningful purposes now we should understand that there is little possibility of our attaining a human form again in the future. To think that one will not practice Dharma in this life but will leave it for a future incarnation is a vain hope. Just as the human form is very noble and powerful, it requires noble and powerful karmic causes.

Three principal karmic causes must be cultivated if one hopes to regain human rebirth after death: pure ethical discipline, the practice of the six perfections, and strong spiritual aspirations. One can only expect to gain a human form again in the future if throughout one's life one is mindful of these causes. Moreover, the potencies of these karmic causes must be nourished and sustained without degeneration. There is little chance of acquiring a human rebirth if one lives the usual samsaric life. Even if one creates a few positive karmic forces, these quickly lose their potency when not protected and cultivated through spiritual practice. The small virtues one performs, which are generated at great effort, are quickly counteracted by the effects of negative activities which seem to arise at the slightest provocation. Goodness overcomes evil only by great exertion and persistence, whereas once the terrible force of negativity enters the mind it can quickly counteract and destroy what little goodness has been acquired, particularly in this degenerate age when most people's practice is feeble and built on weak foundations. Positive karma is generated but rarely and with little strength in our lives, whereas negative actions occur almost continually and with great strength. Even now, when we are experiencing the fruit of positive karma and as humans have met with spiritual masters and the teachings on the path to enlightenment, we nonetheless continue more in negative than positive ways because of the strength of delusion and the agitating conditions around us. This being the case even when we have excellent conditions, one can imagine the unbroken stream of negative karmic forces that one has generated in the countless previous lives during which one had no teacher, teachings, or Dharma wisdom. The imprints of these forces still live on within us and, if not purified during this life, could easily influence us during death and cause us to take a lower rebirth. The three psychic poisons of ignorance, attachment, and aversion have been with us since beginningless time and no doubt have given rise to countless negative actions of body, speech, and mind. That this is so can be known only by looking at our present imperfect state of being. Even now when we have the protection of our Dharma practice the three delusions still dominate us. How much more would they have influenced us when we had no such self-discipline? When we meditate on this fact we experience a strong spontaneous interest in cultivating spiritual attainment and eliminating the psychic poisons and the karmic patterns created by them. Such is the teaching that causes trainees of good fortune to decide to make the most of their human life.

If we ask how we can take the essence of human life, the Third Dalai Lama gives the answer in the following lines of the text.

THE THIRD DALAI LAMA

However, it is of borderline value to listen or to practice Dharma with a motivation mixed with white, black, or gray aspects of the eight worldly dharmas, i.e., the motivation to outdo enemies and protect friends, which is praised by worldly people but actually is shallow; the motivation to selfishly hoard material benefit, a universally condemned motivation; and the motivation of impressing others, which some think good and some despise. If one does not meditate upon impermanence, death, and so forth, and thus pass beyond mundane thought patterns, one runs the great risk of having negative motivations dominate one's mind. On the other hand, if one practices the pure Dharma well and with no pretenses, the foundations of lasting happiness are quickly and firmly laid.

Discard as the husk of a grain all the essenceless, worldly pursuits— works of no positive consequence and spiritually of great peril. Take up the essence of Dharma, so that at the time this pithless human body is left behind, one will not depart from life with regret. Furthermore, think to practice immediately. Drink the waters of meditation now and relieve the thirst of wishing to hold life's essence. As Jey Rinpochey said.

> Human life, found but this one time,
> More precious than the wish-fulfilling gem,
> So hard to regain and so easily lost,
> Is brief as a flash of lightning.
> Seeing this, discard worldly activity like the husk of a grain
> And strive day and night to take life's essence.

FIVE

Three Levels of Spiritual Application

HIS HOLINESS:

All the teachings given by the kind and skillful Buddha Shakyamuni were intended only to benefit beings and to fulfill their spiritual needs. These needs are twofold: the temporary attainment of a samsaric status conducive to progress and joy; and the eternal attainment of either liberation from samsara or omniscient illumination. When we speak of the path of three levels, the first path fulfills the first of these purposes—the temporary attainment of a samsaric status conducive to progress and joy. The second path fulfills the need of liberation from samsara; and the third fulfills the need for omniscient buddhahood. All practices taught by Buddha fit into one of these three paths: certain sections of the teachings aim at producing a high samsaric status, others aim at producing the liberation of nirvana; and still others aim at omniscient enlightenment.

THE THIRD DALAI LAMA:

If one should take the essence of the opportunities provided by a human vessel, how ought this to be done?

Here it is extremely important to have an understanding of the ways of generating actual experience of the general foundations of the paths and practices, and therefore I will briefly explain the process.

This explanation will be done under two headings: how the path of the three levels of spiritual application condenses all the teachings of Buddha; and the reason for leading aspirants through these three levels.

How the Path of the Three Levels of Spiritual Application Condenses All the Teachings of Buddha

Buddha himself first developed the bodhimind—the aspiration to attain perfect compassion, wisdom, and power as the best means of benefiting all sentient beings. In the end, in order to benefit all beings he actually attained full enlightenment. Then, solely for the benefit of beings he taught the holy Dharma.

The practices he taught fall into two divisions: those that aim at giving beings the temporary benefit of a high rebirth as a human or god; and those that aim at giving the two ultimate benefits of liberation from samsara and the attainment of full omniscience.

The first group of practices are known as the practices of the being of initial perspective of spiritual application. Because they are used as a basis to all higher practices, they are called "Common Dharma of Initial Perspective."

The nature of the practitioner of initial perspective is outlined in Atisha's *Lamp for the Path to Enlightenment*,

> Those who by the various methods
> Aim at higher samsaric happiness
> With their own interests in mind,
> Are known as spiritual aspirants of initial perspective.

That is to say, practitioners of the initial perspective are those who do not work for the pleasures of this life, but instead set their minds upon the practices leading to rebirth either in a heaven or as a human being.

The practices that yield ultimate benefit are of two types: those that yield nirvana, or a liberation that is merely a freedom from samsaric suffering; and those that yield the liberation possessed of omniscience. The former of these are known as the practices of the person of intermediate perspective, or "Common Dharma of Intermediate Perspective."

To quote Atisha's *Lamp for the Path to Enlightenment*,

> Those who with the aim of peace for themselves
> Turn their backs on samsaric happiness
> And reverse all negative karma
> Are known as spiritual aspirants of intermediate perspective.

That is to say, intermediate practitioners turn their backs on the securities and joys of higher samsaric positions and take up the practices of the three higher trainings—ethical discipline, concentration, and wisdom—in order to attain for themselves that liberation which is free of all cyclic compulsions, such as karma and delusion.

Finally, in addition to the Hinayana practices outlined above, the methods which accomplish the liberated state of omniscience include all the practices of the Perfection Vehicle [or exoteric Mahayana] and the Vajra Vehicle [esoteric Mahayana, or Vajrayana]. These methods are known as "Exclusive Dharma of Highest Perspective."

To quote Atisha's *Lamp for the Path to Enlightenment,*

Those who see suffering in their own lives
And, realizing that others suffer likewise,
Wish to put an end to all misery,
Are known as the spiritual aspirants of supreme scope.

In other words, supreme practitioners are those who, empowered by great compassion, take up such methods as the six perfections and the two stages of tantra in order to attain full buddhahood for themselves as a method of extinguishing the suffering of others.

This is how the path of the three perspectives of spiritual application condenses all the teachings of Buddha.

The Reason for Leading Aspirants through These Three Levels

Although the practices of all three levels of spiritual application are taught in the *Lam Rim* tradition, this is done only because it is necessary to go through the two lower perspectives of practice as branches leading to the third and highest perspective. In the *Lam Rim* tradition one does not take up the practices of lower perspective merely to gain the samsaric comfort of higher rebirth, nor does one take up those of the intermediate level merely to benefit oneself by gaining nirvana, or liberation from cyclic existence. Both are done purely as preliminaries to the practices of highest perspective. The actual body of *Lam Rim* practice is of the highest of the three.

Why is so much emphasis placed upon the practices of highest perspective? Because there is no door to the Mahayana other than the bodhimind, and this bodhimind is the unique quality of practitioners of highest perspective. One must therefore develop it.

In order to do this, one should begin by contemplating its beneficial effects and thereby generate a longing to attain it. These effects are condensed into two categories: temporary and ultimate. The temporary effect is that the bodhimind ensures the joyous fruit of a high rebirth. The ultimate effect is that it finally gives birth to the liberated, omniscient wisdom of buddhahood. Hence it is indispensable.

As a prerequisite to bodhimind, one must generate great compassion unable to tolerate the sufferings of all sentient beings.

This great compassion for others depends upon an intense awareness of the undesirable experiences and sufferings of one's own
continuum, so one first trains in the practices of lower perspective by contemplating the miseries experienced in the lower
realms. From this contemplation arises a mind which longs for
liberation from such an unsatisfactory existence.

One then enters into the intermediate practices by contemplating the transient nature of the joys of the heavens. From this contemplation arises renunciation of everything in samsara. Finally,
thinking that all mother beings face the same sufferings as does
oneself, one generates compassion [which yearns to see all beings free from suffering], love [which wishes them all to have
happiness], and then the bodhimind, the aspiration for full enlightenment as the best means to fulfill that love and compassion. Thus, leading aspirants to the highest perspective of practice by first training their minds in the two lower perspectives is
a supreme, perfect approach to Dharma.

HIS HOLINESS:

In the *Lam Rim* tradition these three paths are not taught
individually, but rather as interrelated practices. Perseverance in the first path qualifies one to practice the second,
and similarly progress in the methods of the second path
qualifies one to enter the practices of the third. Thus, neither the first nor second paths are final; rather, they are step-
ping stones to the third and highest path, that resulting in
final buddhahood.

Why did Buddha teach the three paths rather than solely
the highest? When the third path is practiced without the
foundation realizations generated on the first two, it can
easily produce the wrong effects in the mind of the practitioner, creating superiority complexes and delusions of gran-
deur. However, in fact the advanced path is not in contradiction to the two lower paths, but rather is a supplement to
and fulfillment of them. Practicing the two lower paths does
not mean moving away from the advanced path. Quite the
contrary. The lower paths strengthen and give a more balanced perspective to the higher practices, making the higher
path more integral to one's life, and thus more wholesome.
Without the first two as preliminaries it is difficult to experience the third path, the essence of which is the bodhimind.

However, although practice of the first two must precede practice of the third, it is useful from the beginning to develop an interest in the bodhimind, as it directs the lower practices into becoming causes of the higher practice. Developing such an interest is done by contemplating the excellence and beneficial effects of possessing the bodhimind.

However, it is not possible to appreciate the deeper implications of the bodhimind without the experience generated by progressing through the first two paths. Unless one has meditated on the precious nature of human life, as well as upon topics such as death, the karmic laws of cause and effect, the nature of samsara as suffering, the meaning of refuge and the three higher trainings, there is little hope of having a realistic attitude toward the bodhimind.

The bodhimind is based on great compassion, or the wish to free the sentient beings from samsaric sufferings. This basis means that one must understand the nature and patterns of the general sufferings that pervade all of samsara, as well as the specific sufferings of the individual realms, particularly the three lower realms. This awareness is generated on the first two paths. Compassion that does not understand the nature of samsaric existence is a half-hearted compassion. Thus the first two paths are very important to a practitioner hoping to enter the highest path.

THE THIRD DALAI LAMA:

> To take the essence of one's human life, there are three actual practices, or levels of practice, to be accomplished, namely, the practices of the three perspectives outlined above.

SIX

Death and the Lower Realms

THE THIRD DALAI LAMA:

The precious human form, difficult to gain and, when found, extremely meaningful, has actually been attained; one is now a human being. However, this life will not last forever, and it is definite that one will eventually die. Moreover, how long death will wait before striking is not known. Therefore, one should immediately exert oneself to take life's essence. One has had infinite previous lives in higher, lower and intermediate realms, but the Lord of Death, like a thief in a rich market place, has stolen them all indiscriminately. How fortunate that he has let one live this long! Generate a mind so filled with the awareness of death that you sit like a person hunted by a desperate assassin.

At the time of death, neither money, possessions, friends nor servants will be able to follow after you, yet the traces of any negative karma created for these objects will pursue you like a shadow. That is how you must go from life. Think it over. At the moment, one is content to eat, drink and consume, yet life, wealth, sensual objects, and food just burn on and on, and nothing is accomplished. One should fully direct whatever remains of one's life towards truly practicing Dharma. Furthermore, one should think to do so from today onward, not from tomorrow, for death may strike tonight.

HIS HOLINESS:

When we contemplate death and the impermanence of life, our minds automatically begin to take an interest in spiritual achievements, just as an ordinary person becomes apprehensive upon seeing the corpse of a friend. Meditation upon impermanence and death is very useful, for it cuts off attraction toward transient and meaningless activities, and causes the mind to turn towards Dharma.

Two principal Sutrayana methods for meditation upon death are the "three roots" technique and the method of repeatedly imagining one's death. Usually the latter of these is practiced for a time before the former.

The former method has three principal subjects of meditation: the certainty of death, the uncertainty of the time of death, and the truth that at the time of death only one's spiritual development is of value.

It is not difficult to recognize the certainty of death. The world is very old, but there is no sentient being we can point to who is immortal. The very nature of our body is vulnerability and impermanence. Beautiful or ugly, fat or thin, we all steadily approach death, and nothing can avert it. Physical power, flattery, bribery, and all things of this world cannot persuade it to turn away.

On hearing that we have a fatal disease we run frantically from one doctor to another, and when that fails we come to the lamas and ask them to do divinations to help us. Eventually we find ourselves eating our last meal, wearing clothes for the last time, and sitting on our last seat. Then our body falls to the ground like a log.

Meditation upon death gives us a type of restlessness, an uneasiness, as though somebody dangerous were watching us. This feeling is very real and useful, for, in truth, the certainty of death looms before us.

The time that death will strike is unknown to us. We do not know which will come first, tomorrow or the hereafter. None of us is able to guarantee that he or she will still be alive tonight. The slightest condition could cause us to have to suddenly part from this world. Even conditions that support life, such as food and medicine, can act as poisons and destroy one's life.

When we die, our body and all its powers are lost. Possessions, power, fame, and friends are all unable to accompany us. Take me, for example. Many Tibetans place a great deal of faith in me and would do anything I ask; but when I die I must die alone, and not one of them will be able to accompany me. All that one takes with one are knowledge of spiritual methods and karmic imprints of one's life's deeds. If throughout one's life one has practiced spiritual methods and learned the meditative techniques that prepare the mind for death, then one will maintain confidence and will be able to deal effectively and fearlessly with the experiences that occur at death. By training during life and cultivating an awareness of the death process, when eventually our breath ceases and the elements of our body gradually dissolve, we will be able to deal with the stages of the process and recognize the clear light of death when it arises. The passing of this clear light consciousness marks the exact moment of death. It is said that prior to the clear light consciousness one falls into a deep faint, and, being confused upon emerging from it, the ordinary person fails to recognize the appearance of the clear light; but someone who has trained in higher meditations recognizes the stages of death and establishes a mindfulness upon entering the faint. Thus one transforms the effects of this very subtle state of consciousness, and when one emerges from it recognizes the clear light of death. Even after the clear light has terminated and one leaves the body to enter the intermediate state, one is able to recognize the bardo as the bardo and to experience the hallucinations and visions that occur with equanimity and insight. At this point the ordinary person falls under the power of anger, attachment, ignorance, etc., and evolves accordingly. The spiritually trained being abides in wisdom and serenity. The clear light of death is transformed into the perfect Wisdom Body, and the bardo experience into the pure Beatific Body. To fulfill their aspirations to benefit beings, spiritually trained persons can then direct their rebirth as desired anywhere throughout the universe.

Those of us who are unable to engage in these yogic practices at death should at least try to apply clear mindfulness throughout the process and to maintain thoughts of love, compassion, and the bodhimind. It is also very beneficial to recollect one's guru and the Three Jewels of Refuge, praying to them for guidance. This will help one to enter the bardo in a spiritual frame of mind, which in turn ensures a high rebirth conducive to further spiritual progress.

We all carry within our mindstream infinitely numerous instincts of both positive and negative past activities. The principal hope of an untrained person is, that by maintaining a positive stream of thought while dying, he or she will activate a strong, positive karmic instinct at the precise moment of death, thus causing this instinct to be the dominating influence throughout the bardo experience. This is the best approach for an untrained person. The yogi and the ordinary being have quite different methods at their disposal.

We should direct our mind at death as stated above. As for our environment, it is important that during or after one's death the room is not filled with crying or lamenting people, or any kind of event that could upset the mind of the dying person.

It is not common for someone who has lived a negative life to have positive thoughts at death or a controlled experience in the bardo. Therefore, from now on we should be mindful of death and should engage in the practices that generate spiritual qualities, qualities that will not only benefit us in this lifetime, but will provide us with the ability to face death and the bardo competently.

Thus, in the "three roots" death meditation, we contemplate that death is certain and resolve to practice Dharma; we contemplate the uncertainty of the time of death and resolve to practice immediately; and we contemplate that only Dharma wisdom is of value at that time and resolve to practice Dharma purely.

Now that as humans we have met with spiritual teachings and have met a teacher, we should not be like a beggar doing nothing meaningful year after year, ending up empty-handed at death. I, an ordinary monk in the lineage of Buddha Shakyamuni, humbly urge you to make efforts in spiritual practice. Examine the nature of your mind and cultivate its development. Take into account your welfare in this and future existences, and develop competence in the methods that produce happiness here and hereafter. Our lives are impermanent and so are the holy teachings. We should cultivate our practice carefully.

How does Dharma help us and non-Dharma harm us at the time of death? The love and compassion of the Enlightened Ones are not sufficient forces to save us. If they were, they would have done so in any of the previous death experiences we have known since beginningless time. To do nothing from our side is like trying to clap with one hand.

THE THIRD DALAI LAMA:

You may ask: If, with the exception of Dharma, nothing helps at the time of death, then how does Dharma help? And how does non-Dharma harm?

At death one does not simply evaporate. Death is followed by rebirth, and whether my rebirth is happy or miserable, high or low, is determined by the state of my mind at the time of death. Now, except for the power of karma, ordinary people are powerless. They must take the rebirth thrown to them by the force of their black and white karmas, or psychic impressions left by previous deeds of body, speech and mind. If at the time of death a positive thought predominates, a happy rebirth follows. If a negative thought predominates, one is born into an appropriate dimension of the three lower realms, where intense pain must be suffered.

What are the torments of the three lower realms? To quote Acharya Nagarjuna,

Remember that in the lower hells
One burns like a sun, and
In the upper hells one freezes.
Remember how ghosts and spirits
Suffer from hunger, thirst, and climate.
Remember how animals suffer
The consequences of stupidity.
Abandon the karmic causes of such misery
And cultivate the causes of joy.
Human life is rare, and precious;
Do not make it a cause of pain.
Take heed; use it well.

As Nagarjuna implies, the sufferings of the hot and cold hells are unendurable, the sufferings of ghosts are horrendous, and the sufferings of animals—eating one another, being domesticated and dominated by humans, being dumb and so forth—are overwhelming. At the moment we cannot hold our hand in fire for even a few seconds. We cannot sit naked on ice in the

winter for more than a few minutes. To pass even a single day
without eating or drinking anything is considered a great difficulty, and merely the tiny sting of a bee seems terrible. How then
will you be able to bear the heat or cold of the hells, the anguish
of a ghost, or the horrors of animal existence?

Meditate on the sufferings of the lower realms until you are
filled with terror and apprehension. Now that you have gained
the auspicious human form, abandon the causes of lower rebirth
and cultivate the causes of a positive one. Determine to apply
yourself to the methods which cut off the road to the lower realms.

HIS HOLINESS:

Some people doubt the existence of the hell realms. However, many independent world cultures speak of these
realms, and there are people with clairvoyant powers who
can perceive them. In Buddhism it is said that through meditation we can develop certain extraordinary powers of
memory ourselves and thus recollect some of our previous
lives, in which case we would be able to remember our own
experiences in hell.

There are many levels of natural law that are beyond the
comprehension of ordinary beings and can only be perceived
by beings with highly developed states of consciousness.
The working of the laws of karma is one of these more subtle
truths.

No two human beings have identical bodies or minds. Each
of us is fully unique, down to the smallest hair, wrinkle or
muscular feature. Why are we so complicated? Why are the
animals and insects individually so unique? This is where
the Buddhist theory of karma and its evolution comes into
focus. But more of that later.

Numerous Buddhist scriptures write of the hells in very
real terms, to the extent that they describe their precise loca-
tions and so forth. Whether or not these realms are exter-
nally real places or whether they are merely states of mind
is a point of debate within Buddhism. Shantideva wrote,
"Who created the guardians and weapons of torture in the
hells? Indeed they are formed from the karmic imprints that
one carries within one's mindstream." However, whether
they are external states or are merely states of mind does

not affect our problem—how to avoid experiencing them. If we find ourselves in the hell realms, the experience of suffering will be inevitable. The types of sufferings characteristic of the hells—intense heat, cold, physical torture, etc.— are not impossible experiences, not something beyond human imagination.

Were the hells and the other realms of suffering not to exist, there would not be much need for Dharma study and practice. But if we look around us we can see that we are enmeshed by suffering on every side. How can we expect similar conditions not to be present with us after the body dies? But then we have no wealth, power, friends or even a body with which to protect ourselves. There is nothing but our positive and negative karmic imprints and our spiritual understanding or lack of it. When one is without wisdom and is carrying the imprints of mainly negative karmic actions, the bardo will transform into hellish visions and one's heart will fill with regret. It would have been better not to have been so proud and confident in the supposed non-existence of the hells when one still possessed the powers of discernment.

The practitioner of initial perspective thus pursues prolonged meditation upon the types of sufferings of the individual hell realms and determines to abandon the causes of these lower rebirths—negative actions performed from a deluded mind. This meditation should be regularly performed, not only for a few days, but for months on end, until one develops a natural aversion to engaging in degenerating activities. At the moment, we make great efforts to protect ourselves from cold, heat, insect bites and so forth. Would it not be wise to also protect ourselves from future sufferings of this nature by avoiding their causes, negative activities of body, speech, and mind?

The scriptures abound in descriptions of the nature of the various hells. They speak of four main types: the eight hot hells; the eight cold hells; the four hells surrounding the lower hells; and the occasional hells where beings have periodic respite. Each of these realms is described as having a different intensity of misery, duration of lifespan and so forth. Their main characteristic is violently intense suffering, and their main cause is negative karma created by violent anger and the harming of others.

I really wish that there were no suffering in this world and no suffering after death. I wish there were no hells or ghost regions. But it would not be wise to believe that these do not exist and to continue in the negative ways that draw the mind down to these realms. The distance between our present existence and the hells could be as short as a single breath.

Negative ways do not have beneficial effects on the mind even in this life. If there is a future life, how can we expect negativity to benefit it? Alternatively, positive ways have positive effects on the mind in this life and lay the foundations for happiness after death. One should contemplate the sufferings of the hells in this light and resolve to avoid the ways that lead to them.

The ghost realms also cannot be seen by ordinary people dwelling in this realm, although there are isolated incidents of inter-realm contact between beings having strong karmic connections. Again, many world cultures have independently spoken of these realms, and many mystics and clairvoyants have written of them.

The principal afflictions of ghosts are intense hunger and thirst. Although they are tortured continually by these cravings, they do not die for many centuries. The main cause for rebirth in this realm is negative karma created out of attachment and greed. One should dwell in contemplation of the sufferings of the ghost realms and resolve to avoid the negative karmas that cause them. At the moment, we find it difficult even to practice a religious fast for half a day; how could we bear a thousand years of such cravings?

The sufferings of the animal realms are obvious to us. Work and farm animals experience being driven, beaten, killed, and eaten by human beings. We would go to an institution and claim our human rights if someone tried to do these things to us, but animals can do nothing but look on pathetically. The fish in the Kangra Lake are not respected as owning the lake; to the humans they are merely sources of food. We forget they are living beings who, like us, grasp at an "I" and aspire to happiness. We forget that they do not want pain and do not want to die, and we pull them out of the water on hooks and in nets, causing them to die in fear and agony. The same is the case with chickens, cattle, goats and so forth. There is nobody they can turn to for help, and they do not have the intelligence to help themselves. This is the karma and suffering of their realm. We should meditate on what we would experience if we were reborn amongst them.

The wild animals, birds, insects and so forth usually suffer even more intensely. Theirs is the jungle law, and the old and the weak are devoured alive. Continually having to chase food and seek shelter, they often experience long periods of deprivation. Their great shortcoming is lack of wisdom, and as a result they are unable to cultivate spiritual progress. Thus their lives are controlled by the forces of karma and delusion, until eventually they die in terror.

We should meditate upon the various sufferings of the animal world and then ask ourselves, "Do I want this suffering? Could I bear it?" If you do not, then make a resolution to avoid its cause, meaningless and deluded activity based upon the ignorant mind.

In this and in many previous existences we have created many karmas that could result in rebirth in any of the three lower realms. We should cease creating such causes and should seek the methods that purify the mind of previous karmic instincts and elevate it from darkness to lasting joy.

SEVEN

Seeking a Place of Refuge

HIS HOLINESS:

A spiritual aspirant requires a model, something he or she can look up to as an ideal and thus find guidance and inspiration. In Buddhism this is the Triple Gem, or the Three Jewels of Refuge: the Buddhas, Dharma and Sangha.

When we think of the fully enlightened Buddhas—the beings who have purified their minds of all stains and obscurations and who have expanded their wisdom to the limits of existence—we feel very attracted and awed; but somehow there always seems to be a great distance between the Buddhas and us. Therefore, there is the refuge of Sangha, the community of spiritual aspirants, the assembly of practitioners dwelling in the various stages of practice and attainment. These beings provide us with a perspective on the path. We have to look up to the Sangha, but not as far as to the Buddhas. The Sangha make us think, "This person is not that far ahead of me. If I just make a bit more effort...." They give us confidence for spiritual practice. Sometimes they make us feel like we can even race them to enlightenment. These are the Sangha of spiritual friends.

Thoughts of the Buddhas make us numb with admiration; thoughts of the Sangha cause us to jump to it and to apply ourselves with zeal to the spiritual path. This path and the methods for traversing it are the third Jewel of Refuge, the Dharma. This is the collection of teachings to be practiced and the realizations to be attained.

THE THIRD DALAI LAMA:

What exactly are the methods which cut off the road to lower rebirth? As explained above, fear of the sufferings of lower rebirth is useful. Also, recognition that the Buddha, the Dharma, and the Sangha have power to guide one away from such rebirth is helpful. Generate this fear by means of meditation and then turn to these Three Supreme Jewels from the depths of your heart.

HIS HOLINESS:

There are different ways to speak of the Jewels of Refuge. In terms of time sequence, the first to appear historically is a Buddha, a fully enlightened one. He gives birth to the Jewel of Dharma, the teachings on the way to enlightenment. From the practice of the Dharma there then appears the community of trainees on the various levels, the Sangha.

How can these Three Jewels benefit us? Buddhas have four qualities that make them effective objects of refuge: they are free from samsaric imperfection together with its fears and sufferings; they have omniscient skill in teaching the paths to enlightenment; they dwell in perfect compassion for every living being; and they have equanimity towards all. The Sangha also possesses these four qualities, although to a limited degree. The Dharma has the capacity to generate the qualities within us.

It is important that all four qualities are present in an object of spiritual refuge. If spiritual teachers are not free from mundane existence, they will not be able to lead others to freedom. If they do not have omniscient skill, they will not be able to lead trainees in accordance with the complexities of their karmic backgrounds and their individual spiritual dispositions. If they do not have great compassion they will choose to dwell in meditative bliss rather than to teach; and if their compassion is partial there is a doubt that they will choose to benefit us at all and, even if they choose to teach us, that they will have the patience to lead us through the challenges of practice.

How did the Enlightened Ones attain the state of omniscient buddhahood? By purifying and expanding their minds through the practice of Dharma, which out of compassion they later teach. Our Buddha Shakyamuni trained under many masters over a string of lifetimes. Eventually his practice of Dharma transported him to enlightenment.

Thus it is said that Dharma is the actual refuge, the Enlightened Ones are the teachers of refuge, and the Sangha the friends of refuge. If we admire the Enlightened Ones, how can we not admire the force that brought them to enlightenment?

Dharma, or the teachings, is not a series of instructions to be believed and followed out of blind faith. The practice of Dharma should be carried out on the basis of reason and contemplation. If one accepts a point of practice or doctrine out of blind faith, one is accepting it for the wrong reasons and in the wrong way. Whenever I myself encounter a contradiction between doctrine and reason, I always give priority to reason. Buddha taught many levels and types of doctrines in dependence upon the quality of his audiences, and we must discern for ourselves what was meant literally and what only figuratively.

THE THIRD DALAI LAMA:

How do the Three Jewels have the power to protect one from the terrors of the lower realms? The Jewel of Buddha is himself free from all fear and, being omniscient, is a master of ways which protect from every fear. Also, as he abides in great compassion that sees all sentient beings with equanimity, he is a worthy object of refuge for both those who are beneficial to him and those who are not. In that he himself has these qualities, it follows that his teachings and the Sangha established by him should also be worthy. This cannot be said of the founders of many religious schools, few of whom were perfect; nor of many doctrines, most of which are filled with logical faults; nor of many religious traditions, most of which are fragmented. Because Buddha, Dharma and Sangha possess these sublime qualities, they indeed are worthy.

How does one go for refuge to the Three Supreme Jewels? Chant three times, "I go for refuge to the perfect Buddha. Pray, show me how to become free from the sufferings of samsara in general and from the lower realms in particular. I go for refuge to the desireless, supreme Dharma. Pray, be my actual refuge and lead me to freedom from the terrors of samsara in general and the lower realms in particular. I go for refuge to the supreme Sangha, the Spiritual Community. Pray, protect me from the misery of samsara and especially from the lower realms." While reciting these lines, generate an actual sense of seeking inspiration from the Buddha, Dharma and Sangha within the depths of your heart.

HIS HOLINESS:

One takes refuge in the Buddhas by recollecting the Enlightened Ones, the supreme beings possessing omniscient wisdom, and by requesting them to turn the Wheel of Dharma and to be one's spiritual guides. Here we take both the causal refuge in the Buddhas as the external model and the resultant refuge of our own attainment of buddhahood.

One then recollects the Dharma, which calms desires and brings one to the state of liberation from all worldly craving. Why is desire specified from amongst the numerous psychic poisons? For although ignorance is more pervasive an affliction than desire, it is said in the scriptures that desire is the force most immediately binding us to samsaric life. As Dharma is the agent erasing samsara, it is thus called "desireless."

The practice of Dharma, which is the fourth Noble Truth expounded by Buddha, gives rise to the Noble Truth of cessation, the third truth, which is the state of nirvana wherein mental distortion is totally pacified. Our actual refuge then is the Dharma, both as the Noble Truth of the path to be practiced and the Noble Truth of cessation to be generated within our continuum.

Thirdly, one turns to the Sangha Jewel, the supreme community, the assembly of spiritual aspirants who rank among the most exalted of the world's beings. Reflecting upon their excellence, one requests them to be one's friends and guides on the path to enlightenment.

Generally it is said that two causes are required in order for one's refuge to be solid: apprehension of the unsatisfactory nature of lower forms of being; and recognition that by relying upon the objects of refuge one will be able to transcend to higher states. If one generates these two causes and reads the lines of the text while recollecting the qualities of the Jewels of Refuge, there is no doubt that a strong sense of refuge will be born.

THE THIRD DALAI LAMA:

However, taking refuge but then not observing the refuge precepts is of very little benefit and the power of having taken refuge is soon lost. Therefore, be always mindful of the precepts. Having taken refuge in the Buddha, no longer rely upon worldly gods such as Shiva and Vishnu, but see all statues and images of Buddha as actual manifestations of Buddha himself. If you have taken refuge in the Dharma, never again harm a fellow sentient being and never show disrespect toward the holy scriptures. And finally, refuge in the Sangha means that you should no longer waste your time with false teachers or with unhelpful or misleading friends, and that you should never show disrespect toward saffron or maroon cloth.

Also, understanding that every temporary and ultimate happiness is a result of the kindness of the Three Supreme Jewels, make a small offering of your food and drink to them at every mealtime, and rely upon them rather than upon politicians or fortune tellers for all your immediate and ultimate needs. As well, in accordance with your spiritual strength, show others the significance of refuge in the Three Jewels and don't ever forsake your own refuge, not even in jest or to save your life.

HIS HOLINESS:

Once one has taken refuge in the Three Jewels one should try to integrate the refuge precepts. Each of the Three Jewels has one precept concerning an activity to be avoided and one concerning an activity to be practiced. If we have placed our refuge in Buddha, we should no longer seek ultimate protection from worldly gods and spirits, although they may certainly be propitiated occasionally for specific needs. However, because they are jealous they could easily harm us and our practice if we become too involved in them, so we should not regard them as ultimate sources of refuge.

The precept to be practiced is the advice to regard all images of the Enlightened Ones as being actual manifestations of the beings they represent and not to regard them as being superior or inferior on the basis of artistic value. All sacred images should be honored as being the Buddhas themselves. Then the image serves the intended purpose. Nonetheless, artists should try to produce high quality works, or they only cause people to create negative karma by being disrespectful. For example, people are constantly bringing paintings and statues to me for consecration, and even though throughout the consecration ritual I should respect the image as being Buddha himself, sometimes I find it hard not to burst out laughing at the sight of crooked noses and drooping jaws. Artists should not take this precept to mean that they need not take care for the quality of their work. A well-made work will have both artistic and spiritual value, whereas a poorly made work is sometimes little more than an embarrassment.

The conduct to be avoided once refuge in Dharma has been taken is the harming of sentient beings. Since the Enlightened Ones teach the Dharma solely out of compassion, anyone with refuge in Dharma should respect this compassion and turn from harmful ways. The precept to be practiced is to regard all scriptures as being embodiments of the Dharma and to treat them with an according respect. Anyone publishing and selling Dharma scriptures should be careful to do so on the basis of benefit for others and not with thoughts of profit.

The activity to be avoided by anyone holding refuge in the Sangha is spending too much time with people who teach or follow wrong paths, and whose influence hinders one's practice and disturbs one's mind. The precept to be practiced here is to regard all beings who wear the monastic robes as embodiments of the Sangha itself and respect them as Arya Sangha beings who have transcended worldly limitations through the wisdom of emptiness. Whenever the great Upasika Drom Tonpa would pass even a discarded piece of cloth of the same color as that of monks' robes, he would pick it up, touch it to his head, and recite the refuge formula. Lay people should try to honor the Sangha in this way, and monks and nuns should be conscientious about this respect and use it to inspire them in practice rather than to become proud and arrogant.

The precept of avoiding spending an excessive amount of time with teachers who expound paths contradictory to Buddhist tenets must be applied with wisdom and tolerance. The point is only to avoid creating unnecessary instability in one's practice. We should respect all other religions and their teachers; but if the teacher is speaking in ways that will disrupt our practice, it will create problems in our path to attainment. When the Fifth Dalai Lama was appointed as the overlord of Tibet in the mid-seventeenth century, he passed laws giving equal rights and footing to the old Bön religion. He also passed laws protecting them from encroachment by the Buddhists. Bön thrived freely in Tibet until the present day, and many Bönpo came into self-exile after the Chinese invasion and persecution of religion. There was also a large Muslim community in Tibet, which had full religious freedom. The Tibetan attitude is that if people do not have a karmic link with the Dharma, one should let them go their own way. Different teachers expound different paths in order to satisfy the variety of human dispositions, not to create discord. The Sangha precept to avoid teachers of wrong paths is not intended in any way to create sectarian attitudes. The aim is to maintain a solid, concentrated, well-directed practice.

Three times during the day and three times at night we should recollect the qualities of the Three Jewels and recite the refuge formula. Never break the refuge precepts even in jest nor use their names derogatorily. When old Tibetans would get angry they would say as an expletive, "Ah, the Three Jewels!" And I am told that after the Chinese invasion, when my name became something of a religious symbol to the people of Lhasa, children picked up the habit of using it as a swear word, "Ah, Yeshin Norbu!" This made the Chinese angry and they told the children that if they wished to curse they should use the name of Chairman Mao instead, "Ah, Mao Tse-tung!" They managed to get a few small children to use his name as a swear-word for a short time. Sometimes the Chinese communists really seem silly.

THE THIRD DALAI LAMA:

With awareness of the need to avoid wasting time on mere words, recite the following refuge formula three times during the day and three times during the night: *NAMO GURU BHYAH, NAMO BUDDHA YA, NAMO DHARMA YA, NAMO SANGHA YA.* While doing so, maintain awareness of the unsurpassed qualities of the Three Jewels, and of their individual uniqueness and commitments.

HIS HOLINESS:

When one meditates on taking refuge in the Three Jewels, one should first generate a recollection of their individual qualities and potencies. This can be an extensive topic, for taking refuge in Buddha means that one should meditate on the qualities, wisdoms and powers of a Buddha's body, speech and mind; refuge in Dharma means that one meditates on all the paths and practices leading to the truth of cessation [of suffering], or the peace of nirvana; and refuge in the Sangha requires an awareness of the twenty types of Sangha and so forth.

As refuge involves all the paths and stages to enlightenment as well as the types of beings dwelling on the paths and beyond, it is a subject that can be explained in brief or expanded into many volumes. One of the best Indian scriptures in terms of its depth and completeness of presentation of the paths, stages, and types of spiritual beings is Maitreya's *Ornament of Clear Comprehension.* When one experiences refuge based on an understanding of the great treatises such as this, one's refuge becomes correct and effective.

One should take refuge in the Three Jewels by understanding their unique natures and individual functions. The function afforded by refuge in Buddha is spiritual guidance; the function of refuge in Dharma is practice; and the function of refuge in the Sangha is spiritual support. With these three aids one has all that is required to traverse the paths and stages and to attain higher states of being, liberation and enlightenment.

EIGHT

The Laws of Karmic Evolution

THE THIRD DALAI LAMA:

One may wonder: Granted, abiding in refuge in the Three Jewels can protect me from the misery of lower rebirth; but how can I produce the causes which bring about a higher rebirth? For this we must consider the four aspects of karmic law: positive and negative deeds plant seeds that will bear respective fruit, i.e., goodness produces future happiness and evil produces future misery; one seed produces many fruits, each of which has many seeds of a like nature; a deed not done produces no result; and every deed one does in body, speech or mind leaves a karmic seed in one's continuum that is never exhausted [unless worked out or neutralized by spiritual exercises]. When one has contemplated these four aspects of karmic law, the importance of living in accordance with the teachings of abandoning negativity and cultivating the good becomes obvious.

To prove the laws of karma solely by means of the force of logic is an extremely difficult and lengthy process, and only a person well versed in logical reasoning could even follow the process. So instead, I will quote a verse from the *King of Absorptions Sutra*,

> Moon and stars may fall to earth,
> Mountains and valleys may crumble
> And even the sky may disappear;
> But you, O Buddha, speak nothing false.

Bearing these words in mind we can consider the following teaching from Buddha himself,

> From evil comes suffering;
> Therefore day and night
> One should think and re-think
> About how to escape misery forever.

And also,

> The roots of all goodness lie
> In the soil of appreciation for goodness.

> Constantly meditate upon how to ripen
> The fruits that can grow therefrom.

HIS HOLINESS:

The main precept of refuge is to develop mindfulness of karmic law. For this one must first gain an understanding of the principles of karma and its evolution, and then try to practice accordingly.

It is said that when one generates clairvoyance one is able to perceive coarser levels of the workings of karma, and that a fully enlightened being sees the most subtle karmic cause of every event. For the ordinary person, however, knowledge of the karmic laws of cause and effect is something acquired only in reliance upon the scriptures. There are a number of logical treatises establishing the theory of karma through the use of reason, but these can only be understood through extensive study.

The Third Dalai Lama gives the quote, "But you, O Buddha, speak nothing false." Before ordinary persons will be able to feel inclined to rely upon the scriptures, they must first gain respect for the Enlightened One. They must be able to open themselves to the teachings. This respect can be generated in some beings by meditating upon the qualities and characteristics of the Buddha, Dharma, and Sangha. But a superior method is to first study the teachings on the two levels of reality—ultimate and conventional—with emphasis upon the subject of emptiness.

The doctrine of emptiness is both vast and profound, and an understanding of it gives one great confidence in the general teachings. In this context Lama Tsongkhapa wrote, "Insight into the teachings on relativity enhances appreciation for all Buddha's works."

The two fundamental spiritual aims are higher rebirth and ultimate goodness. The latter of these means either of two states: the liberation of nirvana or the omniscience of enlightenment. Ultimate goodness is a more sublime goal than higher rebirth, and the teachings on it are all based on logic and reason. The teachings on the laws of karma, the understanding and practice of which results in higher rebirth, can only be presented to the ordinary person on the basis of scriptural evidence. When we study the higher teachings on ultimate goodness and gain an understanding of them by analyzing them carefully with logical reason, contemplating them deeply, and seeing how they coincide with our own experiences in life, we gain a confidence in them that is based on our own reflections. This opens our heart to the teachings of the Enlightened Ones. We come to feel that since Buddha gave such profound, logical instructions on the nature of the self and the deeper levels of truth, then surely his other doctrines will be correct. The study of scriptures dealing with emptiness, the ultimate nature of things, is beneficial not only because it cuts off the ugly head of ego-grasping, but also because it enhances our openness towards all the teachings, including those such as the doctrine of karma, that we will only be able to personally verify as true when we gain higher meditative attainments.

Fundamental to all schools of Buddhism is the doctrine of the Four Noble Truths: the truths that imperfect existence is enmeshed in suffering; that this suffering has a cause; that there is a state wherein there is a cessation of suffering; and that there is a spiritual path leading to the state beyond all suffering. These must also be understood in their sequential order: from the cause of suffering arises the reality of suffering; from the cause of practicing the path arises the reality wherein there is a cessation of suffering. Thus the first two Truths describe samsara and how we wander in it, the latter two refer to ultimate peace and how we attain it.

The initial levels of teachings— those on how to avoid degenerating into the lower states of being and on how to attain the states of a human or god— are thus mostly connected with the first two Truths. Their theme is how to abandon samsaric suffering and gain samsaric happiness. The teachings for gaining liberation and omniscience, the respective goals of practitioners of medium and great perspectives, are mostly related to the second two Truths.

Traditionally in *Lam Rim* literature the teachings of the three perspectives are given in accordance with the nature of the spiritual quality to be experienced by the trainee at his or her specific level of attainment. A problem here is that as the practices of initial perspective are mostly related to the first two Truths, which describe samsara and its evolution, their principal subjects revolve around the doctrine of karma. Now, as I said earlier, unless one has clairvoyance or omniscience one has to rely upon the scriptures in order to formulate an understanding of the laws of karma. Thus, in order to follow the traditional approach we require strong faith, a requirement that somewhat contradicts Buddha's advice always to proceed on the basis of reason.

My own feeling is that as a preliminary to *Lam Rim* practice, one should study scriptures such as Nagarjuna's *Fundamental Treatise on Wisdom* and Chandrakirti's *Guide to the Middle View*. These works are the essential substances of the teachings on penetrative wisdom into emptiness, which are usually given at higher stages of *Lam Rim* training [as in the case of the *Essence of Refined Gold*]. Through studying the wisdom teachings on emptiness, one gains an understanding of how all living beings have an innate grasping at an "I" that simply does not exist in the same mode as it appears. Thus this "I" that appears to us is false, like a rope that we think is a snake. All objects of knowledge—tables, chairs and so forth—are empty of the inherent "I" status that we give to them. The wisdom teachings then describe how this false concept of "I" interferes with our perception of everything and gives rise to the entire host of delusions and negative activities.

When we study the scriptures on these subjects we are encouraged to question and reason to the fullest extent. Nothing is to be taken on faith alone. By persisting in our study, we experience how an understanding of the emptiness of the false "I" pacifies the mind of distortion and lessens delusions, thus enhancing mental peace. This gives one confidence in the last two Noble Truths—the cessation of suffering and the path to cessation—and this confidence in turn renders one's mind more receptive to the first two Noble Truths and the doctrine of karma around which they revolve.

On the basis of this confidence one will be able to accept the Four Noble Truths and engage in the practice of Dharma.

This roundabout way of establishing the validity of karmic law is not perfectly sound, but it is sufficiently convincing to open our mind to the Four Truths to the degree that we will be able to pursue further practice and attain deeper and more conclusive experiences.

THE THIRD DALAI LAMA:

As is here implied, one should in general abandon all negative activity and in particular should contemplate the four unpleasant aspects of the ten non-virtues of the body, speech, and mind: killing, stealing, and wrong sexual activity [such as having intercourse near a temple or near the guru's house, having intercourse on a new or full moon, taking more than five orgasms in one night, etc.]; lying, speaking harshly, slandering others, or indulging in meaningless babble; and holding thoughts of attachment, ill-will or holding wrong views.

To show the four unpleasant aspects of karma by the example of the results of killing: *(i) the main effect* is lower rebirth; *(ii) the effect similar to the cause* is that in a future rebirth you will be killed or will see many dear ones killed; *(iii) the effect similar to the action* is that you will have the tendency to kill again in future lives and thus will multiply the negative karma; and *(iv) the effect on the environment* is that even if you gain a good rebirth your environment will be violent.

The effect is also graded into minor, medium, and heavy degrees, depending upon the object. For example, killing a human results in rebirth in hell, killing an animal results in rebirth as a ghost, and killing an insect results in animal rebirth.

Keep in mind these words from *Chapter of the Truthful One,*

O King, do not kill,
For all that lives cherishes life.
If you wish to live long yourself, respect life
And do not even think of killing.

HIS HOLINESS:

The cause of suffering is said to be negative karma and delusion. In this case, karma refers to the actions that leave an imprint of an according nature upon the mind-stream. A negative action is defined simply as any action that has suffering as its result, and conversely a positive action as any action having happiness as its result. Both positive and negative actions leave karmic instincts on the mind, instincts that lie dormant within us until one day the appropriate conditions manifest to activate them. If the ripening instinct is positive, one experiences happiness; if negative, one experiences suffering.

Karma has four main characteristics. The first is its increasing effect: goodness heralds further goodness and evil heralds further evil. Secondly, karma is definite: in the long run, goodness always produces joy and negativity always produces suffering. Thirdly, one never experiences a joy or sorrow that does not have an according karmic cause. And lastly, the karmic seeds that are placed on the mind at the time of an action will never lose their potency even in a hundred million lifetimes, but will lie dormant within the mind until one day the conditions that activate them appear.

Therefore the first thing the practitioner of initial perspective has to learn at this point is which actions are positive and which negative, which are to be cultivated and which abandoned.

THE THIRD DALAI LAMA:

As said here, one should rely upon an attitude resolved not to entertain thoughts of any evil action, such as killing and the rest of the ten negative deeds. All forms of evil should be abandoned, and one should strive with all one's might to actualize goodness. To quote Jey Rinpochey,

There is no certainty that after death lower rebirth
   does not await you,
But there is certainty that the Three Jewels
   have power to protect you from it.
Therefore, base yourself upon refuge
And let not the refuge precepts degenerate.
Also, consider the working of black and white actions.
Practicing correctly is your own responsibility.

HIS HOLINESS:

The negative courses of action to be abandoned are tenfold. Three of these refer to physical actions: killing, stealing, and misuse of sexuality. Four are of speech: lying, speaking cruelly, slander, and meaningless talk. The last three are mental actions: attachment, harmful thoughts, and wrong views. By avoiding these ten and dwelling in their opposites we practice the ten virtues.

What are the effects of the ten negative courses of action? In the example of killing, violence shortens this life and creates karmic causes for oneself to be killed in a future life. Becoming familiar with killing means that one's mind becomes more prone to engaging in killing in the future. If we kill in this lifetime we are reborn with a pleasure for killing. We can see this reflected in the behavior of young children. Some infants seem to totally enjoy killing. Whenever they see an insect they run up and step on it, laughing with joy. Sometimes they capture animals and torture them to death. Such actions demonstrate a familiarity with killing gained in previous lives. On the other hand, children who show compassion and who cannot bear to see anything harmed reflect the way positive karmic seeds can influence our lives from birth.

As Buddhists we should try to avoid the ten negative karmas throughout this life, or at least to steadily reduce them.

It is difficult to totally avoid the ten negative ways. For example, what if we get bedbugs? If I were to say not to kill them, I doubt that many would take the advice. And I myself would find it unpleasant to live in a bed infested with bugs. Therefore I always recommend prevention of the difficulty as the best solution. Hygiene, cleanliness, simplicity, and conscientiousness can prevent most insect and rodent problems from arising.

Killing and eating meat are interrelated, so do we have to give up eating animal products? I myself once tried to give it up, but health problems arose and two years later my doctors advised me to again use meat in my diet. If there are people who can give up eating meat, we can only rejoice in their noble efforts. In any case, at least we should try to lessen our intake of meat and not eat it anywhere where it is in scarce supply and our consumption of it would cause added slaughter.

Although as a result of the climate and environment of our country we Tibetans have been a race of meat-eaters, the Mahayana teachings on compassion have had a mitigating effect. All Tibetans are aware of the expression, "All sentient beings, my mothers in previous lives." The nomads, who did most of the animal husbandry—who came on pilgrimage to Lhasa wearing long fur overcoats rolled down to their waists even in the middle of winter, a bundle of blessing strings hanging down upon their naked chests— were completely familiar with "All beings, previously my mother." Although they looked rather like a band of robbers and thieves, they were spiritual people with faith in the Mahayana. But they were nomads with no source of subsistence except for animal flesh. They would always kill their animals as humanely as possible while whispering prayers into their ears. In Lhasa a popular meritorious practice was to buy and release an animal destined for slaughter. If ever an animal were to become sick and die, the people could be seen sprinkling holy water on it and making prayers. Throughout the country it was illegal to kill any wild animals with the exception of the wolf, who is the enemy of the nomad, and the rodent, the enemy of the farmer.

The second negative karma is stealing. The negative influence that stealing introduces into society is obvious. Walk up to somebody on the street at random and call them a thief. I doubt that they will be flattered. If there is one thief in a city of 100,000 people, there is one thief too many. As Buddhists we should never consider stealing and we should discourage and prevent others from engaging in it. If we should catch anybody stealing we should advise against it; and, if that person does not accept our advice, we should maintain a sense of compassionate responsibility and threaten them. An orderly society requires people with a sense of personal responsibility for peace and harmony. By permitting people to steal we only contribute to their collection of negative karma and to the degeneration of the society in which we and our children must live.

Instead of stealing, we should give to the poor and to needy causes. This would be far more beneficial for our minds and for the karmic patterns we weave.

Misuse of sexuality mainly refers to adultery, which is a principal cause of family problems. In ancient days entire wars were fought as a result of adultery. It disturbs the life of a palace just as it disrupts the life of the most humble and lowly household. Then there are psychological problems caused in the minds of children of families broken and divided because of adultery, children who do not know their father, who never see his face. Having no father, the child will lack natural paternal warmth and will often feel confused and melancholy. This lack will leave an impression on the mind that will last throughout life.

A Western friend once described to me the lightness with which sexuality is sometimes treated in the West, and asked me what I thought of promiscuity. I replied that I doubt if it ever has much spiritual value and that in most cases I suspect it produces more suffering than joy in the long run. As for specific advice, I told him that personally I think that couples who do not want to live together long enough to raise a family should make every effort not to produce children. Other than that, provided that all parties involved agree and nobody is harmed, people can do what they like. My main concern is the mind of any child who may be involved. Our children are our only hope for the future.

The first of the negative sources of speech is lying. Truth and integrity are valuable characteristics, even if we are not involved in religious training. The understanding of someone who has studied the five great treatises is proved superficial by a single lie. As said in the story of Gyalpo Depa Tenpo, "Truth is everlasting but falsity has no existence." Falsity is based upon fiction, not fact, so it has no solid foundation. On the other hand, truth is based on fact and thus its supports are strong. Therefore, although falsity may benefit us for a while, there is little hope that it can bring about a stable happiness. All members of a society are mutually interdependent, so how does it benefit their lives and the lives of their children if all they do is propagate falsity and distortion? Social harmony relies upon trust, and if we suspect that our neighbors never utter a dependable word it is difficult to establish an acceptable relationship with them. One's mental peace is replaced by doubt and paranoia. Why should we allow ourselves to contribute to these ends? To do so is to dishonor human nature and the kindness of our ancestors and the past masters. Two brothers who lie and cheat one another are like people not born from the same mother. What unpleasant realities we create for ourselves! We should abandon these ways as though they were poison. Let them be objects of human compassion.

The second negativity of speech is slander, or divisive speech. This just further widens the gap between people who are already divided and separates people who are close. We speak freely about high-sounding endeavors like the bodhisattva practices and the tantric methods, but if we are still unable to handle basic exercises such as avoiding divisive speech, there is little spiritual significance in our talk. Rather than ridicule Dharma in this way, we should just fill our mouths with excrement. That would be more appropriate. We have to learn to honor, trust, and respect each other, and to rejoice in others' happiness rather than jealously trying to cause conflicts and disharmony. When our practice just gives us an excuse to self-righteously slander others whom we suspect are not so pure as we imagine ourselves to be, it is time to tie a rope around our tongue for a while.

To be aware of a single shortcoming within oneself is more useful than to be aware of a thousand in somebody else. Rather than speaking badly about people and in ways that will produce friction and unrest in their lives, we should practice pure perception of them, and when we speak of others only speak of their good qualities. If you find yourself slandering anybody, just fill your mouth with excrement. That will break you of the habit quickly enough.

Avoiding these ten negative ways and practicing their opposites gives birth to a state of mental harmony that can act as the basis for all the higher practices, such as meditative concentration, the thought of enlightenment, and the various tantric yogas. However, if one does not have the power of mind to maintain such basic trainings as avoiding the ten negative ways, there is little hope that our application of higher techniques will be very effective. A method is only as effective as the mind of the person using it. Instead of running about looking for the highest and most secret tantric yoga, we should examine ourselves sincerely and discern what level of practice is most appropriate to our level of spiritual qualification.

First we should work on the foundations, which means observance of the laws of karma through practice of the ten disciplines. Otherwise, all we are doing is cheating ourselves. We speak about how many texts we have studied, how many hours we meditate each day, and how many retreats we've done; but we would be better to calculate how many times a day we forget the ten disciplines. A useful practice is to sit quietly each evening and to review one's activities of the day, silently acknowledging any failures and resolving to overcome such challenges in the future. Take refuge, meditate upon the bodhimind, and counteract the negative karmic instincts by applying any of the various meditative techniques. After the mind has been brought into the sphere of purity, one can proceed with one's evening meditations or prayers.

The third negativity of speech is the usage of harsh words, words that cause pain in people's hearts. Even the softest words are harsh if they strike with pain. Spiteful sarcasm is another form of harsh speech. These modes of speech all cause discomfort in the minds of living beings and therefore are to be avoided. It is better to say nothing than to say something cruel. Human life is short enough as it is; there is no need to misdirect and waste what little breath we have.

Meaningless talk is the fourth negativity of speech. Although ostensibly it is rather harmless, as the conversations wander on we eventually end up on a topic that does nothing other than feed delusion and drain us of time and energy. In itself it is not destructive, but as it harbors the seeds of vanity, it is in contradiction to spiritual endeavor.

The three negativities of mind—attachment, ill-will, and holding views contradicting reality—are the sources of all negativities of body and speech. Their relationship is like that of a horse and cart.

The first of these, attachment, is a longing desire for things that are or are not our own. It gives rise to countless negativities of body and speech. From attachment springs jealousy, anger, and all forms of afflicted emotions.

Ill-will is the most immediately destructive of the mental afflictions, resulting in violence, harm, and even killing. Holding views contradicting reality means believing that there is no relationship between one's present activities and future experiences, or that there is no enlightenment nor path to it. These types of views prevent one from leading a wholesome life and from entering the spiritual path.

THE THIRD DALAI LAMA:

> By guarding the ethical discipline of avoiding the ten negative actions one finds a decent rebirth, but if one wishes to go beyond that and gain the eight qualities conducive to continuing along the supreme path to omniscience—qualities such as high status, a good family, a strong mind, a harmonious body and so forth— then one must also produce their causes, which are: to abandon harming any living being, to make offerings of light and so forth to the Triple Gem, to offer clothes, etc., to the needy, and, by means of overcoming pride, to have respect for all that lives. Take the responsibility of these practices into your own hands through the forces of mindfulness and conscientiousness.

HIS HOLINESS:

To attain omniscient wisdom one must engage a powerful method. Through the practice of meditation upon emptiness one generates a store of wisdom, and through the other practices, such as benefiting others and meditating on compassion, etc., one generates a great store of creative energy. The protection of this creative energy is very much based upon the practice of the ten disciplines. Through the application of these ten disciplines we create harmony in this life that brings us peace and happiness and that is conducive to higher spiritual practice; and we lay karmic forces on our mind that shall contribute to providing us with causes for an auspicious rebirth having the eight qualities favorable to further spiritual progress.

Whenever we find that we have contradicted any of the ten disciplines, we should apply purifying meditations such as visualizing the Bodhisattva Vajrasattva and imagining lights purifying our mental stream while we recite the hundred-syllable Vajrasattva mantra; or reading the *Sutra of Purification with the Thirty-five Buddhas*, etc. In this practice one recollects negativity, contemplates its nature, generates apprehension of its karmic implications, and resolves to purify one's mind of the negative traces. On the basis of this resolve one takes refuge, develops the bodhimind and enters the Vajrasattva meditation or whatever method is being used. One can also do exercises such as prostrations and so forth. This concentration of purifying energies destroys the potency of negative karmic imprints like the germ of a barley seed roasted in a fire. Here it is important to begin the meditation session with a contemplative meditation and then to transform this into settled meditation for a prolonged period of time. One abides in the settled meditation until it begins to lose intensity, and then temporarily reverts to contemplative meditation in order to invigorate the mind, returning to fixed meditation once a contemplative atmosphere has been restored.

Generally our mind is habituated to directing all of our energies into things that benefit this life alone, things of no spiritual consequence. By performing these types of meditations, our natural attachment to the meaningless activities of this life subsides and we begin to experience an inner appreciation for spiritual values. When spontaneously one's mind appreciates spiritual rather than mundane goals one has become an active practitioner of initial perspective.

THE THIRD DALAI LAMA:

However, if occasionally you are overpowered by strong mental distortion and commit a breach of practice, you should not be dispassionate but should confess to yourself the unwanted karmic obstacle at the proper time and place and, by means of the four opponent forces, should cleanse all stains of body, speech, and mind. These four are: contemplating the shortcomings of negativity in order to develop a sense of remorse at having committed a wrong; reliance upon the objects of refuge and the bodhimind as forces with the power to purify the mind of karmic stains; generation of a strong sense of resolve to turn away from such negative courses of action in the future; and the power of application of positive counteractive forces, such as the Vajrasattva mantra and so forth.

As Jey Rinpochey wrote,

> Should you not find a suitable rebirth,
> It will not be possible to progress along the path.
> Cultivate the causes of a high rebirth;
> Appreciate the importance of purifying
> The three doors from stains of negativity.
> Cherish the power of the four opponent forces.

By meditating in this way, the mind is turned away from the transient things of this life and takes an unfeigned interest in more lasting things. When this effect has been realized, one is known as the spiritual aspirant of initial perspective.

NINE
Hinayana Realism

HIS HOLINESS:

Through pursuing the meditations of a practitioner of initial perspective, one generates a spiritual interest sufficiently strong to support refuge and observance of the laws of karmic evolution. These practices have the ability to protect us from evolving into lower states and to help us gain a higher rebirth; but are these sufficient attainments? Even in the higher realms we will not be completely beyond suffering, so higher rebirth is not a final goal. When we meditate on the sufferings inherent in the higher realms of samsara, our mind naturally begins to seek a state of freedom from all cyclic existence.

THE THIRD DALAI LAMA:

Training the Mind on the Common Path of the Being of Intermediate Perspective of Spiritual Application

Although by avoiding the ten negative actions and practicing their opposites—the ten disciplines—one can attain a special rebirth in the higher realms, one will not pass beyond the frustrations of cyclic existence. For this reason one must look to the attainment of nirvana, or liberation beyond all frustration and pain.

What is the nature of the shortcomings of cyclic existence? Those of the lower realms have been explained above, and you should meditate well upon them; for once you have done so you will realize that in no way would you enjoy such long and intense misery, and you will automatically give birth to an inclination to work by every possible means to remain free of such unsatisfactory modes of existence. However, even the higher realms are not beyond the reaches of suffering, and to progress along the path one must sooner or later face this truth.

HIS HOLINESS:

Wherever we look in samsara there is only frustration. The intensity of the miseries experienced in the three lower realms have become obvious from our meditations as a practitioner of initial scope. But even attainment of higher rebirth is unsatisfactory, for once that life-form ends there is no guarantee that we will not fall back into lower states. We all carry infinitely numerous karmic seeds gathered over an endless stream of lives since beginningless time, and unless we have generated the wisdom that frees us from the influences of these karmic potencies our higher rebirth will only result in an eventual return to the lower realms.

Maybe we will say that this is not so bad, that there is not much suffering in the higher realms, such as this human world. To do so is merely a defense mechanism. Normally we insulate ourselves from awareness of the sufferings of the human world, but when we meditate upon them, their pervasive nature becomes obvious. The rich and powerful suffer from mental pressure and the poor have physical pressure. Rulers of nations miss their sleep over not being able to fulfill their objectives; the wealthy constantly worry that they will be cheated or reduced to poverty; and the poor suffer from hunger, overwork and so forth. There is no ordinary human being who has not experienced suffering. It is common to all of us.

THE THIRD DALAI LAMA:

A man, for example, is wrapped in suffering. While in the womb he suffers from darkness, constriction, and immersion in filthy substances. When during the last months of the mother's pregnancy the downward pushing energies manifest, the unborn baby feels like a small piece of wood being crushed in a giant vise, or like a sesame seed being pounded for its oil. And after he has emerged from the womb, he feels as though he has fallen into a pit of thorns, even if he has been wrapped in soft garments and placed in a feather bed. Such is the agony of birth.

The baby gradually grows into a youth, and soon he is an old man. His back bends like a bow, his hair turns white as a dried flower and his forehead fills with wrinkles until he looks like a strip of sliced leather. Sitting down is like dropping a heavy load and standing up is like pulling out a tree from its roots. If he tries to speak his tongue will not obey, and if he tries to walk he staggers. His sensory powers, such as sight, hearing, etc., begin to fail him. His body loses its lustre and resembles a corpse. His memory degenerates and he can remember nothing. Powers of digestion fail and he can no longer eat properly, no matter how much he craves food. At this point his life is almost finished and death is rapidly approaching. Such are the sufferings of old age.

In addition to the sufferings of birth and age, throughout life he must continually confront the sufferings of illness. When the elements of his body fall out of harmony, his skin dries and his flesh sags. Food and drink, usually so appealing, seem repulsive, and instead he must ingest bitter medicines and undergo unpleasant treatments like operations, moxabustion, acupuncture and so forth. Should the disease be incurable, he experiences immeasurable suffering from fear, worry, and apprehension; and if the disease is fatal, he must live with death close before his eyes. Thoughts of any evil he may have created during his lifetime cause his heart to fill with regret, and he recollects all that he has left undone. He understands that he soon must leave his body, friends, relatives, associates, and possessions; his mouth dries, his lips shrivel, his nose sinks, his eyes fade, and his breath passes in gasps. Tremendous fear of the lower realms arises within him and, though he wills it not, he dies.

Human beings suffer in many less general ways as well. Some meet with bandits and thieves and lose all their wealth. Their bodies become pierced by weapons or beaten with clubs and so forth. Some suffer heavy punishments at the hands of legal authorities for having committed crimes. Others hear dreadful news or rumors of distant family or friends and suffer terribly, or they fear the loss of their wealth and possessions and suffer with worry. Others suffer from encountering people and situations that they do not wish to encounter, and still others suffer through not getting what they want. For example, although one may try to cultivate a piece of land, drought, frost, hail and so forth may destroy the crop. One may work as a sailor or fisherman, but a sudden gust of wind may result in one's ruin. If one goes into business one may lose one's investment or, after much effort, make no profit. One may take monastic ordination, but then may have to face the sorrow of having broken the vows. In short, having taken a samsaric human form out of the forces of karma and delusion, one must face the sufferings of birth, sickness, old age, death and so forth; and as well one is using one's precious human incarnation largely as an instrument to produce more causes of lower rebirth and greater misery in the future.

HIS HOLINESS:

As Pabongkha Dechen Nyingpo says in *Liberation in the Palm of One's Hand*, "Everyone has many sad tales to tell by the time their life draws to an end." When we see people from a distance they seem very happy and free from suffering, but the closer we come to them the more we become aware of how imperfection and suffering scar their happiness. If you get together with them and exchange stories on the sufferings each has experienced in life, the accounts of personal tragedy become more and more gruesome.

Pain and misfortune are fundamental ingredients of mundane cyclic life. Humans must confront the four great sufferings: birth, sickness, old age, and death. As well as these, there are periodic sufferings of not getting the things one wants, having to face undesirable experiences, having to constantly struggle to get the basic requirements of life, and so forth. These fall on us like waves flowing in from the ocean. The ripening of these events is the suffering of pain.

A second type of suffering is that of changing happiness, or unstable happiness. We want something and work hard to get it, but somehow having it brings more suffering than pleasure in the end. Samsara is such that one is constantly in the situation of being pained by having or else by not having. This is the nature of the dissatisfied mind. There is a Tibetan saying, "If your possessions are the size of a louse, then your sufferings are the size of a louse. If your possessions are the size of a goat, you will have sufferings equal to the size of a goat." To have is to have the suffering of having; not to have is to have the suffering of not having. This is the frustrating nature of changing happiness. We think that if we buy something, possess something, or move to another country, our mind will be satisfied; but there is no satisfaction in the samsaric approach. Unless we develop the wisdom giving freedom from karma and delusion, all happiness is bound to eventually dissolve and be replaced by sufferings.

The very substances from which our body is formed are themselves impure. As is said in the *Red Hat Lam Rim*, "What is our body but the quintessence of a thousand generations of evolution of sperm and ovum?" These come together in the lower regions between the intestines full of excrement and a bladder full of urine and so forth. And then the darkness of the womb must be experienced, where our body grows for nine months, bound and constricted all around. We lie as though strapped in a tight leather bag, experiencing intense heat when our mother eats or drinks hot foods, and intense cold when she eats or drinks anything cold, feeling as though we are being beaten by a stick if she moves suddenly, and so forth. The mother herself experiences much suffering at this time, and toward the end of her pregnancy she feels almost ready to burst. At the time of actual delivery her suffering is so great that she must cry out and wail in pain.

As Shantideva writes in his *Guide to the Bodhisattva's Way of Life*, "If we do not make our life wholesome, our birth is worth only the pain it gave our mother."

Even after birth one is a great problem to one's mother. Because we are unable to do anything for ourselves, she has to serve us day and night for years. Even during her sleep we do not give her peace. We ourselves also undergo much suffering at this time, being unable to express or fulfill our needs or to control our body.

We human beings are not born grandly but in the midst of blood, urine and much pain. Our entrance into life is indeed an ominous sign. "It would seem that this human body is little more than an excrement and pain-making machine," writes Nagarjuna in *A Precious Garland*, and if we do not use our body as a boat for spiritual development this is just what it is—a useless sack of blood, pus, excrement, and bones. Unless our direction is spiritual, the only use in our eating more food is to produce more excrement.

Because a samsaric body is a product of karma and delusion, it is a source of constant anxiety and pain. We usually end up spending most of our lives serving it, feeding it, clothing and sheltering it, washing it, and pampering it when it gets sick and so forth. But unless we use it to develop our mind, there is no benefit in the end. We die and our precious body that we cherished so much, that our mother looked on with such pride, turns cold and becomes the food of worms. This is the reality we have to live with all our lives.

A tantric yogi who has gained control of the subtle energies of the body and the subtle levels of consciousness will have control over the inner and outer elements and consequently can transform his or her ordinary samsaric form into a joyous rainbow body. But until we can do this, we have to accept the fact that our physical basis is a magnet attracting every kind of discomfort and pain.

From the tantric viewpoint, the ordinary human body is the source of much delusion. As the chakras, nadis, white and red mystic drops, vital energies and so forth evolve, the nature of the flow of vital energies which act as the vehicle of mind, itself being impure, gives rise to impure states of mind such as attachment and anger. In the tantric view, mind and bodily energies that support it have this interdependent relationship.

This samsaric body keeps us running all our lives. We have to run to fulfill its endless needs, to keep it away from things that may harm it, and to protect it from anything unpleasant. We have to give it pleasure and comfort. We become ordained, and at first this is very satisfactory; but soon our body makes it so difficult for us that we think our practice would be less disturbed if we were to live as a layperson. So we give up and return to ordinary life; but then we end up with a large family to support, leaving us with no time or energy for meditation. We have the pressing tasks of feeding, clothing, and sheltering our children, and of arranging their education and so forth. Our lives are spent alternating between work and worry, with occasional short periods of pleasure, and then we have to die; but even this we cannot do in peace, for, when we lie down to die, our last thoughts are worried ones concerning the family we are leaving behind. Such is the nature of worldly existence.

Generally the happiest period of our lives is between the ages of five and fifteen, and the most creative is during our thirties. In this decade we are fully mature and can accomplish anything, either worldly or spiritual. Buddha, Milarepa, and Tsongkhapa all gained their realization at this time. I am in my fifties; the sun of my life is at high noon. Soon I will enter my sixties and seventies. My body will lose its strength and vitality, my hair will turn white, and even moving about will become a problem. These are the sufferings of becoming old that all humans must face. How naive to think that it will not happen to us.

The most beautiful people become ugly when old age strikes. Their hair falls out or turns white, their complexions fade. Some become thin like corpses, others become so fat that they cannot stand up without help. Still others become bedridden and helpless. Soon one looks more dead than alive, a skeleton wrapped in a parched, grayish skin. One's reflection in a mirror is difficult even for oneself to bear. Although our family and friends continue to show us kindness, strangers look at us with cold eyes of revulsion. Perhaps the mind is still vigorous and lucid, but the body is unable to serve its wishes. We have to sit and watch ourselves wait for death to come, often with nobody to share our loneliness and sorrow.

To care for our old people—these ones who have given us our body, our life, and our culture—is a sacred duty of humanity. But most humans act more like animals than people, and often we see old people who have been abandoned by their families. Family units were very strong in Tibet, and old people were usually cared for directly by relatives. The national care for the old that we see in the West is something very good, a healthy sign, although perhaps here the spiritual and psychological basis is somewhat lacking.

The suffering of old age is something we all must face, unless we die prematurely. There is nothing we can do about it. Gone will be that false sense of personal ability and strength that made us so proud when we were young. Instead, helpers or friends will bathe us, dress us, spoonfeed us, and have to take us to the toilet. Rather than live under the delusion of permanence, we should engage in spiritual training so that we can enter old age at least with the grace of wisdom.

How can we imagine that the human body is indestructible? Its very basis is impermanence and disharmony. Which one of us has not known sickness, discomfort, and the threat of death? Aryadeva describes it this way in his *Four Hundred Stanzas*, "The elements supporting our body are like a group of poisonous snakes battling for power." Every chemical in our body is a vital force vying with the others in a terrific battle, and only when all the elemental powers are balanced can health be maintained. The smallest germ or incompatible agent can destroy this balance and send us into weeks, months, or years of illness. Then we have to run from one doctor to another, suffering with discomfort and agony, listening to the lies that they tell us out of professional kindness. Sometimes our disease is contagious and even our friends become afraid when they see us coming. At other times our flesh swells or becomes covered with sores that seep with pus, making us so ugly we are too embarrassed to go out of our homes. Some diseases sap our strength and leave us unable to bear even the sight of food; others make us unable to digest or assimilate it. The smallest accident can break our bones, leaving us unable to walk. Often even the medicines we take have nauseating side effects. Perhaps we get cancer and the doctors tell us it is incurable. Tibetan herbal doctors state very proudly that they can cure it, but not being a doctor myself I can only sit and watch. Anyway, a lot of people are dying of cancer.

So we can see that this body indeed causes us much grief in this life and, sadly, in their quest to satisfy its many needs, most people just collect an endless stream of negative karmic instincts that will lead them to lower rebirths in the future.

These are the sufferings of the human world.

The *Essence of Refined Gold* then goes on to describe the sufferings of the realms of the anti-gods, the sensual gods, and the gods of the heavens of form and formless meditation. Again, these are realms of existence that can only be perceived by beings with special perception, although there is evidence of them in the mystical writings of many world cultures. Some *Lam Rim* scriptures describe them in great detail. However, if we have no confidence in the existence of the celestial realms, it is sufficient to meditate upon the human sufferings. These become obvious very quickly when we begin to search for them. The important point here is to become aware of the third type of suffering, the subtle suffering that pervades all imperfect existence, the all-pervading misery concomitant with having a perishable, samsaric base. A god in the highest heaven, a human being, an animal, and also hell beings and ghosts are all enmeshed in suffering because the nature of their body and mind is bound with compulsive cyclic processes. Until we develop the wisdom that is able to free the mind from these compelling forces, there is no doubt that we shall experience suffering throughout our lives, and that we shall continue to wander endlessly in the wheel of birth, life, death, and rebirth where the presence of misery can always be felt.

THE THIRD DALAI LAMA:

A samsaric form is merely a vessel holding the suffering of pain, the suffering of transient pleasure, and the all-pervading suffering. And, in that cyclic existence is by very nature all-pervasive suffering, one never knows any joy or happiness not wrapped in and embraced by misery and frustration. In the realm of the asuras, or anti-gods, the beings suffer from constantly fighting with and killing and wounding one another. Above that, in the realm of the desire gods, when the five signs of oncoming death manifest, the beings suffer more than do the hell denizens. As their splendor fades and they are shunned by the other gods, they know boundless mental anguish. Still higher in samsara are the gods of the realms of form and formlessness, and although they do not experience the suffering of immediate pain, those of the first three levels have the suffering of transient pleasure, and those of the fourth level and of the formless levels must endure the all-pervasive suffering, which is likened to an unruptured boil.

HIS HOLINESS:

Since beginningless time we have been born again and again in the various realms of the universe. If you choose to believe that only humans and animals exist, then when you meditate on the lower realms, do so only on the sufferings of animals, insects and so forth, and when you meditate on the upper realms do so only on the types of imperfections with which human beings are afflicted. The aim in the former meditation is to generate the aspiration to transcend imperfection: to avoid negative behavior, the cause of future suffering, and to dwell in goodness, the cause of higher evolution.

In the latter meditation [upon the unsatisfactory nature of the higher realms of samsara], the aim is to transcend ordinary goodness, which is tinged with grasping at an implied true existence of things and thus is still within the limits of samsara. By replacing this mundane level of goodness with the goodness born from transcendental wisdom, one is able to cut the roots of all compulsive samsaric conduct and enter into the blissful serenity of nirvana. This is liberation from samsara, the third of the Four Noble Truths.

If cyclic existence and the distorted states of mind that give rise to it are elements that cannot be overcome, then there is no need to bother with spiritual practice. But on the other hand, if there is a way to exchange suffering for eternal happiness, one would be very foolish to ignore it. To do so would be a case of the samsaric mind deceiving and cheating us once again.

THE THIRD DALAI LAMA:

You should think over these general and specific imperfections of the various dimensions of samsaric existence and then strive in every possible way to attain the state of nirvana, or liberation from them all. It should be noted that such a state is not causeless or conditionless, and so one should train in the practices which bring about actual attainment of liberation, i.e., the practices of the three higher trainings—ethical discipline, concentration, and wisdom. Furthermore, as the higher trainings of concentration and wisdom depend and are based upon the higher training in ethical discipline, you should first train in it, and because discipline is easily broken when mindfulness and such forces degenerate, you should maintain clear thoughts firmly supported by mindfulness and clarity and thus guard against all possible downfalls. If you ever breach your discipline, don't waste a moment but immediately acknowledge your failing to yourself and resolve to proceed correctly in the future. When a delusion such as attachment, anger, jealousy and so forth arises, meditate upon its opponent, such as non-attachment, love, equanimity, etc. Be your own judge in practice, and do not fall short of your aims. Let nothing you think, say, or do contradict the advice of the spiritual master.

HIS HOLINESS:

How can we eliminate the deepest source of all unsatisfactory experience? Only by cultivating certain qualities within our mindstream. Unless we possess high spiritual qualifications, there is no doubt that the events life throws upon us will give rise to frustration, emotional turmoil, and other distorted states of consciousness. These imperfect states of mind in turn give rise to imperfect activities, and the seeds of suffering are ever planted in a steady flow. On the other hand, when the mind can dwell in the wisdom that knows the ultimate mode of being, one is able to destroy the deepest root of distortion, negative karma and sorrow.

Our grasping at an inherently existent reality is not something with any strong support. The quality of concreteness, which in our ordinary process of perception we project upon everything, has no actual basis in the objects of our knowledge. The sense of inherent self-being that we feel is there in objects is merely a creation of our own mind, and, if we were to investigate for ourselves, it is unmasked as the source of all our suffering. From this grasping at inherent existence stems the entire range of delusion, emotional afflictions, and their ill-directed activities. Alternatively, by eliminating this method of viewing things, we eliminate the direct source of distorted states of mind as well as the activities they produce.

The force that severs this inborn process of grasping at true existence is the higher training in wisdom. This is the most important method in the quest for eternal liberation. However, to intensify and stabilize the higher training in wisdom, one should also cultivate the higher trainings in meditative concentration and ethical self-discipline.

Here the practice of self-discipline largely refers to the vows for individual liberation, such as the five vows of a lay practitioner, the novice and full ordinations of monks and nuns, etc. Any practice done on the stabilizing force of one of these sets of disciplines becomes far more effective. As for the five vows of a lay person—to refrain from killing, stealing, lying, adultery, and alcohol—in Tibet it was common for a lay person to take just one or a few of the five. Generally, every Buddhist should hold at least one of them. The higher the level of ordination, the more firm is the basis of discipline and therefore the more strong becomes all one's other practices, such as the ten disciplines, meditation upon emptiness and so forth.

With a foundation of ethical self-discipline one can then enter into the higher training of meditative concentration. Based on these two forces, our meditation upon emptiness takes on an ever-increasing strength. Throughout our training we should guard our discipline well, and whenever there is a transgression we should recollect the Three Jewels, admit the fault and purify ourselves of it, determining to practice harder in the future. In this way our combined practice of the three higher trainings reaches to the very root of samsaric suffering.

Success in the practice of these three trainings depends upon a correctly directed mind. Therefore we meditate upon the sufferings inherent in even the higher realms of samsara and cultivate an awareness that spontaneously looks upon the highest samsaric pleasures—such as the fame, wealth, power, prestige and so forth of the human plane, or the power and transient pleasures found in the samsaric heavens—in the same way as the tiger sees grass. The spirit of freedom, which is the non-attachment and non-grasping of inner renunciation, inspires us to direct our every energy at transcending all samsaric imperfection.

THE THIRD DALAI LAMA:

To quote Jey Rinpochey,

If you do not contemplate the Noble Truth of Suffering—
the fallacy of samsara—
The wish to be free of samsara will not arise.
If you do not contemplate the source of suffering—
the door to samsara—
You will never discover the means of
cutting samsara's root.
Base yourself on renunciation of cyclic existence;
be tired of it.
Cherish knowledge of the chains that bind you to
the wheel of cyclic existence.

When the thought that aspires to transcend the world arises within you as strongly as the thought of finding an exit would arise in a person caught in a burning house, you have become a spiritual aspirant of intermediate perspective.

TEN

Generating the Bodhisattva Spirit

HIS HOLINESS:

As the exalted master Arya Nagarjuna said, "For those seeking full omniscience, the bodhimind is the wish-fulfilling gem. It should be as stable as Mount Meru, should warm the ten directions with compassion, and should be united with the wisdom which does not grasp at duality."

The first quality we need to generate in order to enter the Mahayana is the bodhimind. And as the bodhimind is a higher form of love and compassion, we must generate these qualities as a prerequisite. Once we have generated the bodhimind, our meditations upon the ultimate level of truth shall contribute to our attainment of omniscient buddhahood rather than the lesser attainment of an arhant's nirvana. This latter is achieved by practicing the three higher trainings without the sublimating influence of the bodhimind. Knowing that we are of little benefit to sentient beings for as long as we remain under the powers of delusion, we enter into meditation upon emptiness not solely in order to remove our own causes of suffering for our own sakes, but also in order to attain enlightenment in order to be of greatest benefit to others. Therefore Nagarjuna made the prayer, "Whoever does not have the bodhimind, may they generate it. And whoever has it, may they increase it."

We have been born as human beings and have the ability to attain tremendously exalted states of spiritual being. It has probably been many lifetimes since we have had such an auspicious conjunction of conditions favorable to progress along the path to higher being, liberation, and enlightenment. Even if we cannot get involved in intensive practice of meditation, at least we should try to accumulate a few positive karmic instincts for further development along the Great Way by occasionally reading the scriptures and trying to incorporate teachings into our daily activities.

At the moment the world's spiritual traditions have greatly degenerated. It is very important in such times that the practitioners themselves make especially strong efforts to gain realization. To permit the lineages of transmission to disappear is to allow the world to plunge into darkness. The great Vasubandhu wrote, "Buddha, who is like the eye of the world, is no longer to be seen. His great successors, who realized the most profound teachings, also have passed away. Who equals them?" It might be asked, who is there today to equal the master Vasubandhu? Who practices as well as did Milarepa? Such people are rare. We should remember that everything but Dharma is useless at death, and instead of wasting our lives on meaningless activities, we should blend our mindstreams with the teachings and with practice. Doing so benefits us as individuals and benefits the world by strengthening its spiritual basis.

Each of us has to be able to feel the pride that we ourselves can reach perfection, we ourselves can attain enlightenment. When even one person indulges in spiritual practice, it gives encouragement to the guardian spirits of the land, and to the celestial deities who have sworn to uphold goodness. These forces then have the ability to release waves of beneficial effects upon humanity. Thus our practice has many direct and indirect benefits. On the other hand, when the people just disgrace and deride the masters and live in ways contradicting natural law, the white protective forces lose their potency and the sinister forces of darkness revive and cause great havoc. Each of us has to do our best on a personal level. There is a saying, "The ways of humans and gods should be in harmony." If we practice the teachings and live the ways of Dharma, all the natural forces of goodness will be behind us. Yet when we look at human beings we can see how few are engaged in serious spiritual training, and if we look at those in training we can see how few are training effectively. We ourselves as humans have a body and mind capable of elevating our spiritual status from its present stage into the most exalted of the supreme. Why miss the opportunity? Once death takes it away, it will probably not come again for thousands or even millions of lifetimes.

THE THIRD DALAI LAMA:

Although by means of the higher trainings in ethical discipline, concentration, and wisdom, one can attain nirvana, or liberation from cyclic existence, this attainment in itself is not sufficient. Of course, for one who has gained nirvana there is never again the need to wander in samsara, yet because only a part of one's faults have been overcome [obscurations to omniscience have not] and only a fraction of perfection has been attained [omnipotence and omniscience have not], one has not really fulfilled oneself from one's own point of view. Also, because one is neither omniscient nor omnipotent, one has not fulfilled oneself from others' point of view. So there is a need to look to the goal of complete buddhahood, which is ultimate fulfillment from both one's own and others' point of view. Moreover, one should not think to gain buddhahood merely for one's own benefit. One should want it purely in order to be able to more efficiently and deeply benefit all sentient beings. Just as you have fallen into the ocean of samsaric misery, so have all others; and they, like you, know only frustration and misery. There is not one of them who previously has not been your father and mother again and again, and who has not shown you unimaginable kindness. It is only justice that if you are to gain liberation and omniscience they too should be freed from anguish. It is primarily to benefit them that you yourself must reach the state of peerless, non-abiding nirvana, and for this you must generate the supreme bodhimind, the enlightened attitude.

HIS HOLINESS:

As practitioners of initial and medium perspectives we turned the mind away from the causes of lower evolution and towards the direction of individual liberation from samsara and its miseries; but is this enough? The answer is to the negative. Those who dwell in nirvana have severed the obscuring influence of the delusions and thus abide in freedom from samsaric existence, but they have not severed the obscurations to omniscience. Consequently, although

they are able to remain absorbed in meditation upon the
ultimate truth and thus to remain free from suffering, they
are not able to simultaneously perceive the infinite diversity of the universe. As a result, their ability to benefit the
world is limited. Moreover, in that they still have subtle
obscurations, even their own purposes have not been utterly fulfilled. Therefore, we should elevate our goal to that
of omniscient buddhahood, the cause of which is the cultivation of the bodhimind.

How did we generate the aspiration to transcend the lower
states of being and attain nirvana, or liberation from all
samsaric misery? Firstly, by contemplating the sufferings of
the lower realms and the causes of evolving into these states;
and secondly by contemplating the sufferings that pervade
all samsaric existence, together with the causes of liberation. However, we did this principally in reference to our
own stream of being. In order to generate the Mahayana
mind, however, one changes the gravitational basis of the
meditations and, instead of contemplating the ways in which
we ourselves do and can suffer, we consider the plight of
the world of sentient beings who live around us. We meditate upon the same sufferings of the lower and higher realms
of samsara as previously, but here we refer them not to ourselves but to others—our mother, father, family, friends,
etc.—until eventually we include all living beings.

All beings suffer in the same way as we do, and some are
even more deeply immersed in sorrow. Yet all of these beings wish to experience only happiness and to avoid all suffering, frustration, and pain. They wish lasting happiness
but do not know how to cultivate its causes, and they wish
to avoid misery but automatically collect only causes of further misery. As Shantideva said, "Although seeking happiness, they destroy their own causes of happiness as they
would an enemy. And although seeking to avoid misery,
they treat its causes as they would a close friend."

Were the countless sentient beings unrelated to us, or were
they not to mind their sufferings, perhaps there would be
no need for us to bother with their welfare. In reality, how-

ever, all are related to us and not one of them wishes to suffer. Over the billions of lifetimes that we have experienced since beginningless time, we have known all the living beings again and again. Sometimes they have been parents to us, sometimes friends or mates, sometimes enemies. Without exception, each of them has been even a mother to us again and again, performing all the kindnesses of a mother. How can we be indifferent to them? Wishing them to have only happiness and its causes and to be free of suffering and its causes, we ourselves should generate a sense of responsibility for their well-being. Finally, as only an omniscient Enlightened One is effectively able to benefit beings in deep, lasting, and ultimate ways, we must quickly attain enlightenment. This is the wishing bodhimind, the inner basis of Mahayana practice. One of the principal methods of generating this mind is the technique called "the seven-point oral tradition of cause and effect."

THE THIRD DALAI LAMA:

The best method to generate the bodhimind is the oral tradition known as the "the seven-point oral tradition of cause and effect." I will explain this first briefly and then in detail.

A Brief Explanation

Of the seven points, six are causes and one the effect. The first cause is the awareness that all sentient beings have been one's mother. From this arises the second cause— mindfulness of the all-embracing, eternal kindness of each and every one of them. This gives birth to the third cause—the wish to repay their kindness. This wish transforms into the beautiful mind engendering the fourth cause—love—and then the fifth cause—compassion. Love and compassion are the forces from which springs the sixth cause—the extraordinary attitude characterized by a sense of universal responsibility, the cause which eventually ripens as the one effect, bodhimind. This is the seven-spoked wheel that rolls on to the omniscient state of perfect enlightenment.

HIS HOLINESS:

This seven-point oral tradition of cause and effect is one of the most effective methods for generating the bodhimind; but in order to utilize it we must first develop the smooth mind of equanimity. Our present attitudes towards others are rough and inconsistent. We regard some with affection and wish them happiness; others with indifference to their happiness and sufferings; and others we dislike and hope that they come to sorrow. This discriminating mind cannot meditate effectively on love, compassion, etc., without casting these into a discriminating perspective. Any sense of the bodhimind that arises will be unbalanced and easily disturbed. Therefore as a preliminary to using the method of the seven-point oral tradition of cause and effect we must train the mind in the meditations that develop equanimity.

THE THIRD DALAI LAMA:

As a preliminary to all seven of these meditations, however, one must make the mind level by means of meditation upon equanimity for all sentient beings. If the mind sees some beings as dear, some as alien, and some as neutral, it is not sufficiently mature to be able to meditate upon all beings as having been one's own mother. If the mind has no equanimity, any love or compassion generated will be biased and unbalanced. Therefore one must first practice equanimity meditation.

Begin this by visualizing various "neutral" people—those who have neither harmed nor helped you in this life. From their side, each of them wants only happiness and does not want suffering. From your side, each one of them is like a member of your family and has been your father and mother in many previous lives. Think, "In some lives I have held them dear and have helped them, whereas in others I have held them as alien and have harmed them. This is hardly correct. I should meditate now in order to generate an attitude of equanimity for them all."

Once you have meditated like this upon neutral people, then consider those who have helped you in this life and whom you therefore hold as dear, and those who have harmed you in this life and whom you consequently hold as alien. Develop equanimity toward them both. Finally, generate equanimity toward all sentient beings of the six realms.

HIS HOLINESS:

Why do we like some beings, dislike others, and feel indifferent toward even others? Because of actions done or not done in this life. We like the beings who have helped and supported us, dislike those who have harmed us or who threaten our existence in any way, and feel indifferent to anyone unrelated to us, who has done nothing either pleasant nor unpleasant to us.

If we meditate on the people whom we dislike, the superficial nature of our reasons for disliking them become very obvious. Some merely smiled at us strangely, frowned at us or said something against us at one time. Others happen to play an unfortunate role in our lives. On the other hand, our reasons for liking the people whom we choose as friends are usually just as silly. Most people change their emotions towards others as quickly as the weather changes. Such a mind is a cause of laughter, even by worldly conventions. How much more inappropriate is it to the spiritual path?

It would be reasonable to call one person a friend, another an enemy, and a third a stranger if they had held this status throughout the billions of lives we have experienced since beginningless time. But this is not the case. All beings have been friend, relative, and even parent to us again and again. Each time they have showered us with a rainfall of kindness, protecting us from harm, and providing us with much happiness. This is in the past. As for the future, until we attain liberation or enlightenment we shall continue to spin on the wheel of life with them, meeting with them again and again in relationships of friend, relative and so forth.

Similarly, the people whom we like and love in this life have not always been our friends. In many previous lives they have killed us, stolen from us, and harmed us in many ways. As for the future, until we attain enlightenment we will continue to meet with them in life upon life, each time our relationships with them dramatically changed. There is nobody who has always played the role of ally in our lives, and nobody who has always played the role of antagonist. Nor is there anyone who has always been a stranger. As the wheel of karma rolls on, the beings fulfilling these functions constantly change positions with one another.

When we meditate on these facts and apply the experiences of our meditations in our daily exchanges with people, the smooth mind that looks on all beings with equanimity is quickly generated. This lays the foundation for the actual practice of the seven-point cause and effect meditation technique.

THE THIRD DALAI LAMA:

A More Detailed Explanation

The first cause: developing awareness that all beings have been one's mother. Because there is no findable beginning to sentient life and cyclic existence, one must have had an infinite number of previous lives; and all other beings must share this same situation. Thus it follows that there is no place in which we can say we have not taken birth and there is no sentient being we can say has not been our parent. In fact, each and every sentient being has been our parent countless times. If we search throughout the endless round of birth, death, and rebirth, a being who has not been our mother will not be found. All sentient beings have shown kindness towards us equal to the kindness of our mother of this life. Consequently they should be seen as being only kind.

HIS HOLINESS:

The kindness of the mother is chosen as the example of the intensity of kindness that all beings have shown us, because generally in samsara the mother's concern is something very strong and obvious. We can see the kindness of a mother not only in humans but in animals, birds and so forth. A mother dog will starve herself to feed her pups and will die to protect them. In the same way, even if our mother were strange to us in some ways she still would have instinctively and unconsciously shown us great kindness. All beings have loved us in this very same way, sacrificing their food for us and even dying to protect us because their love for us was so strong. The people who are friends, enemies, and strangers to us in this life showed us the great kindness of a mother in countless previous lives.

Actually, there is no imperative that mother love be the model used here if doing so should cause a problem. If we have serious problems in our relationship with our mother, or if we were orphans and an aunt or uncle brought us up, we could just as easily take whomsoever we feel has been most kind to us and use him or her as an alternative model in this step in the meditation. We then contemplate how all sentient beings have been born into this same relationship with us in countless previous lives and have shown us these same kindnesses. We have to learn to see all sentient beings in that person's image.

As a result of this meditation one gains a feeling of spontaneous familiarity with all other sentient beings, a recognition that they are somehow very close to us and very precious.

THE THIRD DALAI LAMA:

The second cause: mindfulness of the kindness of the infinite sentient beings. How has the mother of this life shown you kindness? When you were in the womb she thought only about how to protect and tend you. After you were born she took you and wrapped you in soft garments, held you in her arms, gazed on you with eyes of love, smiled on you affectionately, out of mercy gave you milk from her breasts, and held you to her flesh to keep you warm. Then for year upon year she prepared your food for you and cleaned the mucus and excrement from your body. Even if she was mortally ill and you contracted merely a minor disease she would think solely about you. She shielded and protected you from every difficulty, gave you whatever she could to help you accomplish your wishes, and anything you could not do by yourself she did for you. In fact, she protected your life and person in every possible manner. You should in this way repeatedly contemplate how your mother has greatly helped you and has been extremely kind to you.

Then simultaneously visualize all three categories of people: those close to you, such as your family and friends of this life; neutral people with whom you have had no real contact; and alien people, or those who have harmed you in this life. Consider how each of them has been your mother uncountable times in the past. Uncountable times have they given you even a human rebirth, protecting you as much as has the mother of this life, showing you immeasurable kindness, and helping you limitlessly again and again.

HIS HOLINESS:

The kindness of a mother is boundless and overwhelming. She wants everything for her children. Could she give enlightenment to them, she would rush to do so. If we watch how mother birds sacrifice themselves to protect their children, how in order to feed their offspring they even starve themselves until their feathers fall out and the flesh falls away from their body, we can appreciate the tremendous kindness all sentient beings have shown us when they were reborn as our mothers in countless previous lives.

Whenever anyone harms us we should think to ourselves, "In many past incarnations this being was my mother. As my mother she fed me, cleaned my body, and protected me from every harm. I slept in her lap and drank milk from her breasts. At that time this person only benefited me and shared all possessions with me. The harm this person is now bringing to me is due only to the forces of negative karma and delusion."

THE THIRD DALAI LAMA:

The third cause: the wish to repay them. However, these mother sentient beings who have nurtured us with kindness so many times are disturbed by demons of mental distortion and delusion. Their minds are uncontrolled and they are as though insane. Their wisdom-eye is made blind with the smoke of ignorance, and they have no way to see the paths leading to high rebirth, personal liberation, or omniscience. Most of them, not having a spiritual master who can lead them to the city of freedom, are like blind beggars with no guide. Every day they further divorce themselves from happiness because of unskillful karmic actions of body, speech, and mind. Like members in a drunken procession staggering towards a cliff, they are stumbling over the precipice of evil into the sufferings of cyclic existence and the lower realms. Think, "If I do not do something for these pathetic, feeble beings, who will? If responsibility for them does not fall upon my shoulders, upon whose will it fall? Were I to ignore these kind beings and work only for my personal liberation from samsara, what lack of conscience and consideration!

"Furthermore, were they to attain the various pleasurable states of samsara, such as the states of Brahma, Indra or the like, their peace would not be eternal. I should from now on think less of myself and more of mitigating the samsaric suffering of living beings as vast as space, and by every possible means I should work for enlightenment so as to be able to place them in the joy of peerless liberation."

HIS HOLINESS:

Just as a mother has responsibility towards her child, the child has responsibility towards the mother. Since all sentient beings have been our mother countless times, our sense of responsibility towards each of them should be equal. What is the difference between a debt from last week and one from last year? We should dwell in this sense of responsibility towards others. When a mother falls into difficulty, who should be more concerned for her than her own child?

THE THIRD DALAI LAMA:
> *Causes four and five: love and compassion.* Think, "Why should these mother beings, bereft of happiness, not have happiness? May they be happy. May I in every way contribute to their happiness. Also, why should the mother beings who are aching with misery not be separated from misery? May they be separated from it. May I contribute to their being separated from it."

HIS HOLINESS:

How can we repay the kindness of sentient beings? Through showing them immaculate love and compassion.

Immaculate love is the thought, "May they have happiness and its causes." Compassion is the thought, "May they be free of suffering and its causes." In that to obtain happiness and to avoid suffering are the two most primordial, inborn instincts of all that lives, love and compassion are the supreme gifts.

What does it mean to give happiness? What does it mean to remove suffering? Of course we can help materially in small ways, but compared to the depth of the suffering in which the beings of samsara are immersed, this will provide only short and superficial benefits. All beings have had every happiness, pleasure, and power that exists in samsara, for their previous lives are countless; yet these have proved to be more deceptive than beneficial to them. Therefore the thought adds, ". . .and the causes of happiness." Ultimately speaking, in order for the beings to have lasting happiness they require its causes. They must be inspired in goodness and wisdom. Similarly, the "causes of suffering" reflects the thought not only must beings be freed from the specific states of suffering in which they presently struggle, but in order to gain lasting freedom from suffering they must be inspired to purify their mindstreams of negative karmic instincts and to counteract the force of delusion by cultivating profound wisdom.

In his *Three Principal Practices of the Path,* the great Tsong-khapa wrote, "Sentient beings are swept downstream by the violent rivers of the four sufferings and are tightly chained by the powerful bonds of compulsive karmic activity. Trapped in the iron mesh of ego-grasping, they are lost in the darkness of confusion. Thus they repeatedly live and die, wandering endlessly throughout cyclic existence with the three terrible sufferings as their constant companions. Yet they all want only to attain happiness and to avoid suffering."

The problem is one of negative karma and delusion. The only way they can gain lasting happiness and freedom from suffering is by overcoming these two negative forces within themselves and by generating their opposites. Until they do so, suffering and more suffering will remain the nature of their future.

THE THIRD DALAI LAMA:

Cause six: the extraordinary attitude, and the one effect, the bodhi-mind. Think, "However, do I have the power to accomplish these two wishes? Not to mention all sentient beings, I don't have power to free even one from suffering nor place even one in transcendental happiness. For that very reason I made the resolve to attain perfect buddhahood, and if I now give up that resolve surely I will fall into the lower realms. Yet I can do nothing to free beings from suffering and place them in peerless happiness until I have myself attained full buddhahood. I should immediately start working in every conceivable way to realize the state of complete, perfect enlightenment, *samyaksambodhi,* taking as the basis the thought to be able to free sentient beings from even the deepest suffering and bring them to ultimate joy."

HIS HOLINESS:

If the child does not take responsibility for the mother in times of need, who will do so? Thus we meditate that we ourselves should generate a personal sense of universal responsibility for the welfare of others, each of whom has been our mother many times over.

However, do we have the wisdom, skill, and power to benefit them? Not being free from samsaric processes ourselves, we can hardly speak of doing anything for anyone else on anything but mundane levels. Who is able to benefit others most effectively in ultimate ways? Only someone with omniscient enlightenment, with full powers of compassion, wisdom, and ability. Such a being in communicating with others instinctively perceives their entire karmic background, spiritual propensities and so forth; and as a result, a single word from that being is more useful than a thousand words of discourse from an ordinary person. A teacher must speak from his or her own experience. There is little benefit in merely parroting Buddha and the Indian masters. Just as to give someone directions to a distant place that one has never visited can easily lead to confusion and error, so in order to be effective as an unmistaken guide one must first gain realization oneself. Without spiritual attainment, there is really very little we can do for ourselves, let alone for anyone else.

Although the aim of the bodhimind is to attain enlightenment in order to be able to benefit others, this does not necessarily mean acting as a teacher in the formal sense of the word. After attaining enlightenment, one can manifest in many ways to benefit sentient beings, just as the bodhisattva Maitreya appeared in the form of a worm-ridden dog to Asanga in order to cause his compassion to rise and overflow. Similarly, Tilopa appeared to Naropa as a half-mad beggar eating live fish. The scriptures contain a wealth of accounts of beings who have manifested their enlightenment in totally mundane ways in order to benefit beings. Sometimes they appear as someone who says a few words to us that solve a difficulty confronting our lives, sometimes as a book when we are in need of information, and even as a bridge for someone stranded in distress. Such is the wondrous power of the omniscient state.

Understanding that we are striving for enlightenment in order to benefit all living beings, a subtle change in our attitude toward them is immediately effected. Our compassion takes on an added depth and richness, and our meditation upon emptiness takes a new dimension. This is the first of the twenty-two stages of development that the bodhimind undergoes as it gradually evolves into the omniscient mind of perfect enlightenment.

The bodhimind experienced by the ordinary person is something of a negative bodhimind. We reason to ourselves, "In order to gain full omniscience I require the bodhimind, and as the basis of the bodhimind is great compassion and the cherishing of others, I must also cultivate that." The innate self-grasping nature of the mind is used as a force in order to overcome self-grasping and to replace it with love and compassion for others. In the beginning, however, it is really practiced more for the benefit of oneself than for others. Thus it is the bodhimind in name only; although by persistence in practice, this negativity is eliminated because of the nature of the technique.

Once we have developed some experience in meditation upon the bodhimind, it is very useful to request a master to convey the ceremony of the aspirational bodhimind pledge. Sealing our experience in the presence of a master by making a pledge to always hold the altruistic aspiration for the highest enlightenment as most precious, we make its foundations solid. Then, having taken the pledge of the aspirational bodhimind, we should practice the four associated trainings and should avoid the four black dharmas.

THE THIRD DALAI LAMA:

However, merely meditating upon the bodhimind is not enough. One should also maintain the following four trainings:

(i) The training of recollecting the beneficial effects of the bodhimind. This aims at generating enthusiasm for developing the aspirational aspect of the bodhimind, and ensures that the resolve one has taken does not degenerate in this life.

(ii) The training of giving rise to thoughts of the bodhimind six times a day. This aims at increasing the practice aspect of the

bodhimind, or the actual bodhimind.

(iii) The training of not mentally abandoning any of the beings for whom one has taken the vow of the bodhimind.

(iv) The training of increasing one's inner spiritual force.

To Go Into These in Greater Detail:

(i) The training of recollecting the beneficial effects of the bodhimind means that one should maintain a constant awareness of the following teaching [condensed] from Shantideva's *Guide to the Bodhisattva's Way of Life.*

The moment one develops the thought of enlightenment, the bodhimind, one becomes an object of worship for humans and gods alike. By means of fundamental nature one surpasses the brilliance of the shravaka arhants and pratyekabuddhas, or the practitioners of the Hinayana. One passes beyond the reach of diseases and evil spirits. The tantric accomplishments—the powers to pacify, increase, overpower, annihilate and so forth— are attained without difficulty. One will no longer be born into any of the three miserable realms—hell, ghost, or animal. Even should one not attain enlightenment in this lifetime but be reborn in samsara, one will quickly gain freedom. And the karmic seeds of even the gravest of one's past negative karmic actions will be instantly crushed.

Were the beneficial effects of developing the bodhimind to take form, the sky could not contain them. Think, then, not to degenerate what bodhimind you have already developed, and to increase it evermore.

(ii) Giving up the enlightened attitude towards even a stranger has a heavier negative karmic consequence than that created by a monk who breaks one of his four root vows—not to kill, steal, feign spiritual qualities, or engage in sexual activity. Do not give up the bodhimind until buddhahood has been actualized. Until then, recite the following verses three times each day and three times each night:

> To Buddha, Dharma, and the Supreme Community
> Until bodhi I turn for refuge.
> By the power of my practicing the six perfections,
> May buddhahood be attained for the sake of all.

(iii) We are developing the enlightened attitude in order to be able to benefit all sentient beings. Therefore, no matter how any of them relates to us, we should from our own side never abandon relating to them on the basis of the bodhimind.

(iv) If one develops a spark of the thought of enlightenment even once, one should try to prevent it from degenerating. Also,

try to further it by amassing meritorious energy through such techniques as contemplating the qualities of the Three Jewels, making offerings, meditating and so forth.

The cause of not losing the power of the bodhimind in future lives arises from the practice of abandoning the four black dharmas and relying upon the four white dharmas.

The Four Black Dharmas Are:

(i) Lying to or deceiving one's abbot, teacher, or any worthy being. Neither lie to them nor deceive them.

The opponent force to this black dharma is not to speak falsely to any sentient being whatsoever, not in jest or to save your life.

(ii) Causing someone who has done something good to regret that deed.

The opponent force to this black dharma is to direct anyone to whom one may give spiritual instruction towards the Great rather than the Small Way.

(iii) Speaking harshly and with anger to someone who has developed the Mahayana enlightened attitude.

The opponent force to this black dharma is to regard all Mahayana practitioners as one's teachers and, when the occasion presents itself, to praise their good qualities. Also train yourself to see all living beings as pure and noble.

(iv) Being hypocritical and false with sentient beings. Avoid this and be constantly sincere with everyone.

HIS HOLINESS:

This aspirational bodhimind is like the trunk of a tree. Able to support the branches and leaves, which are the practices of actual bodhimind, or the bodhimind that engages in the six perfections, the four ways of amassing trainings and so forth, it is the very foundation of the path to enlightenment. The presence of the aspirational bodhimind qualifies us as Mahayanists, and to lose it is to fall from the Great Way. Whether or not one is a Mahayanist is determined solely by one's possession or lack of the wishing bodhimind.

This mind is like a magical elixir able to transform iron into gold, for it directs all activities of those who possess it into causes of golden omniscience. It is a mind from which can be drawn forth every virtue, for all virtues on touching it become multiplied many times over. Thus one should make every effort to generate, protect, and increase it. It is useful to read scriptures describing the nature and development of this mind, such as Nagarjuna's *Precious Garland* and Shantideva's *Guide to the Bodhisattva's Way of Life.* One of my own teachers, the late Kunnu Lama Tenzin Gyaltsen, also wrote an interesting little text on the subject, *Treatise on the Bodhimind;* but I don't believe this has been translated into English yet. These types of scriptures are both useful and inspiring.

THE THIRD DALAI LAMA:

To quote Jey Rinpochey,

Development of the bodhimind,
The thought of enlightenment,
Is the central pillar of Mahayana practice,
The foundation of the bodhisattva activities,
An elixir producing the gold of merit and wisdom,
A mine holding the infinite varieties of goodness.
Knowing this, courageous followers of the Buddhas
Hold it tightly at the center of their hearts.

ELEVEN

Practice of the General Mahayana

THE THIRD DALAI LAMA:

These are the trainings to generate the aspirational bodhimind. But it may be asked, is this discipline sufficient? The answer is no. One should also take up the commitment of the actual bodhimind and train in the vast activities of a bodhisattva: the six perfections, which one practices in order to ripen one's own continuum; and the four ways of benefiting trainees, which one practices in order to ripen the minds of others.

The Six Perfections

(1) How to train in the perfection of generosity

Basing oneself on the motivation born from the thought that one must oneself attain buddhahood in order to be of benefit to all sentient beings, one should abide in the practice of giving correct teachings to those destitute of Dharma instruction; giving protection to those oppressed by the wrath of kings, soldiers, etc., and to those frightened by sentient forces such as ghosts, demons, wild animals, snakes and so forth, and to those frightened by inanimate forces like burning, crushing, drowning, suffocation, etc.; and giving food, drink, healing medicines and so forth to those in need. In brief, with a free heart dedicate your body, all possessions, and the meritorious energy of the past, present, and future for your attainment of enlightenment for the good of the world.

To quote Jey Rinpochey,

> The perfection of generosity is the magic gem
> to fulfill the hopes of the world,
> The best tool with which to cut the knot
> of miserliness constricting the heart,
> The bodhisattva practice giving birth to the unfailing
> powers of the spirit,
> The foundation of beneficial reputation.
> Knowing this, the wise rely upon the practice
> Of dedicating their body, possessions, and merits.

HIS HOLINESS:

We should practice giving the three types of gifts: spiritual inspiration, material objects, and protection from fear. The perspective of the application is given by Shantideva,[7] "If the perfection of generosity is the alleviation of the world's material poverty, then how have the past Buddhas accomplished it? Do not living beings continue to starve? Therefore the perfection of generosity is said to be the attitude of generosity, the thought of being generous to living beings, together with the actions that spring from this thought. It is basically a state of mind."

Generosity is a magic gem fulfilling one's own and others' hopes, for by being open and generous with others one fulfills their needs and in the process collects karmic causes for future well-being for oneself. It is a sharp weapon destroying the binding ropes of miserliness, which causes a beggar to fear losing his bowl and renders a millionaire unable to spend her own wealth even to benefit herself or her relatives. Miserliness is like a tight knot binding the heart, giving birth to a tremendous amount of unnecessary pain to both oneself and others.

In the beginning of practice one cultivates an awareness of other people's needs and performs simple acts of generosity, such as mindfully giving leftover food to animals or birds, giving small gifts to good causes, showing kindness to someone in need, and so forth. It is interesting to observe how this affects the heart and spirit. Eventually one's every breath, movement, and word becomes an act of giving, an expression of generosity towards the world.

THE THIRD DALAI LAMA:
(2) How to train in the perfection of ethical discipline
One must attain enlightenment for the sake of all sentient beings. In order to do so, one should maintain an attitude having the qualities of mindfulness, mental alertness, conscientiousness, humility, modesty and so forth, and should practice the three types of ethical discipline: the discipline of virtuous conduct, with which, even under the fear of death, one would not indulge in evil; the discipline of tethering oneself away from mistaken modes

of being, which is the basis of furthering one's practice of the six perfections; and, founded upon the above two, the discipline of working ethically to improve the world.

To quote Jey Rinpochey,

Ethical discipline is water to clean away the stains of evil,
Moonlight to cool the heat of delusion,
Radiance towering like a mountain
    in the midst of sentient beings,
The force peacefully to unite humanity.
Knowing this, spiritual practitioners guard it
As they would their very eyes.

HIS HOLINESS:

Three types of ethical discipline are to be practiced: the generation of goodness; the avoidance of mistaken activities; and the accomplishment of the needs of sentient beings. As for the nature of the application, Shantideva says, "Those who wish to maintain a practice should guard their mind carefully. An unguarded mind is an unguarded practice. Wild elephants cannot harm me as much as could an undisciplined mind, and when the elephant of the undisciplined mind is bound firmly by the rope of mindful awareness, all causes of fear subside and all virtues arise. By binding the mind with discipline, all wild animals and harmful agents become bound. The world is subdued by the subduing of one's own mind."

Bodhisattvas practice ethical discipline in order to gain full enlightenment for others' benefit. Their activity is without the stains of self-interest and thus is like water to wash away the potency of negative karmic instincts.

From the very beginning of practice, discipline is like moonlight to cool the wild mind that is burning with anger, attachment, ignorance, jealousy and so forth. One becomes calm, concentrated, and magnificent, towering over ordinary beings like Mount Meru rising above the world. Others will be drawn to one's strength and will find great inspiration and confidence in it. It pacifies our own being, and it brings peace into the way other people and sentient beings relate to us. Thus wise practitioners protect their discipline as they would their eyes.

THE THIRD DALAI LAMA:

(3) How to train in the perfection of patience

When people harm you, anger is not a worthy response, for the harm that they do to you is just the karmic product of a harm that you previously inflicted upon them. Also, as they have no mental control and are helplessly overpowered by anger, it would be inappropriate to become angry with and hurt them. As well, because one moment of anger destroys the three roots of the three bases of merit accumulated over many aeons, on no account permit thoughts of anger to arise. This is the practice of patience unmoved by harm.

When one experiences pain and suffering because of harms done to oneself by another, negative attitudes like pride, arrogance and so forth are dispelled and the mind which renounces samsara is strengthened. Remember that the experience of this unwanted harm has arisen from previous negative actions done by you yourself, and that if you respond with negative, unskillful actions based upon anger, you are creating the conditions for further violent karmic patterns. Remember also that no effect arises if it has no cause, and that if you meet this harm with patience, not only will the previous negative deed that has given birth to this difficulty be depleted, but also you will create a positive karmic pattern by the skillful practice of patience. By avoiding the further non-virtue of anger, you avoid future suffering for yourself. Furthermore, by meditating upon patience when others harm you, your practice of the other perfections develops and matures. For these and many other valid reasons, the gurus have advised us to face harm with meditation upon patience. Remember their teachings and practice the patience which views suffering delivered by others as great kindness.

Finally, recognizing that the power of the Three Jewels and of the Buddhas and bodhisattvas is inconceivable, appreciate the value of the activities of a Buddha Child, and also appreciate meditation upon egolessness. Practice the patience which is certain of Dharma and wishes to train as do the bodhisattvas.

To quote Jey Rinpochey,

> Patience is the best ornament of real heroes,
> A supreme self-mortification to overcome delusions,
> The garuda bird to destroy the snake of anger,
> Armor to protect one from arrows of criticism.
> Knowing this, in every way familiarize yourself
> With the armor of supreme patience.

HIS HOLINESS:

The practice of patience is a great asset to all spiritual paths, and particularly to those related to the generation of qualities such as love and compassion. Its application is taught in great detail in Shantideva's *Guide to the Bodhisattva's Way of Life* with many engaging lines of reasoning that are to be pursued in meditation, as well as contemplations on how and why to apply these to life situations.

Three types of patience are to be practiced: patience towards harmful beings; patience in facing the sufferings and hardships that arise throughout life; and patience in cultivating an awareness of emptiness.

As for the value of the perfection of patience, Shantideva says, "The number of unkind and uncontrolled beings equals the measure of all space. Who could possibly defeat them in battle? But by overcoming anger from within ourselves we overcome all external enemies. Where is there enough leather to cover the face of the earth? Yet by wearing leather shoes we experience the same effect. Likewise, although it is not possible to tame the world with external forces, simply to tame one's own mind will tame one's entire world."

THE THIRD DALAI LAMA:

(4) How to train in the perfection of joyous perseverance

If one has not meditated upon disillusionment with samsara as well as with desire for low-quality happiness such as that gained by lassitude, indulgence, sleep and so forth, one will continue to live in apathy.

Abandon all causes of apathy and devote yourself solely to noble works of body, speech, and mind. In order to alleviate the suffering of even one living being, practice the three types of joyous perseverance: armor-like perseverance, which does not abandon difficult practices for any reason whatsoever; based on that, perseverance which rests in wholesome Dharma and furthers one's practice of the six perfections; and by means of the above two, the perseverance which works for the good of others by striving for the goal of enlightenment of all sentient beings.

To quote Jey Rinpochey,

If one wears the armor of unrelenting perseverance,
Qualities of learning and insight will increase
like the waxing moon,

All activities will become meaningful,
And all works begun will reach completion.
Knowing this, bodhisattvas apply themselves
To vast perseverance, dispeller of apathy.

HIS HOLINESS:

Shantideva asks, "What is joyous perseverance? It is the [secondary] mind that delights in wholesome activities. Its opposites are laziness, attraction to negativity, and lacking confidence in oneself."

Joyous perseverance, or energetic application, is an indispensable ingredient to successful spiritual training. Intelligence without perseverance leads to no great progress, whereas perseverance without clear intelligence can study and practice until the limitations of a dull mind are transcended. It causes one's qualities of learning and realization of the holy teachings to increase like the waxing moon. Perseverance lends strength and purpose to every task, giving one the ability to complete every work undertaken.

Of the three forces mentioned above that counteract perseverance, lacking confidence in one's personal abilities to generate spiritual qualities and to progress along the path is particularly dangerous. In this context Shantideva wrote, "Even flies, mosquitoes, and other insects will win peerless enlightenment when they make spiritual effort in some future life. Why should I—who am born as a human and have the human capacity of a differentiating awareness able to discern skillful from unskillful ways—not be able to attain it?"

THE THIRD DALAI LAMA:

(5) How to train in the perfection of meditative concentration

With the bodhimind as motivation, divorce consciousness from agitation and torpor and train in both worldly and transcendental concentrations. Or, from the viewpoint of direction, train in the various mental quiescence concentrations, penetrative insight concentrations, and the concentrations combining meditative quiescence and insight. Or, from the point of view of function, train in the concentrations which abide in physical and mental joy realized and experienced in this very life, the concentrations which actualize higher qualities such as clairvoyance, magical powers, etc., and the concentrations which accomplish the needs of the world.

To quote Jey Rinpochey,

Meditative concentration is the king to rule the mind.
When stabilized, it sits like a mountain,
When directed, it can enter all virtuous meditations.
It leads to every physical and mental joy.
Knowing this, great yogis always rely upon it,
The destroyer of the inner enemy mental wandering.

HIS HOLINESS:

There are a number of ways to divide the types of meditative concentration. Some people will be content to hear their names, but those who want an immediate inner experience of the efficacy of Dharma will attempt to develop such concentration within themselves.

When we are engaged in activities and so forth that require a flowing, rather than a concentrated awareness, our mind seems very supple and pliant. But try and apply it to an object of meditation and see how wild and unruly it becomes. The untrained mind is very coarse, uncontrolled, and difficult to correct. We barely catch a glimpse of our object of concentration due to the intensity of our inner conversations and mental wanderings. Then, if we do manage to calm the mind for a few seconds, we just fall asleep. At this point it no longer seems so supple and malleable. Conversely, a mind possessing meditative concentration can focus on any object of contemplation for as long as is desired and will maintain clarity, joy, and control as the sphere of absorption.

Meditation based upon this type of a mind will naturally be far more effective than that based on a chaotic mind. The undisciplined mind just wastes itself on distractions and rarely enters into meditative clarity. With meditative concentration one can enter deeply into absorption for days and weeks on end without any mental wandering. This causes our resources of energy and wisdom to blossom at a greatly accelerated rate. Once we have gained concentration, we can then easily develop minor psychic powers such as the ability to recollect previous lives and so forth. These are not particularly valuable in themselves, but they provide the trainee with a solid basis of confidence in the laws of karma, and both stabilize and strengthen one's practice. The master Atisha taught in *A Lamp for the Path,* "A day of meditation practiced with special perception born from concentration is like a hundred years of conventional meditation. We should cultivate it within ourselves."

THE THIRD DALAI LAMA:

(6) How to train in the perfection of wisdom

Taking the bodhimind as motivation, one should train in the following three types of wisdom: wisdom which sees the ultimate mode of existence—the point of suchness, emptiness, shunyata—and thus pulls out the root of samsara; wisdom which understands conventional realities (such as the Four Noble Truths); and, by means of the previous two wisdoms, the wisdom which accomplishes the needs of sentient beings.

To quote Jey Rinpochey,

Wisdom is the eye to see thatness,
The practice which pulls out samsara's root,
The treasure of excellences praised in all scriptures,
The supreme lamp to dispel dark ignorance.
Knowing this, the wise, seeking freedom,
Dedicate every effort to generating it.

HIS HOLINESS:

Wisdom is praised in all the scriptures as being the most profound method of freeing oneself and others from the sufferings of samsaric experience. Therefore, we should train in the three types of wisdom: the wisdom understanding the ultimate level of reality; the wisdom understanding conventional reality; and the wisdom that expresses the above two wisdoms in order to fulfill the needs of the world.

The deepest cause of samsaric suffering is ignorance that grasps at the inherent existence of the concepts we impute upon things, the way we perceive things. We conceive ourselves and the objects around us as being very solid and real. We superimpose a quality of inherence upon everything and, as a result, our perception is distorted. We attribute to our perception of things qualities that do not exist, and then make discriminations of good and bad, and so on. Based on these falsely applied labels we then experience attachment, anger, and so forth. The qualities inspiring these emotions, however, have no real existence. They are like the child who dies in our dream and like a magician's creations.

Sometimes when we look back upon something that caused us attachment or anger, we can almost laugh at ourselves for how confused we became because of our method of grasping at, and our misapprehension of, the nature of the event. Something becomes mixed into our perception, emotional balance, and karmic action. This is how the twelve-linked chain of dependent origination evolves and how samsaric frustration is sustained. We can cut the chain at its first link by cultivating the wisdom able to abide in an understanding of the ultimate level of reality, the wisdom of emptiness. This eliminates the primordial distortion of grasping at true existence.

The four great schools of Indian Buddhism—Vaibhashika, Sautrantika, Chittamatra, and Madhyamaka—differ largely in their interpretation of the theory of emptiness and the two truths. The study of these topics is difficult and requires intense effort, but its effects are profound.

First we must gain an intellectual comprehension of what the scriptures mean by emptiness, and then meditate and cultivate a direct understanding within our own mindstream. This method is the approach to the perfection of wisdom.

THE THIRD DALAI LAMA:

The Four Ways of Benefiting Trainees

Taking as motivation the thought that one must attain enlightenment for the sake of all sentient beings, *(i)* one practices supportive generosity toward one's entourage of trainees. Then, *(ii)* in order to inspire them, one shows them a smiling face and speaks to them gently. Thirdly, *(iii)* one teaches them the Dharma—the six perfections and so forth—and encourages them to actually practice it. Finally, *(iv)* one lives and practices in accordance with the teachings one has given.

You should in every possible way develop these four profound methods of benefiting others.

HIS HOLINESS:

The six perfections essentially function as causes to ripen one's own stream of being. The four ways of benefiting trainees ripen the mindstreams of others. Therefore, to enhance the bodhimind one should practice the four: helping trainees materially; showing kindness to and care for them; encouraging them in the practice of the Dharma; and then living in accordance with the teachings oneself. These four cause the mindstreams of others to mature and evolve.

THE THIRD DALAI LAMA:

Combining Samadhi and Wisdom

Moreover, because ego-grasping is the root of samsara, a single-pointed concentration which does not travel a path contradicting that grasping does not have the ability to sever samsara's root. Alternatively, wisdom able to cognize non-true existence but divorced from mental quiescence able to dwell unwaveringly and single-pointedly on objects of meditation, will never turn back mental distortion, no matter how much it searches. In order to attain liberation forever free of psychic distortion, one must mount the horse of mental quiescence meditation that does not waver when placed in the view able to fathom the depths of emptiness, the ultimate and unmistaken meaning of existence. Riding this horse and brandishing the sharp weapon of the four great methods of Madhyamaka reasoning free of the extremes of eternalism and nihilism, one should generate wisdom which understands the actual mode of existence, the force which destroys all grasping at extremes, and forever expand the clear mind able to perceive the ultimate.

HIS HOLINESS:

Although cultivation of the wisdom understanding emptiness is a most profound method, if not conjoined with meditative concentration it will not develop into the strength of penetration that cuts at the deeper roots of grasping at true existence. Similarly, although with meditative concentration one can attain the ability to focus the mind on any object of contemplation for prolonged periods of time and can gain mental and physical bliss, clairvoyant powers, miraculous abilities and so forth, which will give one great freedom and power in this life as well as result in rebirth as a god in one of the realms of form or formless absorption after death, if this concentration is not well-trained in the methods of wisdom it will not eliminate the subtle grasping that causes even the highest gods one day to fall back into the lower realms of being. The practice of emptiness conjoined with meditative concentration can transport one across the four stages of the path of application—which are distinguished by their level of penetration into emptiness—and bring one to the path of vision, which is a direct, non-conceptual experience of the ultimate nature itself.

One generates an awareness of emptiness in meditation by applying methods such as the four keys of Madhyamaka reasoning, and when a sense of emptiness has been aroused one enters into fixed meditation upon it. If we do not have meditative concentration, then the awareness that we have so painstakingly generated is quickly lost. The method will lack real strength and we will never get beyond the preliminary exercises. Neither clarity nor sustaining abilities will be present, and a deeper understanding can never be generated because mind will not dwell upon the subject with sufficient intensity.

As is said in the scriptures, "Whether the Buddhas manifest or not, the ultimate level of truth is always present." Emptiness of inherent existence is not merely a philosophy or doctrine invented by the Buddhas, it is the ultimate nature of ourselves, our body, our mind, and the world we experience. Whether the Buddhas are here or not, and whether we are aware of it or not, the ultimate nature of existence surrounds and permeates our world at all times. All we have to do is to cultivate an awareness of it. But, unless this awareness is based upon a reliable method such as the Madhyamaka techniques and is practiced on the basis of meditative concentration, one will not be able to attain deeper levels of understanding.

Ultimate reality was not created by the Enlightened Ones; nor was it produced from the contaminated karmic activities of samsaric beings. The very basis of the conventional world is the ultimate truth of emptiness. It is a secret phenomenon in that it is something not known to the ordinary mind, but it is an object of valid perception, for it is seen by the Enlightened Ones as well as the transcended ones who have evolved along the paths. To generate the wisdom able to dwell in knowledge of emptiness is to gain liberation from mental distortion and the negative karma and misery that arise from erroneous states of mind.

The problem with our perception is that we always exaggerate the nature of the phenomena we perceive. Either phenomena seem overly solid and static or they seem overly ethereal and non-existent. We either see something in the objects of our perception that simply is not there or else we miss seeing something that is. We put the object too high or too low. This fundamental error gives rise to every other problem afflicting living beings. Therefore, a Madhyamaka trainee begins the practice of emptiness by applying reasoning to the objects of perception. We try to get a clear idea of how the object—such as the "I" or any other phenomenon—appears to the mind, and then we investigate the basis of this appearance. For example, when we analyze the nature of the self that appears to the mind as "I," we ascertain the nature of this "I" and then search the body, mind, and beyond to find a possible basis for it, applying lines of reasoning that each time render obvious the impossibility of the subject under analysis being a basis for this false "I." Eventually, our meditation generates a very profound suspicion that both we and the world appearing to us in fact in no way exist as the ordinary mind conceives. This doubt shakes our entire being, causing the objects that normally grip our mind to lose their overpowering effect upon us. Therefore, Aryadeva wrote, "Merely suspecting emptiness causes samsara to be torn asunder."

We should seize the sharp sword of wisdom, mount the stallion of meditative concentration, and attack the very source of the distorted mind.

THE THIRD DALAI LAMA:

To quote Jey Rinpochey,

> But the power to cut samsara's root
> Lies not in single-pointed concentration alone,
> And wisdom divorced of the path of meditative calm
> Reverses not delusion, though it may try.
> Wisdom searching for ultimate truth should ride
> The horse of unwavering samadhi
> And with the sharp weapon of Madhyamaka reason
> Should destroy grasping at extremes.
> With vast wisdom that searches thus,
> Expand the mind understanding suchness.

HIS HOLINESS:

Concentration that is devoid of awareness of the ultimate will always have some degree of distortion; conversely, awareness of the techniques instilling knowledge of ultimate reality will never have sufficient strength when devoid of meditative concentration. Taking emptiness of inherent existence as the object, concentration becomes sublimated and pacified of its distorting elements, and the methods of generating awareness of emptiness become very powerful. Thus to combine them is to enhance the excellence of both. One's samadhi takes on a new dimension and one's knowledge of emptiness steadily increases. Eventually one's concentration on emptiness develops into an overwhelming space-like experience in which all ordinary concepts disappear and only the radiance of ultimate truth is perceived. This radiance then gradually nullifies the very roots of karmic instincts and delusion.

This space-like awareness should not be confused with a conventional thoughtless state such as is generated by suppressing mental processes through concentration. It arises not from suppression but from the gradual absence of the binding negative thought patterns that teach us to cling. When we discover how these have been completely deluding us, causing us to see a reality that does not exist and at the same time blinding us to the very truth, mind no longer goes to them and they subside, leaving one's processes of thought open to experience the sphere of deeper knowledge.

This is space-like emptiness, devoid of the clouds of conventional thinking, and has very little to do with the nihilistic concept of nothingness.

THE THIRD DALAI LAMA:

As stated, merely accomplishing the concentration that abides calmly when placed unwaveringly upon its object is not a sufficient attainment. A mind placed in the posture which rests in one-pointed concentration and made to analyze with wisdom able to distinguish the various levels of reality—-able to discern the mode of suchness—gives birth to a concentration which rests firmly and unwaveringly in the significance of emptiness, the way things are. Seeing this, appreciate how wonderful is the effort made to accomplish concentration combined with wisdom. Make a sublime wish toward this end yourself, and thus plant its seed forever.

To quote Je Rinpoche,

One-pointed meditation brings a samadhi
    fantastic beyond description;
Yet do not stop there; for that, combined
    with distinguishing awareness
Able to discern the modes of being,
Gives birth to a samadhi which rests firmly
    and unwaveringly upon the ultimate.
Understanding that, see as wondrous
Efforts made in samadhi joined to wisdom.

HIS HOLINESS:

Thus during meditation periods one concentrates one-pointedly upon the subject of emptiness. The effects of our meditation, however, do not end with termination of the sitting. Due to having dwelt meditatively upon emptiness and having thus pacified the gross levels of distortions, in the periods between meditation sessions we will continue to doubt the way phenomena appear. One should cultivate this awareness by constantly applying the Madhyamaka reasonings to the various objects that appear to us, such as houses, people, and mountains. Normally these things appear to the mind with a strong impression of truly existing, of being ultimately real. But, the Madhyamika practitioner continues the process of analysis even after meditation sessions while going about the activities of daily life. One investigates the nature of the things that appear to one's mind, searching for a basis for their appearance. Not being able to find one, the practitioner is sustained in the vision that sees the world as a rainbow, a magician's creation, and the events of a dream.

The external objects that we perceive appear to our mind as though palpably truly existent and self-powered, as though they possessed a substantial basis of their own. They appear as though they were free of causes, conditions and so forth. But nothing has this self-existence. All phenomena exist only by way of causes and conditions. For example, when we search for the basis of a cart, in its individual parts, in the collection of parts, or anywhere outside these two possibilities, a basis for our image of a truly existent cart cannot be found. Even the smallest atom is without the least tinge of substantiality. The way an object depends upon its parts, its materials, and the arrangement of these parts and so forth, demonstrates that the cart has no self-existence. It appears to truly exist, but is an illusion created by the accumulation of various conditions, much in the same way that a rainbow appears to be substantial, but in fact has no solid basis. What we have to do is take the conventional appearance of things and mix it with an awareness of their non-inherent nature. This is the essence of the training for cultivating an awareness of emptiness in the post-meditational periods.

It is very important, however, that this practice of wisdom is kept within the sphere of the bodhimind, which is the basis of the Mahayana method. For, as Chandrakirti wrote, "Just as the king of geese stretches his two strong wings and leads his flock to their destination, so should we stretch the wings of method and wisdom and fly to omniscient enlightenment for the benefit of others."

Also, the master Atisha wrote, "Wisdom is the cultivation of an awareness of emptiness. Method includes all other practices." Therefore, the basis of the bodhisattva's method is the bodhimind, supplemented by the practices of the first five perfections and so forth. Meditating upon emptiness from within the sphere of the wish to attain enlightenment for the sake of all, the bodhisattva conjoins this with the other aspects of method, such as perseverance and meditative concentration. Such a one does not detour into a partial path, such as that aiming at higher rebirth or liberation; for by wisdom the bodhisattva gains liberation from all samsaric experience, and by the force of the bodhimind's great compassion, the bodhisattva shuns the complacence of mere liberation. Thus the bodhisattva's goal is said to abide in neither samsara nor nirvana. This is the non-abiding nirvana attained by a practitioner who takes as his or her fundamental approach the practice of the bodhimind as method conjoined with the wisdom understanding emptiness. Supporting this conjunction with the other range of methods, such as the thirty-seven wings to enlightenment, he or she steadily progressses through the ten stages of a superior being and attains the exalted state of full omniscience.

THE THIRD DALAI LAMA:

During meditation sessions, place the mind evenly in concentration and penetrative vision, and focus single-pointedly upon emptiness, which is as free of extremes as the sky is of tangible hindrances. Between sessions, watch how things, though not inherently existent, manifest, like a magician's creations. In this way one takes up the practices of wisdom and method combined— true meditation upon emptiness, grasped by great compassion and the bodhimind—and goes to the other side of a bodhisattva's practices. Understanding this path well-worthy of praise, train in ways not satisfied by method or wisdom alone, but which combine the two on a balanced basis. Such training is the spiritual legacy of beings of good fortune. Apply yourself to it.

To quote Jey Rinpochey,

Meditate single-pointedly upon space-like emptiness.
After meditation, see life as a magician's creation.
Through familiarity with these two practices,
    method and wisdom are perfectly united,
And one goes to the end of the bodhisattva's ways.
Understanding this, be not satisfied by a path
    exaggerating either method or wisdom,
But stay on the road of the fortunate.

TWELVE

Vajrayana

THE THIRD DALAI LAMA:

These are the practices common to the Sutra and Tantra Vehicles. Once you have gained solid experiences of them, you should cast aside all doubts and enter into the way of secret mantra, the Vajrayana. The gateway to this secret path is an appropriate initiation, gained from a fully qualified tantric master in order to ripen your mindstream. At the time of initiation one pledges to carry out certain practices and to avoid certain modes of conduct that contradict tantric attainment, and these pledges should be honored. If you gain initiation into any of the three lower divisions of tantra—*Kriya, Charya,* or *Yoga*—you should go on to practice their systems of "yoga with symbols" and then "yoga without symbols." If you are initiated into the highest division of tantra—*Mahanuttarayoga* tantra—you should first master the generation stage practices and then those of the completion stage.

To quote Jey Rinpochey,

Having generated experience in these practices common
    and fundamental to the two Mahayana vehicles—
Sutrayana's "Cause Vehicle" and Vajrayana's
    "Result Vehicle"—
Rely upon a wise guide, a tantric adept,
And enter into the ocean of tantras.
Then, basing yourself upon the complete oral teachings,
Give meaning to the human birth you have gained.
I, a yogi, practiced like that;
You, O liberation seeker, should do likewise.

HIS HOLINESS:

All the subjects discussed so far in the *Essence of Refined Gold*—from cultivating a relationship with a spiritual friend up to developing meditative concentration with emptiness as the object of absorption—belong to the Sutrayana classification of doctrine. These Hinayana and Mahayana practices are called the common or general path because they generate the basis for higher tantric training within the mind of the spiritual aspirant. Thus they are shared in common with the Vajrayana. Anyone wishing to approach the Buddhist tantras must first refine and mature his or her mindstream through gaining experience in the Sutrayana methods, which is done not merely by reading a few books or mumbling a few prayers; rather, what is required is an inner experience in each of the meditational topics.

The four great sects of Tibet—Nyingma, Sakya, Kagyu, and Geluk—all hold more or less identical views concerning the Sutrayana trainings. There are minor differences in certain terminologies used, in details of how the various practices are arranged and so forth, but all four Tibetan traditions teach all the above Hinayana and general Mahayana trainings as preliminaries to entering into the secret Vajrayana. The Kagyu speak of them as "the four ways to turn the mind," the Sakya as "separating from the four attachments," and so forth, but the subject, nature, and aim are the same in each case. Milarepa's principal disciple, Gampopa Lhaje, himself wrote a *Lam Rim* text *[The Jewel Ornament of Liberation]* that is studied by most Kagyupa trainees even today.

There are a number of ways to classify the various tantric lineages. The new sects [Sakya, Kagyu, and Geluk] mostly speak of four classes of Tantras, whereas the Nyingma further subdivide these into six. The *Essence of Refined Gold* follows the fourfold division into *Kriya* or Action tantras; *Charya* or performance tantras; *Yoga* or union tantras; and *Maha-anuttarayoga* or great highest yoga tantras. This division becomes twofold by classifying the first three as "lower tantras." Once one has progressed through the Sutrayana trainings one can consider taking up a Vajrayana method from amongst these four divisions.

Which classification of the Vajrayana we should practice and, within that classification, which specific tantra, is to be determined by the nature and disposition of our body, mind, karmic background and so forth. Within Highest Tantra, the nature of our bodily energy channels, mystic pressure points, vital energies, genetic impulses and so forth are important factors to be taken into consideration. These are topics to be discussed with one's teacher before adopting a tantric method.

Once one has ascertained which tantric system would be most suited to one's needs, one should enter the doorway to the Vajrayana by gaining the complete initiations from a fully qualified holder of the lineage. Because the basis of all attainment is the guarding of the pledges and commitments made at the time of initiation, one should be mindful of these at all times. For example, in the two lower classifications of tantra one takes the refuge and bodhimind pledges, and as well makes various commitments such as not eating meat and other black foods. In yoga tantra the nineteen commitments of the five buddha families are added to these, and in order to enter Highest Tantra one must also cherish the twenty-two tantric pledges as well as various commitments of practice associated with the specific tantra one is pursuing. Practitioners of Mother Tantra, for instance, should begin all movements from the left, and, on the tenth and twenty-fifth days of the lunar cycle when the dakas and dakinis perform their mystic dance within the channels, drops and pressure points of the body, they should make the secret offering symbolizing the union of male and female energies.

Constantly maintaining the disciplines of the tantra that one has adopted, one applies oneself to the yogas of the two tantric stages. In the lower tantras, these are the yoga with symbols and the yoga without symbols. In highest tantra division, these two levels of yoga are called the generation and completion stages. These are the paths walked by the great Buddhist yogis and mahasiddhas of the past. The principal method that they ascertained and applied—the stages of deity yoga—is particularly powerful because it is something that can be effectively applied every moment of our lives.

In order to apply the tantric techniques, one first must be personally qualified by having a free spirit of renunciation, the Mahayana mind of great compassion, and a correct understanding of the doctrine of emptiness. Without the free spirit of renunciation one will be too constricted by sensual grasping and overpowering biological impulses to be able to maintain the tantric disciplines. This prerequisite of renunciation is particularly important in Highest Tantra, which is expressed in very sexual imagery.

The presence of the second quality mentioned by Tsongkhapa, the bodhimind's great compassion, is necessary in order to transform the practice into a cause of omniscience. Also, as much of the imagery in Highest Yoga Tantra is violent, a practitioner not saturated with great compassion could easily get the wrong idea.

The third quality, an understanding of the doctrine of emptiness, is fundamental to tantric practice. Every sadhana begins with, is structured around, and ends with meditation upon emptiness. To practice Vajrayana without the wisdom of emptiness can be very dangerous. For example, a main tantric technique is the cultivation of a subtle divine pride, a confidence that one is an enlightened tantric deity, the Lord of the Mandala. One's mind is the Wisdom Body of a Buddha, one's speech is the Beatific Body, one's form is the Perfect Emanation Body, and the world and its inhabitants are seen as a mandala inhabited by the various forms of tantric deities. Thus we have to utterly change our sense of "I." To do so involves the subject of emptiness. To practice the yoga of divine pride without an understanding of emptiness will not only be useless, but could lead to identity problems and other undesirable psychological effects. Therefore it is said that although the Vajrayana is a quick path when correctly practiced on the proper spiritual basis, it is dangerous for the spiritually immature. This type of danger area is one of the reasons why the Vajrayana must be practiced under the supervision of a qualified vajra acharya.

If one does not yet have the three qualifications—the free spirit of non-attachment, the great compassion of the bodhimind, and the wisdom understanding the emptiness of our concepts of reality—then one should cultivate the practices of the Sutrayana for some months or years until they arise as stable, inner forces. However, we should hope to be able to practice the Vajrayana as quickly as possible and should strive with great zeal to qualify ourselves. The Sutrayana methods divorced of Vajrayana aids will not be able to bring us to full enlightenment in one lifetime, whereas application to the Vajrayana within the framework of a mind that has extracted basic spiritual stability and experience from the common Sutrayana can bring enlightenment within the space of a few years. There are many examples of Indian and Tibetan yogis who have attained enlightenment in one lifetime. The reason Tibetans repeatedly mention the name of Milarepa is not because he was the only Buddha we produced. There are books with the lists of names of yogis who have attained full realization in one lifetime. Milarepa is just especially close to our hearts and tongues because he was the people's Buddha. His exchanges with the populace during his many wanderings is something we love to remember and to speak about. To us, Milarepa embodies the spirit of spontaneous individuality that we Tibetans so love and prize as a national characteristic.

If we can accomplish both generation and completion stage yogas of Highest Tantra, enlightenment in one lifetime in this body is definite. Even should we only complete the generation stage yogas, all purposes of this life become fulfilled and great attainment is still possible at the moment of death or in the after-death state. In the generation stage one practices the deity yoga of divine pride and radiant appearance mainly in relation to the meditative process known as "taking the clear light of death, the after-death state, and rebirth respectively as the Wisdom Body, Beatific Body, and Perfect Emanation Body of a Buddha." This practice prepares one's mind for the sophisticated tantric yogas of the completion stage and plants the seeds of the three perfect kayas of a Buddha. Application to the completion stage yogas will later cause these seeds to ripen and mature into the actual three spheres of a Buddha. Should we not have time to complete the second stage before death falls upon us, then our generation stage training in taking the clear light of death as the Wisdom Body, the after-death state as the Beatific Form, and the rebirth as the Perfect Emanation Body will provide us with three occasions for gaining great realization and controlling our future evolution. Moreover, once we master the generation stage yogas we are able to perform many of the various tantric activities of the mandala in order to benefit living beings. The practice of deity yoga is both vast and profound, encompassing all teachings given by Buddha and all types of situations that may come to us.

Competence in the generation stage yogas is like a certificate permitting one to register with the school of completion stage yogas. Even if we cannot develop the subtle level of generation stage mandala meditation techniques, at least we should gain stability in the coarse generation stage meditations before seriously attempting the completion stage practices. There is also a tradition of performing certain completion stage meditations throughout generation stage training in order to develop familiarity with the material and to lay instincts upon the mindstream that will prove useful later when we engage in intense application to the completion stage yogas.

The highest tantras, such as Heruka, Guhysamaja, Kalachakra, Hevajra, Yamantaka and so forth, teach a full range of tantric techniques of body-based meditations in which the vital energies of the body are brought under control and directed into the central energy flow. These energies are then focused upon mystic pressure points of the body where the various energy channels meet, with the aim of untying the knots that hinder the free flow of vital currents. Here one must gain control over the primordial drop composed of male and female genetic substances from which our body was originally formed and draw this through the pressure points in order to purify and stimulate them. This is the process called *tsa-tig-lung*, or "channels, drops and vital energies." In the tantric view of things, the vital energies of the body are the vehicles of the mind. When the vital energies are pure and subtle, one's states of mind will be accordingly affected. By transforming the bodily energies we transform the state of consciousness.

How does one use the *tsa-lig-lung* technique? One directs the vital energies into the central energy flow and withdraws the primordial male and female drops from their seats in the pressure points at the crown and the navel respectively, bringing them into union at the pressure point at the heart. The very subtle level of energy that is produced gives rise to a very subtle level of consciousness. We then encourage this special level of consciousness to arise in the nature of the wisdom of emptiness. The benefits of one day of meditation from within the sphere of this extraordinary level of mind and supporting physical energy exceed those of years of conventional meditation, and therefore it is said that in the Vajrayana one can achieve in a few years what would take lifetimes by the conventional Sutrayana methods.

In order to attain omniscient buddhahood, we must gain the causes of both a Buddha's mind and form. In the Sutrayana, the cause of a Buddha's form is the practice of method as explained earlier in the discussion of the six perfections, and the cause of his or her Wisdom Body is meditation upon emptiness. This is all done within the framework of a conventional physical and mental state. In Highest Tantra one generates the subtle energy basis of an illusory body and the subtle consciousness of a clear light mind; and then the subtle energy upon which the mind rides and also the images on which we focus the subtle consciousness in meditation become causes of the Rupakaya, or manifest form of a Buddha; and the subtle consciousness and our absorptions upon emptiness become cause of the Dharmakaya, or Wisdom Body. We let the subtle energy arise in the form of an illusory rainbow body and then direct the subtle consciousness that it produces into awareness of only thatness.

This is the purpose of the teachings on the *tsa-tig-lung*. The crux of gaining great attainment in this lifetime through tantric practice lies in actualizing the primordial subtle mind. With this primordial subtle mind of clear light as the basis, buddhahood in one lifetime can easily be attained through exclusive tantras such as Kalachakra, or popular tantras such as Heruka and Guhyasamaja. We can even attain the state of enlightenment without remainder, in which one's ordinary physical aggregate transforms into the mystic rainbow body. There are many stories of great tantric yogis who attained this state. When they died their bodies turned into rainbows and disappeared, usually leaving behind only hair and nails.

THIRTEEN

A Summary of the Path

THE THIRD DALAI LAMA:

This is how the complete body of the path that condenses all the principal points of the sutras and tantras is to be approached, and how the opportunities afforded by human rebirth are rendered meaningful. By practicing in this graduated way, one uses the precious Buddhadharma most effectively for the benefit of oneself and others. Jey Rinpochey himself took the experience of these practices into his heart, and it is his advice that those who would follow after him do likewise.

Keeping this in mind, [pause from reading for a moment and] visualize that Jey Rinpochey is sitting before you, exhorting you with a calm, powerful, penetrating voice to practice as described here and to accomplish his words by means of actually using his teachings to tame your mindstream.

HIS HOLINESS:

Such is the range of doctrines contained in the *Lam Rim* teaching compiled by Jey Rinpochey in the form of a short poem that, as he states in a following verse, he wrote not only in order to further acquaint his mind with the teachings of Buddha, but also for the benefit of those with the karmic fortune to appreciate it.

When we speak of the city of enlightenment it sounds very near and very easy to attain; but when it comes to practice, suddenly it seems very difficult to attain, very far in the distance. This is the contradiction between our thoughts and our application. Instead of becoming disheartened by this realization, we should gather our energy and concentration, and focus them on the spiritual practices. Persistence, mindfulness, determination, and an ability to enjoy the art of dwelling in discipline are all that are required in order for steady progress to be generated.

A common mistake in practice is to have expectations of quick results. Of course we should practice as intensely and purely as we can, but unless we have generated the subtle levels of bodily energy and consciousness as mentioned in the previous chapter, I feel it is more wise to practice without eyes anxious for signs of quick enlightenment. First we should try to generate some signs of small attainments. By thinking of enlightenment as something far away, one's practice remains stable and calm. To expect immediate progress is to hinder progress, whereas to practice without expectations makes all attainments possible.

What is progress? How do we recognize it? The teachings are like a mirror before which we should hold our activities of body, speech, and mind. Think back to a year ago and compare the stream of activities of your body, speech, and mind at that time with their present condition. If we practice well, then the traces of some improvement should be reflected in the mirror of Dharma.

The problem with having expectations is that we usually do not expect the right things. Not knowing what spiritual progress is, we search for signs of it in the wrong areas of our being. What can we hope for but frustration? It would be far better to examine any practice with full reasoning before adopting it, and then to practice it steadily and consistently while observing the inner changes one undergoes, rather than expecting this or that fantasy to become real. The mind is an evolving organism, not a machine that goes on and off with the flip of a switch. The forces that bind and limit the mind, hurling it into unsatisfactory states of being, are impermanent and transient agents. When we persistently apply the practices to them, they have no option but to fade away and disappear. Ignorance and the "I"-grasping syndrome have been with us since beginningless time, and the instincts of attachment, aversion, anger, jealousy and so forth are very deeply rooted in our mindstreams. Eliminating them is not as simple as turning on a light to chase away the darkness of a room. When we practice steadily, the forces of darkness are undermined, and the spiritual qualities that counteract them and illuminate the mind are strengthened and made firm. Therefore, we should strive by means of both contemplative and settled meditation to gain stability in the various *Lam Rim* topics.

There are many ways to approach the stages of practices found in the *Lam Rim*. There was a tradition in Tibet with some teachers to give each of the *Lam Rim* meditations separately to a trainee, the next higher topic not being taught until experience in the previous subjects had been gained. I don't think this means, however, complete development of each successive meditation, but rather that we should cultivate a degree of familiarity with each subject before going on to the next. For instance, the meditation on cultivating an effective relationship with a spiritual master has different levels of training in the exoteric Sutrayana than in the esoteric Vajrayana. One will have a different attitude towards the teacher before and after one has developed qualities such as meditative concentration, inner experience of the nature of emptiness and the self, etc. Even within the highest tantra division, perception of the spiritual master differs within the generation and completion stage yogas. Thus we obviously cannot complete the first *Lam Rim* step—the training in guru yoga—before proceeding to the second step, the meditation on the precious opportunities of the human incarnation. What one does is try to gain a basic meditative experience of the main points in the specific subject on which one is presently working. In the case of guru yoga, this means that we meditate upon the two main points outlined in the *Essence of Refined Gold:* firstly, we should learn to regard the spiritual master as being a Buddha, or a personal representative of the Enlightened Ones, coming as an ordinary being into our lives in order to perform their work for us; and secondly, we should consider the nature of the great kindness of the guru, and the beneficial effects that a correct relationship with a master can cause to ripen upon us. When our mind spontaneously appreciates the spiritual friend as being a messenger of the Buddhas and recognizes the ways by which he or she is able to help us unlock the spiritual gateways within our streams of being, we have a sufficient basis for proceeding to the second meditation, that on the preciousness and rarity of a human incarnation endowed with infinite spiritual potential. One then makes this topic one's main subject of meditation for some time, until there arises an appreciation of the human body as being a spiritual vessel, a boat with which to generate inner qualities that shall have eternal benefits. The ordinary samsaric mind sees the human body as just a tool with which to chase material, social, and biological needs, all of which satisfy only superficial levels of the spirit. Their effects do not pass beyond the gates of death. We have to learn to appreciate the intrinsic spiritual quality of human nature, to have a subtle confidence in the positive, creative aspect of our being. It is difficult to enter spiritual training if one regards one's life as having no purpose other than the pursuit of ephemeral, transient goals, as does a rat who builds a strong nest and then drags home all sorts of trinkets to it. In order to break the mind of this vain, mundane attitude towards life, we sit in meditation and contemplate first the eight freedoms and ten endowments as described earlier, and then the meaningful and rare nature of a human incarnation. This contemplation imbues us with a sense of spiritual dignity that subtly transforms our way of relating to ourselves and our existence. We cease to see ourselves merely as animals uncontrolledly chasing after the immediate cravings of the senses in a vicious circle of jungle law; and we come to appreciate the quality of penetrating awareness and the capacity for spiritual development that distinguishes humans from animals and insects. This causes the thought of extracting the essence of life to arise with a joyous intensity.

The next meditation—that on death and impermanence— inspires us to appreciate the basis of this hope and joy within the context of its transient nature. We must be constantly aware that at any moment death can rob us of our life and that if we have not generated spiritual knowledge we will be helpless and empty-handed.

As Tsongkhapa wrote in *The Three Principal Practices of the Path*, "Understanding the rare and precious nature of human life and the brief length of its span will shatter our illusions concerning superficial, worldly goals in this life. Repeated contemplation of the infallible laws of karmic evolution and the unsatisfactory nature of cyclic existence will shatter illusions concerning worldly goals in future lives. When our mind is cultivated to the point that it no longer yearns for samsaric indulgence but day and night aspires only to dwell in the serenity of liberation, the free spirit of renunciation has been produced."

As we can see here, when Tsongkhapa abbreviates the *Lam Rim* into its three most essential practices—those for cultivating the free spirit of renunciation, the altruistic bodhimind, and the wisdom of emptiness—he somewhat rearranges the structure and order of their sequence. The meditations upon the preciousness of human life, and upon impermanence and death are the only two initial perspective mediations used in the initial perspective context of cutting attraction to spiritually insignificant pursuits and generating an interest in attaining higher states of being. The meditation upon the laws of karmic evolution is used in the middle perspective context of transcending hopes for higher states of being and instead aiming for the liberation of nirvana. The fourth initial perspective meditation—that on the vicious nature of the three lower realms—is subsumed under the middle perspective practice of contemplating the unsatisfactory nature of all cyclic existence. The fifth initial perspective meditation—that upon the objects of refuge—is not formally incorporated at all.

Thus, in this system only two of the five initial meditations are used in the traditional approach: the meditations on the precious nature of human life and on the omnipresence of death. One pursues these until gross attraction to vain habits and ways subsides and then adopts the second two meditations mentioned above: those on the laws of karmic evolution and the unsatisfactory nature of all cyclic existence. Although the meditation upon the suffering-producing nature of the three lower realms is subsumed under this latter topic, there is actually no need in the system of *The Three Principal Practices of the Path* to meditate upon these realms at all, because the aim of the meditation now is solely to cut attraction to samsaric experiences, and not to develop aversion to lower states of being, as was the case in the initial perspective. Nobody is particularly attracted to the lower realms, so there is no real purpose in contemplating them here. Meditation upon the laws of karmic evolution and upon the unsatisfactory nature of even the highest realms of samsaric existence are themselves sufficiently far-reaching contemplations to give rise to a well-based aspiration to total spiritual freedom. The sign of progress in the meditations is that the aspiration to freedom begins to exert a steady influence upon the mind, day and night.

This yearning for spiritual liberation now becomes an important propelling force. We see that the deepest power behind cyclic life is the "I"-grasping ignorance, the inborn habit of identifying ourselves with something that has no basis in reality; and we also see how this gives rise to the endless flow of mental distortion, afflicted emotions, and mistaken activities of body and speech. We see how this distortion and the suffering and confusion that it brings upon us are baseless fabrications that are easily eliminated by awareness of the deeper nature of our mind and the objects of our perception. When we understand the deeper nature of our being, the mind's innate grasping at false realities is eliminated and all distortion is overcome. To comprehend this deeper nature of all things is to attain the third of the Four Noble Truths—the serenity of nirvana, wherein all suffering has ceased.

All phenomena arise and disappear from within this deeper nature of existence, which is the dharmadhatu free from all obscurations and stains. By arising within the dharmadhatu wisdom, the mind frees itself from conventional stains and limitations. Even a partial understanding of this deeper level of truth greatly pacifies the flow of negative karma and delusion that plague our stream of being. One therefore here applies oneself in the ways that reveal the profound nature of the deeper truth, and thus enters the higher training of wisdom, using the trainings in discipline and meditative concentration as supports.

Up to this point in training, the emphasis in one's meditations has been directed at oneself, one's own sufferings and one's own liberation. This is because the forces of ego-grasping and self-cherishing are extremely strong in the beginning of our practice, and so it is very easy to stimulate the mind to take an interest in personal liberation. Once this interest becomes firm and one's cultivation of wisdom has cut the bindings of the more gross levels of ignorance, one can begin to bring one's practice into a more universal perspective. In *Essence of Refined Gold* this is done by generating great compassion and the altruistic bodhimind through the seven-point technique of cause and effect as described earlier in the chapter on the trainings of high perspective. Another method is that called "exchanging self [awareness] for [awareness of] others" which is taught in Shantideva's *Guide to the Bodhisattva's Way of Life* and, much earlier in Indian history, in Nagarjuna's *Precious Garland*. The former of these two treatises seems to be a general commentary to the essential meanings of the latter. A study of these two sacred works is a great help in the task of inspiring us to generate the Mahayana attitude of great compassion, which seeks personal enlightenment as the best means of benefiting all living beings.

Persistent application to the meditations of either the seven-point technique of cause and effect or the method known as exchanging self [awareness] for [awareness of] others causes one's concern for the liberation and happiness of the living beings to become very powerful and eventually to transform into the wishing bodhimind. On the basis of this, one then engages in the activities of the actual bodhimind such as the six perfections and so forth, as explained in *Essence of Refined Gold*. However, in the sequence of practice given here by Jey Rinpochey and the Third Dalai Lama, one cultivates meditative concentration, the nature of which is samadhi, in conjunction with penetrative insight, the nature of which is vipashyana, as preliminaries to entering tantric practice. Most practitioners these days do not follow this procedure but instead, after developing familiarity with the six perfections and so forth, go directly to the Highest Tantra and develop meditative concentration conjoined with penetrative insight in accordance with the methods of the Vajrayana's generation stage. This is a more effective approach in producing quick enlightenment. One then accomplishes at least the coarse level of generation stage yoga and engages in the powerful completion stage yogas to give birth to the illusory body, the subtle mind of clear light, and the stage of great union. Thus is full enlightenment actualized in the short span of one human life.

THE THIRD DALAI LAMA:

> Jey Rinpochey then concludes his *Song of the Stages on the Spiritual Path* as follows,

> > In order further to acquaint my mind with the paths
> > And also to benefit others of good fortune,
> > I have herein explained in simple terms
> > All stages of the practices pleasing to the Buddhas,
> > And have made the prayer that any merits thus created
> > May cause all beings never to separate
> > From sublime ways always pure.
> > I, a yogi, have made this prayer.
> > You, O liberation seeker, should do likewise.

> Bearing in mind these teachings of Jey Rinpochey, [conclude each meditation session with the following prayer:]

> > From now onward, in this and future lives,
> > I will make devotions at your lotus feet
> > And apply myself to your teachings.
> > Bestow upon me your transforming powers
> > That I may practice only as pleases you
> > With all actions of my body, speech and mind.
> > And by the power of mighty Tsongkhapa
> > As well as of the Lamas from whom I
> >   have received teachings

May I never be parted even for a moment
From the sublime path pleasing to the Buddhas.

[The Third Dalai Lama concludes his text with the following
verse:]

By any merits of my having written this text
Condensing without error the principal points
Of the stages on the path leading to enlightenment—
The essence of the teachings of Dipamkara Atisha
    and Lama Tsongkhapa—
May all beings progress in the practices pleasing
    to the Buddhas of the past, present and future.

The Colophon: Thus is concluded the *Essence of Refined Gold*, an
exposition of the stages in the practices of the three levels of spiritual application. Based upon Jey Rinpochey's *Song of the Stages
on the Spiritual Path* and arranged in a format easy to follow, it is
in the tradition of clarified doctrine and therefore is well worthy
of admiration and interest. It was written at the repeated request
of Docho Choje from the eminent abode of Omniscient Sherab
Palzang, by the Buddhist monk and teacher Gyalwa Sonam
Gyatso at the Great Site of Dharma Activity, the mighty Drepung
Monastery, in the room called "Swirling Sunbeams in the Palace
of Sublime Joy."

Gyalwa Sonam Gyatso, even while only a baby, received the
omens of being in communication with Jey Rinpochey [and therefore was fully qualified to write this commentary to Jey
Rinpochey's *Song of the Stages on the Spiritual Path*]. May it cause
the quintessence of mystic lore to flow into the ten directions.

HIS HOLINESS:

If we correctly engage in all these meditational practices—
from cultivating correct attitudes towards the spiritual master up to the final completion stage tantric yoga resulting in
perfect enlightenment—then there is no doubt that we can
progress along the spiritual path. However, we must be very
careful at every step, for our samsaric mind is always looking for ways to trick and cheat us. To make mistakes in any
of the basic meditations—such as cultivating correct attitudes toward the guru, establishing the foundations of discipline, etc.—will lead to an equivalent distortion in all
higher practices. Therefore, one must train mindfully, constantly observing one's stream of thought and activities and

relating them back to the teachings. As Buddha himself advised, "Work out your own salvation." We must practice with clarity, humility, and a sense of personal responsibility for our own progress. Then the path to enlightenment is something that we hold in the palms of our own hands.

As the Fifth Dalai Lama wrote, "Enlightenment is not that difficult. Just as the master artist has no difficulty in taking clay and forming it into the image of a perfect Buddha, when we gain skill in the practices we can easily shape the clay of our samsaric body, speech, and mind into the three supreme bodies of a fully omniscient being."

Appendix I
A Lam Rim Preliminary Rite

Translator's note: The following prayer is included by the Third Dalai Lama in the opening section of *Essence of Refined Gold* in his explanation of how to practice guru yoga. His Holiness the present Dalai Lama gave a detailed description of the prayer in his 1976 discourse, but I have not included that in this volume as his commentary was directed at committed practitioners. However, I thought it would be useful to include the Third Dalai Lama's text because it shows the lineage of transmission of *Essence* and reveals the attitudes that are to be generated as the basis for meditation.

It should be observed that there are many liturgical works of this nature in Tibetan, some for beginners and others for more advanced practitioners. Often a text such as this would be expanded in accordance with the meditator's related practices, or condensed to fit time limitations. It is not uncommon to leave out or add complete sections, nor to replace certain sections with similar materials from other sources.

A Lam Rim Preliminary Rite

In a quiet place pleasing to the mind, erect an altar with an image of your teacher, a statue of Buddha, a stupa, and a scripture. Upon this altar daily arrange offerings both fresh and pure. Fix a comfortable meditation seat for yourself, and either four or six times a day sit there in the seven-point posture of Vairochana, perform the following liturgy, and meditate as instructed.

Begin by blending the depths of your mind with the meaning of refuge by reciting the following formula three times—

NAMO GURU BHYAH,
> to my Teachers I turn for refuge.

NAMO BUDDHA YA,
> to the Buddhas I turn for refuge.

NAMO DHARMA YA,
> to the Teachings I turn for refuge.

NAMO SANGHA YA,
> to the Spiritual Community I turn for refuge.

Then contemplate the four immeasurable thoughts in accordance with the following verses:

May all sentient beings have happiness
and its causes,
May all sentient beings be separated from suffering
and its causes.
May they never be separated from the happiness
beyond suffering,
May they abide in that equanimity beyond
attraction for the near and aversion for the far.

Now recite the verse of specifically Mahayana refuge:

To the Buddhas, Dharma, and the Supreme Community
Until bodhi I turn for refuge;

By the merits of my practicing the six perfections
May buddhahood be attained for the sake of all.

OM SVABHAVA SHODDAH SARVADHARMA SVABHAVA SHODDOH HAM
*[All dharmas become seen as that emptiness which is the empti-
ness of inherent existence.]*

From the sphere of emptiness in the space before me appears a large and vast jewelled throne supported by eight
lions. Seated there upon a lotus and a moon seat is the lama
who is guiding me through the stages in spiritual practice.
His physical form is that of Buddha Shakyamuni and he is
surrounded by the lineages of gurus from whom come the
teachings on the vast bodhimind activities and the profound
emptiness. Outside this group are the Buddhas of the ten
directions, the bodhisattvas, the sravaka arhants, the
pratyekabuddhas, the dakas, the dakinis, and the dharma
protectors.

Then invite the Wisdom Beings:

Though wavering not from perfect dharmadhatu,
Out of compassion you watch the countless beings.
Lama and entourage, carry out the magic work
Of all Buddhas; I request you to descend here.

Lords and protectors of all that lives,
Buddhas who crush the forces of evil,
Embodiments of every knowledge,
Bhagawans and retinues, I request you to descend here.

*Visualize that they come from their natural abodes to the space
before you. Then:*

JAH HUM BAM HOH: The Wisdom Beings merge into
the Symbolic Beings.

*Now visualize a bath house, offering water, towels, clothes, and
ornaments, in accordance with the following verses:*

A bath house of fragrance sweet,
A crystal floor clear and blazing,

Pillars of radiant gems alluring,
A canopy made brilliant with pearls.

Then offer the mystic water:

Just as when Buddha took birth
The gods appeared and bathed him in water,
Mystic water I now myself
Offer to this visualized assembly.
OM SARVA TATHAGATA ABHISHEKA SAMAYA SHRI YE AH HUM

To the Form born of a million virtues,
Speech which fulfills infinite beings' hopes,
And Mind perceiving life as it is:
To Buddha Vajradhara I offer this water.
OM SARVA TATHAGATA ABHISHEKA SAMAYA SHRI YE AH HUM

To the lineage of bodhimind's vast action,
To the lineage of profound emptiness,
To the blessed tantric practice lineage:
To the lamas of these three lineages I offer water.
OM SARVA TATHAGATA ABHISHEKA SAMAYA SHRI YE AH HUM

To Buddha, the founder of the lineages,
To Dharma, which saves the mind,
To the Sangha, who help on the way:
To the Three Jewels, the protectors, I offer water.
OM SARVA TATHAGATA ABHISHEKA SAMAYA SHRI YE AH HUM

Now, with unmatched fragrant cloth
I dry and clean their bodies.
OM HUM TRAM HRIH AH KAYA VISODHANAYE SVAHA

With the best of oils and perfumes
Found throughout the three worlds,
I annoint the bodies of the powerful ones;
Just like a smith polishes gold.

Clothing soft, fine, and light I offer
To those possessing undying vajra body.
With undivided faith I make this offering,
So that I too may attain the diamond state.

The Buddhas, being adorned with the 112 marks,
Have no need of my ornaments;
Yet supreme ornaments I offer them,
So that all beings may gain signs of perfection.

O conquerors, out of compassion for me and all others,
Use your powers to emanate magically
And remain with us and work for the world
For as long as we continue to propitiate you.

Recite these verses from Shantideva's Guide to the Bodhisattva's Way of Life *while pursuing the requisite contemplation. Then recite the following verses, known as the seven-limbed puja, which condense the points of purification and collection of merits:*

To my lama, who embodies all Buddhas,
Who in nature is Vajradhara, and
Who is the root of the Three Jewels,
Ah, to my lama I bow down.

To all-compassionate Buddha Vajradhara,
The perfect seers Tilopa and Naropa,
The glorious Dombipa and Atisha;
To the tantric practice lineage I bow down.

To Maitreya, Asanga, Vasubandhu, Vimuktisena,
Paramasena, Vinitasena, Shrikirti, Singhabadra,
Kusali the Second, and Dharmakirti of the Golden Isles—
To the lineage of bodhimind's vast action I bow down.

To Manjushri, destroyer of grasping at "is" and "is not,"
And to Nagarjuna, Chandrakirti, Vidyakokila the Great,
Buddhapalita and the other exalted teachers;
To the lineage of the profound teachings on emptiness
    I bow down.

And I bow to the glorious Atisha,
Who in the presence of Buddha was Badrapala,
In Tibet was called Dipamkara Atisha
And now, in Tushita Heaven, as Namkha Tri-ma-me,
Like a magic jewel works the good of the world.

And to the feet of the perfect friend and master,
The bodhisattva who performed the work of Buddha,
A precious source fulfilling the two needs:
To the feet of the spiritual friend Drom I bow.

To Lama Tsongkhapa, crown jewel of Tibetan sages,
Who was an incarnation of the three Bodhisattvas—
Avalokiteshvara, treasure of unapprehendable compassion,
Manjushri, lord of the stainless wisdom,
And Vajrapani, destroyer of Mara's armies:
To Tsongkhapa, Lobzang Drakpa, I bow down.

And to the Lineage Gurus past and present
Who train us in the mystic lore,
Teach us the sutras, tantras, commentaries,
   and oral traditions
And bestow initiations and blessings, I bow down.

Homage to the Guru, embodiment of the Three Jewels:
The precious Buddhas, peerless teachers,
The precious Dharma, a peerless saviour,
And the precious Sangha, a peerless guide.

To Buddha Shakyamuni, Lord of the Shakyas,
Who out of wise compassion was born a prince,
Invincible one who crushed the forces of evil:
To he whose body is a golden mountain I bow down.

O lions amongst men,
Buddhas past, present, and future,
To as many of you as exist in the ten directions,
I bow with body, speech, and mind.

On waves of strength of this king
Of prayers for exalted, sublime ways,
With bodies numerous as atoms of the world,
I bow to the Buddhas pervading space.

On every atom is found a Buddha
Sitting amidst countless bodhisattvas.
In this infinite sphere of mystic beings,
I gaze with eyes of faith.

With oceans of every possible sound
In eulogy of the perfect Buddhas,
I give voice to their excellent qualities:
Hail those passed to bliss.

Garlands and supreme flowers I offer them;
And beautiful sounds, supreme parasols,
Butter lamps and sacred incense,
I offer to all Awakened Ones.

Excellent food, supreme fragrances,
And a mound of powders as high as Mount Meru
I arrange in mystic formation
And offer to those who have conquered themselves.

All these peerless offerings I hold up
In admiration for those gone to bliss.
In accord with exalted and sublime ways,
I prostrate and make offerings to the Buddhas.

Then perform either the long or short versions of the mandala offering:

OM VAJRA BHUMI AH HUM, I lay the powerful golden base; OM VAJRA REKHE AH HUM, circling outside, the iron fence; in the center, the King of Mountains; in the east, the continent Lupakpo; in the south, Jambuling; in the west, Balangjo; in the north, Draminyan; off the east continent are the islands Lu and Lupak; off the south are Ngayab and Ngayab Zhan; off the west are Yodan and Lamchokdro; off the north are Draminyan and Draminyankyida.

[Above this I place] the jewel mountain, the wish-yielding tree, the magical cow, the untouched harvest, the precious wheel, the precious jewel, the precious queen, the precious minister, the precious elephant, the precious horse, the precious general, the vase filled with a great treasure, and the goddesses of beauty, garlands, song, dance, flowers, incense, light, and perfume. And I place the sun, the moon, a jewelled umbrella, the banner symbolizing total victory, and at the center, the best things of gods and humans.

All this I hold up and offer to all the holy teachers—my kind Root Guru and all the gurus of the lineage—and also to Lama Tsongkhapa, who is both Buddha Shakyamuni and Buddha Vajradhara, as well as to the myriads of deities and retinues. For the sake of living beings accept it with compassion and, having enjoyed it, bestow your transforming powers.

Earth blessed with flowers, incense, and scented water
And adorned with the King of Mountains, the four
  continents, and the sun and moon,
I offer to this field of Awakened Beings.
May all beings enjoy this pure sphere.

The body, speech, and mind of both myself and others,
Our possessions and masses of goodness of the past,
  present, and future,
And the precious mandala of the King of Mountains
  and so forth,
Together with Samantabhadra's peerless offerings,
I mentally claim and offer as a mandala to the lamas,
Yidams, and the Three Precious Jewels;
Out of compassion please accept them
And bestow upon me your transforming powers.
IDAM GURU RATNA MANDALAKAM NIRYATA YA MI

May these clouds of offerings
Which cool the sufferings of living beings—
Offerings made with sounds gentle and entrancing—
Remain until samsara is ended.

The General Purification:

So be it!
O lamas, great Vajra Holders, and all the Buddhas and bodhisattvas who abide in the ten directions, as well as all the Venerable Sangha, gaze upon me.

I, who am called ...., circling in samsara since beginningless time until this present moment, overpowered by mental distortions such as attachment, aversion, and ignorance, have, by means of body, speech, and mind, created the ten negative karmas, have engaged in the five boundlessly evil deeds and five negative ways bordering thereon, have transgressed the pledges of individual liberation, have contradicted the trainings of a bodhisattva, have broken the tantric commitments, have dishonored the kind parents, masters, spiritual friends and those following the pure paths, have committed actions harmful to the Three Jewels, have ignored the holy Dharma, have stolen from the Sangha, and have harmed living beings. These and many other negative deeds I have done, have sought to do, and have rejoiced in seeing others do. In short, I have created many obstacles to my own higher rebirth and spiritual freedom, and have planted countless seeds for further wanderings in samsara and the miserable states of being.

All of these I now face in the presence of the gurus, the great Vajra Holders, and all the Buddhas and bodhisattvas who abide within the ten directions, as well as the venerable Sangha, the High Ones. All this negativity I lay bare, leaving none concealed, opening all; and I vow to refrain from recreating it in future time. For by facing and acknowledging it I know I am turning to that place that is in communion with happiness; whereas, by concealing and hiding from it, true happiness cannot be.

Recite this short text three times to purify your continuum of negative tendencies. Then return to the seven-limbed prayer—

Long overpowered by attachment, anger, and ignorance,
Countless negative deeds I have committed
With acts of body, speech, and mind:
Each and every one of these I acknowledge.

In the perfections of Buddhas and bodhisattvas
And the arhants' training and beyond,
And in the potential of every living being
I lift up my heart and rejoice.

O lights unto the ten directions,
Buddhas who have found the stage of enlightenment,

To all of you I turn in prayer:
Turn the incomparable Wheel of Dharma.

Enter not into parinirvana
But work for the good of living beings.
For as many aeons as there are specks of dust
Stay with us and teach us, I pray.

By whatever small merits I may have amassed
By prostrating, making offerings,
Purifying, rejoicing, and asking the Buddhas
To remain and teach the Dharma,
All of it I dedicate now
To supreme and perfect enlightenment.

Now recite the following prayer to the lamas of the Lam Rim
*lineage while maintaining clear visualization of and profound con-
viction in them:*

O precious, holy Root Guru,
Sit upon a lotus and moon at my head;
Hold me within your great compassion
And bestow siddhis of body, speech, and mind.

O peerless teacher, transcended Buddha,
O holy regent, invincible Maitreya,
And Asanga, who was prophesied by Buddha,
To Buddha and these two bodhisattvas I bow.

O Vasubandhu, crown jewel of Indian sages,
And Vimuktisena, who achieved the Middle View,
And Vimuktisenagomin, in whom I place faith:
To these three, who have opened the world's eyes, I bow.

O Paramasena, wondrous and splendid one,
O Vinitasena, master of the profound path,
And Vairochana, treasury of vast deeds:
To these three friends of the living I pray.

O Haribhadra, propagator of the profound
   wisdom-teachings,
O Kusali, holder of oral traditions,

And Ratnasena, saviour of the living beings:
To these three spiritual guides I bow.

O Serlingpa, who found the heart of bodhi,
O Atisha, upholder of this great vehicle,
And Drom Rinpochey, elucidator of the good path:
To these three pillars of the doctrine I bow.

O peerless teacher Shakyamuni,
O Manjushri, embodiment of all Buddha's knowledge,
And Nagarjuna, seer of the profoundest meaning:
To these three crown ornaments of teachers I bow.

O Chandrakirti, clarifier of Nagarjuna's thought,
O Vidyakokila, the great disciple of Chandrakirti,
And Vidyakokila the Second, a second son:
To these three lords of the lineage I bow.

O Atisha, upholder of this great vehicle,
Who sees the profundity of dependent arising,
And O Drom Rinpochey, elucidator of this good path:
To these two ornaments of the world I bow.

O Gonpawa, lord of mystics,
O Neuzupa, whose support is deep samadhi,
And Takmapa, upholder of the teachings on discipline:
To these three lights amongst barbarians I bow.

O Namseng, whose practice is spontaneous,
O Namkha Gyalpo, he blessed by the holy,
And Sang-gye-zang, he free of worldly passions:
To these sublime sons of Buddha I bow.

O Namkha Gyaltsen, who is blessed
And guarded by the meditational deities
And who is a supreme spiritual friend
To the beings of this dark age: to you I bow.

O Potowa, image of Buddha himself,
O Sharawa, whose intellect is beyond challenge,
And Chekhawa, teacher of the bodhimind:
To these three fulfillers of hope I bow.

O Chilpupa, lord of scriptures and insight,
O Lhalung Wangchuk, a supreme sage,
And Gonpo Rinpochey, saviour of the three worlds:
To these three great ones I bow.

O Zangchenpa, who radiates with control,
O Tsonawa, lord of the scriptures on discipline,
And Mondrapa, master of abhidharma:
To these three navigators of the world I bow.

O Dholyob Zangpo, glorious lama
Who has found the vast and profound Dharma,
Who upholds the doctrine through enlightened action,
And protects the fortunate: to you I bow.

O Tsultrim Bar, lord of the siddhas,
O Shonnu Od, who relied well on many masters,
And Gyer Gonpa, whose mind is one with the Mahayana:
To these three sons of Buddha I bow.

O Sanggye Won, treasury of marvelous qualities,
O Namkha Gyalpo, he blessed by the holy,
And Sang-gye-zang, he free of worldly passions:
To these three gentle Bodhisattvas I bow.

O Namkha Gyaltsen, who is blessed
And guarded by the meditational deities
And who is a supreme spiritual friend
To the beings of this dark age: to you I bow.

And to Tsongkhapa, crown jewel of Tibetan sages,
Who was an incarnation of the three Bodhisattvas—
Avalokiteshvara, the treasure of unapprehendable
    compassion,
Manjushri, lord of the stainless wisdom,
And Vajrapani, destroyer of Mara's armies:
To Tsongkhapa, Lobzang Drakpa, I bow.

And O Jampal Gyatso, lord of siddhis,
O Khedrub Gelek Pal, a son amongst adepts and teachers,
And Baso Jey, a mine of ear-whispered lineages:
To these three peerless lamas I bow.

O Chokyi Dorje, he attained to great union,
O Gyalwa Wensapa, he who is three buddha-*kayas*,
And Sang-gyey Yeshey, lord of scriptures and insight:
To these three sagely adepts I bow.

O eyes through whom the vast scriptures are seen,
Supreme doors for the fortunate who would cross
    over to spiritual freedom,
Illuminators whose wise means vibrate with compassion:
To the entire line of mystic friends I bow.

Then, Tsongkhapa's *Foundation of All Perfections, a petition to the Lineage Gurus for instant realization of the stages on the spiritual path:*

Following a kind master, foundation of all perfections,
Is the very root and basis of the path.
Empower me to see this clearly
And to make every effort to follow him well.

Precious human life gained but once
Has great potential but is easily lost.
Empower me to remember this constantly
And to think day and night of taking its essence.

I must remember that death is quick to strike,
For spirit quivers in flesh like a bubble in water;
And after death one's good and evil deeds
Trail after one like the shadow trails the body.

Understanding that this most certainly is true,
May I discard every level of wrong
And generate an infinite mass of goodness;
Empower me to be thus continually aware.

Sensual gluttony is a gate to suffering
And is not worthy of a lucid mind.
Empower me to realize the shortcomings of samsara
And to give birth to the great wish for blissful freedom.

And empower me that with mindfulness and alertness
Born from thoughts ultimately pure,

I may live in accord with the holy Dharma,
The ways leading to personal liberation.

Just as I myself have fallen into samsara's waters,
So have all mother sentient beings.
Empower me to see this and really to practice
Bodhimind, that carries the weight of freeing them.

Yet without habituation with the three spiritual disciplines,
Thought-training accomplishes no enlightenment.
Empower me to know this deeply, and intensely to train
In the various ways of the great bodhisattvas.

And empower me to pacify distorted mental wanderings
And to decipher the ultimate meaning of life,
That I may give birth within my mindstream
To the path combining concentration and vision.

The one who trains in these common Mahayana practices
Becomes a vessel worthy of the Supreme Vehicle, Vajrayana.
Empower me that I may quickly and easily
Arrive at that portal of fortunate beings.

The foundation of what then produces the two powers
Is the guarding of the pledges and commitments of tantric
    intitiation.
Bless me so that I may have uncontrived knowledge of this
And guard my disciplines as I do my very life.

And bless me so that I may gain realization of
    the main practices
Of the two stages of Vajrayana, essence of the tantric path;
And, by sitting relentlessly in four daily sessions of yoga,
Actualize just what the sages have taught.

Empower me that the masters who have unfolded the
    sublime path within me
And the spiritual friends who have inspired me
    may live long;
And that the myriads of inner and outer interferences
Be completely and utterly calmed forever.

In all future lives may I never be parted
From the perfect gurus or the pure ways of Dharma.
May I gain every experience of the paths and stages
And quickly attain the stage of Holder of Diamond
    Knowledge.

Having thus made your mind into a vessel suitable for the reception of spiritual attainment, engage in meditation as instructed.

This liturgy, a preliminary to the study and practice of the Lam Rim *tradition in general and to relying upon a spiritual master in particular, should be performed either four or six times a day.*

The last meditation session of the day should conclude with:

The visualized assemblies return to their natural abodes.

If one 's practice of Lam Rim *meditation is done in conjunction with this recitation rite, there is no doubt that realization will quickly be attained.*

Appendix II
Biography of the Third Dalai Lama

Biography of the Third Dalai Lama

[Abbreviated from *The Lives of the Lam Rim Preceptors* [Tib., *Lam-rim-bla-brgyud*] by Tsechokling Yongdzin Yeshey Gyaltsen]

Homage to the great guru Gyalwa Sonam Gyatso,
Holder of the white lotus of compassion.

The omniscient Sonam Gyatso was born amidst inconceivably wondrous omens in the village of Khangsar of the Toung Valley on the twenty-fifth day of the *Chi* month[1] of the Water Hare Year. Depa Namgyal Drakpa was his father's name and Paldzom Butri his mother's. He emerged from the womb while still in his protective water sac, like a white crystal jewel glorious in its brilliance. The sac opened like a white lotus at sunrise, to reveal a tiny body as untarnished and clear as crystal, and adorned with countless marks and signs of perfection.

During his birth the sky became filled with rainbows, and the divinities caused flowers to fall like rain from the sky. Immediately afterwards his parents gave him milk from a white goat, recited numerous verses and prayers of good fortune, and gave him the name Ranu Shicho Palzangpo.

From the moment of his birth the child began to recite the mantra OM MANI PADME HUM. He exhibited the most extraordinary manner of behavior as an infant and did not play as do ordinary children. Instead, he spent his time making mystical hand signs, such as that of teaching the holy Dharma, and would fold his legs into the meditation posture and pretend to enter samadhi for long periods of time. When he learned to speak, he continually mentioned the deceased [Second Dalai Lama] Gyalwa Gendun Gyatso, describing events from the life and times of Gendun Gyatso with uncanny accuracy and behaving in ways similar to those of the deceased Lama; at the time he was in his third year.

The unusual qualities of the birth and behavior of the boy did not go unnoticed, and before long it became widely believed that he must be the reincarnation of the omniscient Gendun Gyatso. Eventually a delegation of monks and officials from Drepung Monastery came to examine him. Satisfied that he was indeed the reincarnation of their late teacher, in the Fire Horse Year they formally made offerings to him from the entire assembly of Drepung and invited him to come and live in the monastery. In this same year he came to Drepung and was placed on the great Lion Throne of the Ganden Podrang, the residence in Drepung that had been built by his predecessor Gyalwa Gendun Gyatso.

Here the young Lama was entrusted to the care of Panchen Sonam Drakpa,[2] and from him received the basic *upasika* ordination. It was at this occasion that he received the name Sonam Gyatso Palzangpo Tenpai Nyima Choklenamgyal [or, in brief, Sonam Gyatso, the name by which he was to be known throughout his life].

On the third day of the fifth Tibetan month he left Drepung to go on a pilgrimage to Gyal Monastery.[3] Thousands of devotees lined the road as he went, hoping to see or hear him, or perhaps even to be touched by his holy hands. Consequently he did not arrive at Gyal Metoktang until the fifth day of the following month. At the time of his arrival a number of miracles occurred in the vicinity. Here the young Lama made offerings to the sacred images housed in the monastery, especially to that of the protective deity Palden Lhamo.[4] He also offered vast prayers for the well-being of the Doctrine and the living beings, and gave the assembly of monks a discourse on the holy Dharma.

After spending a short time in the Gyal area he returned to Drepung to continue his studies.

On the full moon of the auspicious fourth month of the Earth Bird Year the boy took the ordination of a novice monk, with Panchen Sonam Drakpa acting as the abbot of the ceremony and Sangpu Choje Lekpa Dondrub as assistant abbot. Having in this way laid the basis for monastic life, the child now entered into intensive study.

Firstly he received numerous tantric initiations from Panchen Sonam Drakpa in order to place the seeds of blessings of the lineage masters on his mindstream. Included in these initiations were those of the Amitayus longevity empowerments of the Siddharani lineage; the Vaishravana tradition; the initiation of Palden Lhamo; the Mahakala transmissions from Khedrub Palden Senggey, as well as the four-armed Mahakala system; and the external Dharma-raja empowerments.

Then from Lingto Choje Lekdon he received: the Vajrabhairava initiation; a commentary on Ashvagosha's *Fifty Verses on Guru Yoga* (Skt., *Gurupanchashika)*; the great and intermediate *Lam Rim* treatises of Tsongkhapa; Atisha's *A Lamp for the Path to Enlightenment* (Skt., *Bodhipathapradipa)*; the great and abbreviated commentaries to Vinaya; Nagarjuna's *Root of the Middle View (Mulamadhyamakakarika shastra)*, together with Chandrakirti's *Entering into the Middle View (Madhyamakavatara)*; Tsongkhapa's commentaries to these; Dharmakirti's *Treatise on Valid Knowledge (Pramana-varttika)* and the general commentaries to it; Vasubandhu's *Treasury on Metaphysics (Abhidharmakosha)* together with the First Dalai Lama's commentary to it; the *Mulasutra* [on abhidharma]; Tsongkhapa's *Differentiating Between Direct and Interpretive Teachings* (Tib., *Dran-nges-legs-bzhad-snying-po)*, together with the Second Dalai Lama's commentary to it; the Kadampa *Book of Similes* (Tib., *dPe-chos)*; Nagarjuna's *Five Stages* (Skt., *Panchakrama)* with various commentaries to it; miscellaneous lineages from Khedrubjey, and also his *Ocean of Attainments* (Tib., *sGrub-thabs-brgya-mtsho)* commentary to the generation stage mandala meditations; and numerous other profound transmissions.

In addition, from Shartse Lekdon he received many important tantric lineages. Included in these were the mandalas of White Manjushri; four-armed Avalokiteshvara; the secret practice of Hayagriva; White Tara; Sarvavidya; Ucharya; the five longevity traditions; Kurukulla; the Twenty-one Taras; Vaishravana; Shramana; Yamantaka in both red and black forms; the combined peaceful and wrathful Manjushri mantric recitation technique; Guhyasamaja-manjushri-vajra; the thousand-armed Avalokiteshvara tradition; the Sixteen Kadampa Heart Drops; the Kadampa *Collection of Excellent Teachings* (Tib., *Gegs-'bam);* and many others.

These are but a few of the transmissions he received at this time. With each individual tradition he first ascertained the meaning of the particular teaching by means of study and contemplation, and then arrived at the heart of the matter through intensive practice. Every day he dedicated much of his time to meditation, and periodically he entered into intensive retreat.

For some time after this Sonam Gyatso divided his time between Drepung and Gyal, practicing and studying under his various masters. As he traveled back and forth he would visit the monasteries along the way to give blessings and teachings, and to offer prayers in the temples.

In the Water Mouse Year he took up residence with Panchen Sonam Drakpa and was placed on the Golden Throne of Drepung, being entrusted with the responsibility to maintain both the material and spiritual well-being of the monastery.

In the Water Ox Year he presided over the Great Prayer Festival at Lhasa, in the morning delivering the traditional discourse on Aryasurya's *Jatakamala* and in the afternoon leading the prayer session. Thus he honored the tradition. Countless miraculous signs occurred that day, indicating the pleasure of the forces of goodness.

After this he again engaged in intensive study and training under Panchen Sonam Drakpa. Here he received initiation into the mandala of Guhyasamaja Akshobyavajra, together with the full discourse. He also received the oral transmissions of the Kadam history, and the root text and commentary to the Kadam scripture entitled *The Blue Vase* (Tib., *Beu-bum-sngon-po);* the *Karmashatum;* the history of the Ganden patriarchs; and several other such works.

From the great yogi and accomplished meditation master Ngarampa Gendun Tashi he received various Avalokiteshvara lineages, and also the three- and nine-deity mandalas of the Amitayus transmission.

At this time in Tibet there were numerous transmissions of the *Vajramala* set of initiations, but the most exalted of these was the lineage of forty-five mandalas united with the *Kramasamucchaya* system. However, with the exception of Choje Dorjechang Ehvampa, no one had really achieved complete mastery of this precious tradition. Gyalwa Sonam Gyatso dedicated himself with special intensity to the study and practice of this system and achieved realization of it, thus preserving it for future generations.

Furthermore, during this phase of his life Sonam Gyatso received the Zurka set of initiations; both the Arya and Jnanapada lineages of the *Guhyasamaja Tantra;* the Luipa lineage of the sixty-two deity mandala of Chakrasamvara; the Gandhapada body mandala of the five-deity Chakrasamvara; the *Samphuta Tantra;* the *Man-nga* and *Dok* traditions of the *Hevajra Tantra;* the fifteen-deity mandala of the dakini Nairatmya; the Rva Lotsawa lineage of Vajrabhairava; Krishnayama; the forty-nine deity practice of the Zhang tradition; the thirteen-deity mandala of Red Yamantaka according to the Shridhara lineage; Mahachakra; Achala; Ushnishavijaya; Sitatapatra; the Maitri yogin lineages of Avalokiteshvara; the Kalachakra initiations; the five-fold Vajrapani mandala; the Siddharani lineages of Amitayus; Jambhala; the Saraha tradition of six-armed Mahakala; the thirteen Mahakalas; the four Devi practices; and many other such tantric lines of transmission.

In brief, during this early phase of his life he filled the vase of his knowledge with all the principal traditions of both the Sutrayana and Vajrayana Vehicles that existed in Tibet at the time, fathoming these teachings and initiations by means of listening and contemplation, and then integrating them into his experience by means of meditation and yogic endeavor.

At this time he was asked to visit the Hor area of Northern Tibet, which was inhabited by wild and violent tribes of nomads. He accepted, and through his work there succeeded in turning the people away from their sinful ways and induced them to embrace the path of peace and the ten ways of goodness. In this way he enhanced the practice of the Buddhadharma in the snowy lands of Tibet, and, in particular, spread the pure teachings of Lama Tsongkhapa.

After returning from Hor he was invited to visit Radeng Monastery. Here he offered prayers in front of the many sacred images housed in this holy monastery. He also taught from the *Kadam Lek Bum*[5] and *Nyingpo Don Sum*,[6] as well as several other essential scriptures. All were astounded by the learning and wisdom of this young lama.

Sonam Gyatso then returned to Drepung in order to meet with and study under Tolungpa Palden Dorje, one of the three chief disciples of Gyalwa Wensapa. Each of these three had allegedly attained full enlightenment in one lifetime and had manifested the esoteric rainbow body as a sign of their accomplishment. Under Tolungpa, he received all the ear-whispered traditions coming from Lama Tsongkhapa.

On the full moon of the fourth month of the Wood Mouse Year—the day established as the annual commemoration of Buddha's birth, enlightenment and passing away—Sonam Gyatso took the complete precepts of a fully ordained monk. The former Ganden Throne Holder, Khedrub Gelek Palzangpo, acted as the Ordaining Abbot, and the Throne Holder Gendun Tenpai Dargye, an incarnation of Geshe Potowa, acted as the Assistant Abbot. Shang Gepel Choje was the Confidante, and Lhatsun Sonam Palzang the Observer. The prescribed number of elder monks were also in attendance as witnesses.

In this way Sonam Gyatso honored the monastic tradition as established by Buddha. During the ordination ritual he made extensive offerings to the Sangha as a sign of his respect for the monkhood. More importantly, from the time of his ordination he always maintained with purity the precepts and disciplines to which he had committed himself, never allowing himself to transgress even a minor aspect of the trainings. Thus he raised on high the victory banner of Buddha's Way.

After his ordination, a letter of invitation came from Tashi Lhunpo Monastery of Southern Tibet, asking him to come to Tsang to teach the holy Dharma. Subsequently he left for Tsang. However, travel was slow, for thousands of devotees lined the road as he went, hoping to see him and receive his blessings, and thus gain the karmic seeds of higher being and liberation.

On the way he stopped at Wen Monastery in order to offer prayers and to meditate before the image of the mighty yogi Gyalwa Wensapa. At the request of Khedrub Sanggyey Yeshey he stayed there for some time and gave several discourses to the assembly of monks.

When he arrived at Tashi Lhunpo he was greeted by an enthusiastic crowd of devotees, who made extensive and colorful ritual offerings. Tens of thousands of people had gathered to welcome him. Here he sat upon the Lion Throne and gave numerous discourses on the holy Dharma.

After leaving Tashi Lhunpo he went to Nartang, the monastery founded by Atisha and the early Kadampa masters, and famed as the principal seat of the sublime Kadam teachings. Here he made offerings and prayers in front of the many sacred images, and gave several discourses to the monks and lay people of the area.

Next he visited Gangchen Chopel, where he performed the ritual invocation of Palden Lhamo and delivered a discourse on the Dharma to the people assembled there.

After leaving Gangchen Chopel he visited Tropu to make offerings and prayers before the famous image of Maitreya Buddha housed in this monastery.

Next he visited Sakya Monastery to make offerings and prayers before the sacred images housed in this holy sanctuary. At the time there was a famous mask of the terrifying protector Sedrabpa in the Protector Temple of this monastery, which was said to possess tremendous magical properties. Nobody had been able to touch this mask in years due to its overwhelming power. Sonam Gyatso walked up to it, picked it up and began to clean and polish it. It is said that while he was cleaning it the eyes of the mask blinked several times, indicating the protector's great pleasure with Sonam Gyatso's activities. Numerous miracles and auspicious signs manifested in the area during Sonam Gyatso's visit.

Sonam Gyatso also visited Khau Monastery, where he performed the ritual invocation of Mahakala before the sacred Mahakala image housed in its temple. Again, many auspicious signs and miracles occurred during his stay in the vicinity.

He then set out on the long road to Drepung, on the way giving teachings and blessings to the many thousands who collected to see him. In this way he upheld the glorious Doctrine of Truth and greatly inspired those with the good fortune to meet him.

Not long after returning to Central Tibet an invitation arrived from the illustrious Sera Monastery asking him to come there to teach the sutras and tantras. Similarly, teaching invitations came from all the other great monasteries of Central Tibet. He attempted to fulfill all their requests, thus dedicating himself untiringly to the well-being of the Buddhadharma. Wherever he went, the faithless were placed on the firm ground of faith; those who delighted in evil were moved to turn away from their negative ways and to pursue the path of goodness and joy; and all practitioners were inspired to increase their efforts on the spiritual path. His mere presence in an area would cause evil and conflict to subside, and also cause peace and happiness to increase. Thus he revived and strengthened the life of the Buddhadharma in Tibet and, in particular, increased appreciation for the lineages collected and elucidated by Lama Tsongkhapa.

Especially, Sonam Gyatso's life and work had a tremendous impact on the two monasteries Drepung and Gyal. These were his two principal residences, and he divided his time equally between them. Due to the energy and attention he gave to them they greatly increased in stature and well-being in both spiritual and material terms during his lifetime.

Even though he was required to travel and teach almost without respite during this period of his life, in order to set an example of intensive practice for his disciples he constantly maintained an extensive daily meditational schedule of both Sutrayana and Vajrayana methods. Every day he would wake up long before dawn and perform the six preliminary practices such as ritual washing, cleaning his meditation area, taking refuge in the Three Jewels, making prostrations and offerings, etc. He would then perform an extensive *Lam Rim* meditation. When these Sutrayana foundations had been completed he would engage in his daily Vajrayana practices.

These were too numerous to list in full. To mention but a few of them: the longevity yogas associated with Mahakala; the yogas of the four longevity deities, together with the training in consciousness transference; the sadhana practices of the black and orange forms of Manjushri; the special guru yoga, bodhimind and relaxation yoga meditations; the higher tantric practices such as the Heruka Chakrasamvara mandala meditation, together with recitation of a hundred of the root mantras as well as three hundred of the heart and proximate mantras; the sadhana of Akshobyavajra, together with a hundred recitations of the long dharani; the sadhanas of the four principal Kadam tantric deities, together with a hundred of each of the mantras; and various prayers, hymns and auspicious verses from each of these traditions.

Each day he would also perform both generation and completion stage yogas of the Amitayus longevity trainings, as well as the longevity meditations associated with White Tara. He also daily performed the sadhanas of Manjushrivajra; White Sarasvati; Vajrayogini; those of Chakrasamvara-caturpitha; etc.

The meditations that he performed on a daily basis were too extensive to describe or enumerate in detail. However, fundamentally his practice was built from the union of the Sutrayana and Vajrayana methods. By dedicating himself to the *Lam Rim* trainings he daily extracted the essence of all the Sutrayana techniques. As for the Vajrayana, his practice included a range of traditions from the four levels of the tantras, and especially focused on the two yogic stages of Highest Tantra conjoined with the Chöd (Tib., *gcod*) tradition from Padampa Sanggyey, and the propitiation rituals for the various Dharma Protectors such as Mahakala.

In the Iron Sheep Year an invitation arrived from Altan Khan, king of the Tumed Mongols, who had heard of Gyalwa Sonam Gyatso and had experienced profound feelings of faith toward him. In turn, Sonam Gyatso himself felt that he possessed a karmic link with the Mongolians that would enable him to civilize them and cause them to abandon their warlike ways. With this thought in mind he sent the great Khan a promise to come at a later date, in the meantime sending as his representative his personal disciple Lama Tsundru Zangpo to establish a legation at Tsokha.

The news of Gyalwa Sonam Gyatso's prospective visit to Mongolia caused considerable consternation amongst the Tibetans, who feared for his safety and well-being on a precarious journey of this nature. When eventually he left from Drepung, a large assembly of high monks, officials and devotees set out on the first step of the journey with him for auspicious purposes. Both the former and present Ganden Throne Holders were there, as well as the chief monks from Ganden, Sera and Drepung. Included in the group were a large number of renowned masters, such as Rinchen Pokar, Tsangpa Panchen Rikpa Senggey, Sanggye Yeshey of Wen Monastery, Ponlob Tashi Rikpa, and Karpa Ponlob Namkha Jampa of Gyal Monastery. In brief, there were representatives of all the great monasteries, as well as of all the secular official leaders and chieftains, together with hundreds of ordinary people. In one voice they begged him not to go, and instead to change his mind and stay in Tibet. Yet he remained firm in his decision and the journey began.

First he went as far as Radeng, from where he asked most of the group to return to Lhasa and to allow him to go on alone. As he left Radeng, the Depa Tashi Rabten grabbed hold of the stirrup of his horse and, tears streaming from his eyes, offered the following prayer:

O great Guru, glorious embodiment of Dharma,
May you live for long.
May the earth be covered
By masters such as you.

However, by the time he had completed these words he was so overcome with sadness at Sonam Gyatso's departure that he began to choke with tears and was unable to complete the couplet, but could only hold the stirrup to his head in reverence as cries of anguish welled up from within him.

Therefore Sonam Gyatso placed a gentle hand on his devoted disciple's head and finished the couplet for him, changing its context accordingly:

May there always be faithful and
Devoted patrons of the Dharma such as you;
And may there be auspicious signs
Of the Dharma flourishing for long.

In this way, with the chieftain Tashi Rabten sobbing tearfully and clutching Sonam Gyatso's stirrup, the group proceeded on its journey.

When the party arrived at the Drichu River [i.e., the Yangtsey], the evil spirits and hindering demons used their magical powers to cause the river to rise and become violent, and it seemed as though the group would be unable to ford it. However, Gyalwa Sonam Gyatso merely cast an occult glance at it and made the magical hand gesture of wrath. Immediately the waters calmed and subsided, and within a few moments the party was able to cross over to the other side with ease.

Eventually they arrived at Nya-tso-to. Here, thousands of monks and lay people had gathered to greet Sonam Gyatso.

They made extensive offerings to him of three thousand measures of silver and many rolls of silk brocade. He stopped at the monastery for some days in order to rest from his journey and to give blessings to the crowd, giving a discourse on guru-yoga and a transmission of the six-syllable mantra. He also consented to lead an ordination ceremony, and almost a thousand youths took the precepts of a monk from him at this time. Thus he placed countless people on the path to liberation and enlightenment.

Traveling on once more, the group came to the Machu [i.e., the Yellow River]. All the members of the party were dismayed and apprehensive, for the river was extremely high and seemed impossible to cross. Sonam Gyatso told them not to fear, and that they would be able to ford it the following day. That night they camped on the river bank. To their amazement, when they awoke in the morning the mighty Machu River had almost completely dried up, and was no bigger than a tiny stream. Everyone in the party was overwhelmed with faith in Sonam Gyatso and his extraordinary spiritual power. They crossed with ease and continued on their way.

After some time they arrived at Ahrik Karpatang, where a camp had been set up to receive them. Here the people showed tremendous faith in Sonam Gyatso and made elaborate offerings to him including a thousand horses and ten thousand herd animals. During his stay, the sky was continually filled with rainbows and the divinities of goodness sent down rainfalls of flowers from the sky. The karmic seeds of liberation were placed on the mindstreams of innumerable people at this time.

While the group was staying at Ahrik, a convoy of five hundred horsemen sent by Altan Khan arrived to meet them. Led by Choje Tsundru Zangpo, whom Sonam Gyatso had earlier sent as his personal envoy to Altan Khan's court, the convoy also included the translator Lotsawa Goshri. This was to be their escort for the remainder of the journey.

The travelers now proceeded with great regalia, banners fluttering in the wind and the sound of the high-pitched *gyaling* trumpets filling the air. They moved as though of one body, swaying to and fro like a mighty elephant leisurely crossing a pond, their numbers steadily increasing as they went until the master was surrounded on every side by many thousands of horsemen from Mongolia, China and the borderlands of Tibet. They covered the earth like a living blanket slowly floating northward.

Finally they arrived at the camp of the mighty Altan Khan, whose power equalled that of a chakravartin of the kaliyuga. To symbolize his intention to bring the civilizing light of Buddhism to his dark nation, Altan Khan was dressed in a white robe. More than ten thousand of his people had gathered with him, including his wife and her entire entourage.

The reception ceremony prepared for Gyalwa Sonam Gyatso was extensive, and the offerings extremely elaborate. Firstly they presented him with a mandala made from five hundred silver coins, and a golden bowl four hands wide and four deep, filled with precious gems. Next they offered him a hundred rolls of silk brocade, twenty each of the five auspicious colors—white, yellow, red, green and blue. Then they gave him a hundred horses, each fully adorned with an exquisite saddle and bridle. They also offered him ten rolls of silks of the five colors, a thousand silver coins, dozens of rolls of cotton cloth and innumerable other gifts.

After the reception ceremony, Gyalwa Sonam Gyatso and Altan Khan walked together to a tent specially prepared for the master. The two shone like the sun and the moon, the thousands of devotees in the crowd surrounding them like stars in the sky. The Lama was seated on a golden throne and was asked to teach the holy Dharma, with Goshri Bakshi serving as his translator.

Actually, this was not Mongolia's first contact with Buddhism, nor Altan Khan's only connection. More than two centuries earlier under Kublai Khan, who had exerted tremendous influence over all of Mongolia, China and Tibet, the Mongols had been briefly introduced to Buddhism by the illustrious Sakyapa Lama Pakpa, known as Sakya Pakpa.

But Kublai's successor Timur Khan had objected to the paci-
fying influence of Buddhism, and from the time of his rule
Mongolia had rejected Buddhism and reverted to its old religion and the bloodthirsty ways that it advocated. Once
more Mongolia had become a land of darkness, taking joy
in evil ways and delighting in the sight of rent flesh and
blood. She became an island in a sea of blood that she herself had spilled.

Altan Khan was descended from the same Chakhar tribe
to which Kublai had belonged, and he wished to bring his
people back to the gentle ways of the Buddhadharma. It was
his deepest prayer that Gyalwa Sonam Gyatso would be the
man with the spiritual power to accomplish this feat.

Indeed, it was the kindness of the concerted efforts of
Gyalwa Sonam Gyatso and Altan Khan, who were like the
sun and moon in an age of darkness, that the path of Buddhism was introduced into Mongolia and the era of bloodshed that had characterized this nation for so long was
brought to an end. The sea of blood was transformed into
milk, ushering in an age of peace and prosperity.

In his first discourse Gyalwa Sonam Gyatso pronounced
the new law to all those present—Mongolians, Chinese and
borderland Tibetans alike. They must, he told them, learn to
abandon evil and to follow in the ten ways of goodness prescribed by Buddha. Killing, stealing, taking the wives of others, and so forth must be forsaken, and they must instead
learn to respect the lives, property and rights of others.

In particular, he asked the Chakhar Mongols to leave behind their lust for blood. It had been the tradition in
Mongolia that whenever a man died, many living beings
would be sacrificed as an offering to the gods, the number
of blood sacrifices depending on the status of the deceased
in life. Often his wife [or wives], servants, horses and herds
would be put to death as an offering. Gyalwa Sonam Gyatso
ordered them to give up this horrific custom, and instead to
make simple offerings of a portion of the deceased's possessions to religious causes, such as temples and monasteries,

etc., as a source of merits; and to offer virtuous prayers and auspicious wishes instead of blood. The practice of blood sacrifies, he ordered, must be totally given up. Were any family to make a human sacrifice, such as of a widow or servant, the punishment should be death to the offender. As a punishment for the making of an animal sacrifice, all the offender's possessions should be forfeited to the state. If anyone were to retaliate against these injunctions by harming the monkhood or destroying temples or monasteries, as a punishment his house and fields were to be seized by the state.

Also, previously in Mongolia the evil god Ongghon would be invoked on the full, half and new moon days of the month, and on special annual occasions. He would manifest in the form of a deceased family member and would be asked to describe how large and what type of blood sacrifice should be made for the specific occasion. Gyalwa Sonam Gyatso ordered all images of this deity to be burned or destroyed, and the blood sacrifices to him abandoned. Anyone caught making animal sacrifices to him should be fined ten times the number of animals sacrificed. If anyone were to be caught with an image of this deity, his house should be destroyed as a punishment. Gyalwa Sonam Gaytso asked them to replace these evil statues with images of the Wisdom Protector Mahakala, the wrathful six-armed emanation of the Bodhisattva of Compassion, and to see Mahakala as their national protective deity. All blood sacrifices were to be given up, and offerings limited to simple foodstuffs, such as the three white [milk, curd and butter] and three sweet [honey, sugar and rock candy] substances.

In general, the Lama requested, everyone should strive in the ways of goodness. In particular, on the days of the new, half and full moon the people should take the *upasika* precepts of self-purification and devote themselves to spiritual practice.

Especially, the Mongolians should cease making raids of pillage into China, Tibet and other areas of Mongolia, instead dedicating their energies to the ways of peaceful co-existence. In brief, they should attempt to emulate the gentle ways of Central Tibet, and to integrate the Buddha's teachings into their way of life.

These and many other such laws were set forth by Gyalwa Sonam Gyatso and were instituted by Altan Khan.

After giving the Chakhar Mongols their new code of life, Sonam Gyatso imparted to them a transmission of the Avalokiteshvara meditation, together with the six-syllable mantra of compassion [OM MANI PADME HUM]. His entire discourse was rendered into Mongolian and Chinese by appointed translators, so all those present could know exactly what was expected of them. He asked them all—high and low alike—to recite the six-syllable mantra as much as they could.

During his discourse the sky became filled with rainbows, and flowers fell from the heavens. All who were present were deeply inspired by the profundity of the Buddha's teachings, the sublime nature of the lineages collected by and transmitted through Lama Tsongkhapa, and the power of Gyalwa Sonam Gyatso. Countless miracles and auspicious signs occurred in the area at the time, indicating the pleasure of the forces of goodness.

On the site where Gyalwa Sonam Gyatso met with Altan Khan and gave this discourse, the people erected a temple and monastery. Sonam Gyatso himself performed the consecration rite.

At the conclusion of the discourse, the Mongolians again made elaborate offerings as a sign of their acceptance of his advice. Altan Khan personally offered him a hundred sets of winter meditation robes, a hundred rolls of silk brocade, a hundred rosaries made of precious gems, a hundred animal skins, seven golden vessels filled with pearls and decorated with silver dragons, a large vase made from a thousand silver coins, as well as a large number of monk's robes and golden hats. The members of the crowd then individually made offerings to him in accordance with their means. Here he received seven silver tea cups with silver saucers, each made from three silver coins; a hundred pieces of silver shaped like the feet of horses and sheep, each made from five silver coins; a thousand rolls of cotton cloth; a hundred horses bedecked with saddles and bridles, amongst them three white stallions with silver saddles and bridles embellished with gold and precious stones; and innumerable other such gifts to symbolize their faith in him and their willingness to follow his teachings.

In return he spoke in depth with them on the holy Dharma, advising each to practice in accordance with his or her capacity.

Thus he placed the Mongol nation on the firm ground of immutable faith for Buddha, Avalokiteshvara and Lama Tsongkhapa. His impact was such that he completely transformed the spiritual landscape of the country. Whereas previously the Mongols had delighted only in bloodshed and violence, now they were pledged to the way of peace. Previously whenever anyone would die the event would be followed by human and animal sacrifices due to their shamanistic beliefs; now they had been convinced that such practices were not only useless but in fact were harmful to the welfare of the deceased for whom they were being made, and that these misguided methods should be replaced by creative activities such as building temples and monastic colleges, offering auspicious prayers, performing meditation upon and recitation of the six-syllable mantra of Avalokiteshvara and the five-line mantra of Tsongkhapa known as the *Miktsema* prayer.[7] No longer were they to live off the spoils of war, pillage and violence that for so long had caused their neighbors to live in constant fear.

Gyalwa Sonam Gyatso then traveled to the provinces of Amdo and Kham in Eastern Tibet. Here he built several monasteries, including one at Litang and another at Kumbum, the birthplace of Lama Tsongkhapa. At Lama Tsongkhapa's birth, a drop of blood from his umbilical cord had fallen to the earth, and from this a mystical sandalwood tree had sprung forth. Famed as the "Tree of Great Merits," this tree had come to be one of the holiest pilgrimage objects in Tibet. Gyalwa Sonam Gyatso now built a silver stupa around it to protect it from the elements. Beside it he built Kumbum Monastery, or Kumbum Jampaling, a monastic college dedicated to the study and practice of the Sutras and Tantras taught by Buddha. Kumbum was destined to quickly become one of the largest and most influential monastic colleges in Eastern Tibet, causing the profound lineages of Lama Tsongkhapa to rise like an umbrella over the border regions of the east.

Due to the many activies of Gyalwa Sonam Gyatso in the remote areas of Tibet and in Mongolia, Jetsun Lobzang Chokyi Gyaltsen [the First Panchen Lama] wrote:

> The great Lama Gyalwa Sonam Gyatso
> Traveled to the remote border regions of Tibet
> To civilize those whom earlier teachers
> Had been unable to subdue,
> Thus taking to fulfillment the ocean [Gyatso]
> Of wisdom and merits [Sonam] of the Buddhas
> And Bodhisattvas of the ten directions.
> Therefore I sing this praise to him.

Also Panchen Yeshey Gyaltsen [the Second Panchen Lama] wrote,

> Homage to Gyalwa Sonam Gyatso, who
> Tamed those difficult to tame
> And placed them on the path to freedom
> By teaching with wise and skillful means.

Although Gyalwa Sonam Gyatso dedicated so much of his life to travel and teaching and therefore could not write as extensively as had the two earlier Dalai Lamas, he nonetheless found time to pen a number of important texts. The most famous of these undoubtedly is his *Essence of Refined Gold*, a treatise on the stages of the spiritual path to enlightenment. In addition, he composed several distinguished prayers, hymns, practice manuals and spiritual poems. Most of these are short in length but profound in meaning, revealing the extent of his insight into the wonderful

Buddhadharma. After his passing, his writings were collected together. They formed only one volume; yet although small in quantity, in quality they fathom the depth of Buddha's thought. After he had spent several years traveling, teaching and building monastries in Mongolia and Eastern Tibet, his disciples in Central and Southern Tibet began to become restless with the length of his absence. The monastic communities of Sera, Drepung and Ganden were particularly upset, for he was one of their most important teachers and initation masters. Consequently a river of requests began to pour in to him asking him to return to Lhasa. From his own side, he several times expressed a wish to return to Central Tibet and see his old disciples again.

Simultaneously, strong requests came to him from the King of Kharachin[8] asking him to come and to teach there. At first Gyalwa Sonam Gyatso declined the king's invitation on the basis that he had already dedicated considerable energy to the northeast and wished to return to his homeland. The king, however, persisted with increasing intensity in his request, until eventually Gyalwa Sonam Gyatso felt compelled to acquiesce.

In Kharachin, Gyalwa Sonam Gyatso was housed in the Shangto Palace, that in the olden days had been the residence of the great kings of Hor. Here he gave the initiation of the Hevajra mandala to the king and his ministers, and to the general public gave an introductory discourse on the nature of spiritual life, placing many on the *upasika* path. At the conclusion of the teaching the king offered him a two-pillared house built of silver. The Lama refused the offering, but in order to establish an auspicious karmic connection with the king, agreed to stay in the house for a few days. The king nonetheless made him extensive offerings of gold, silver, brocades, horses, yaks and so forth, which the Lama accepted in order to build a temple and monastery for the peoples of the area.

During the first month of the Earth Mouse Year he led an extensive prayer festival. At the end of the month a letter arrived from the Emperor of China requesting him to visit the Chinese capital. The invitation was written in gold and delivered in a palanquin carried by eight men. In order to establish an auspicious karmic connection the Lama sent an affirmative reply, promising to come at a later date. However, in the Nakpa month[9] he showed signs of being slightly ill. Knowing that his life was drawing to an end and that he had placed on the spiritual path and had matured all those with whom he held the karmic link, he wrote a long letter of advice to his many disciples whom he had not been able to see before his death. This was his final teaching.

At dawn of the twenty-sixth day of the same month he sat up in meditation and ceased breathing. After this he transmigrated to the Tushita Pure Land, where he met with Maitreya Buddha and Lama Tsongkhapa to discuss where he should reincarnate and what should be his next work for the benefit of living beings.

Such is the account of the life, studies, practice and activities of Gyalwa Sonam Gyatso. We who practice the *Lam Rim* or *Lojong* traditions of spiritual training that come through him and who hope to achieve enlightenment should take our inspiration from the example set by his biography. We should make prayers to be able to emulate the standards of energetic endeavor that he laid out.

In particular, we should heed the spiritual advice Gyalwa Sonam Gyatso has left for us in his wonderful composition *Essence of Refined Gold*,[10] which so skillfully condenses all the principal points of Buddha's teachings on the path to enlightenment. We should take its contents as advice intended directly for us and should apply ourselves to the spiritual exercises that it sets forth. There is no better way to repay the kindness of this unsurpassed lama than to practice his teachings and thus achieve enlightenment. He himself dedicated every moment of his life to the cause of enlightenment, the supreme way of benefiting the world, so for us to dedicate ourselves to the path of enlightenment would be the supreme offering to him. We should make every effort to make this dedication, for the benefit of ourselves and all living beings.

Glossary

ANIMAL: All forms of visible life other than humans, e.g., insects, fish, birds and mammals. Symbolically, animals represent the short-sightedness of humans.

ARHANT: Lit., "foe destroyer." Generally used to indicate one who has completed the Hinayana path, or "destroyed the foe" of delusions such as attachment, anger, ignorance, etc., as well as their instincts. When used in a general sense, it can also include high bodhisattvas and Buddhas, for they, too, have destroyed these elements.

ARYA: Lit., "High One." One who has a direct realization of emptiness.

AVALOKITESHVARA: Tib., *sPyan-ras-gzigs*. The Bodhisattva of Compassion, of whom the Dalai Lamas are considered to be incarnations. In the tantric systems, Avalokiteshvara becomes the symbol of a yogic means for the accomplishment of enlightenment.

BARDO: The state between death and rebirth, of which there are three phases: the bardo of death, the bardo of reality, and the bardo of rebirth.

BEATIFIC BODY: Skt., *Sambhogakaya*. The ethereal body of a Buddha, which is perceivable only by those with knowledge of emptiness.

BODHIMIND: Lit., "the awakened mind." This is of two main types: conventional and ultimate. The former is also of two types: that which aspires to highest enlightenment as a means of benefiting the world, and that which engages in the practices leading to enlightenment. Ultimate bodhimind is the latter of these placed within an understanding of emptiness.

BODHISATTVA: A Mahayana adept. Bodhisattvas are of two types: ordinary bodhisattvas, who have embarked on the path but have not yet gained direct perception of the meaning of emptiness; and Aryas, who in meditation can directly experience it.

BODHISATTVAYANA: The path of a bodhisattva, the Mahayana.

BUDDHA: Tib., *Sangs-rgyas*. *Sangs* means one who is purified of the obscurations to liberation and omniscience; *rgyas* indicates one who has expanded his or her mind to encompass all excellences and knowledges.

BUDDHAHOOD: The state of full enlightenment, wherein all negative aspects of mind and being are transcended, and compassion, wisdom, power, and spiritual qualities are fully attained.

COMPLETION STAGE: See TWO STAGES OF HIGHEST TANTRA.

DAKINI: Tib., *mKha'-'gro-ma*, or "Sky-goer." The class of tantric female deities embodying wisdom.

DELUSION: Skt., *Klesha*. The three principal delusions are ignorance, aversion, and attachment. The destruction of these and their instincts bestows nirvana.

DEVELOPMENT STAGE: Also, generation stage. See TWO STAGES OF HIGHEST TANTRA.

DHARMA: The Doctrine of Buddha, which incorporates both scriptural and realization traditions. Also any object of knowledge.

DREPUNG: The monastery in which the early Dalai Lamas were educated. Tibet's largest monastery at the time of the Chinese invasion of the 1950s, it housed more than ten thousand monks.

EMANATION BODY: Skt., *Nirmanakaya*. The coarsest of the four mystic bodies of a Buddha. This is the only Buddha-aspect perceivable by ordinary beings.

ENLIGHTENMENT: Tib., *Byang-chub*. *Byang* refers to the total purification of the two obscurations; *chub* refers to the expansion of wisdom to the encompassment of the two levels of truth.

FOUR CLASSES OF TANTRA: *Kriya*, which uses many external rituals, such as washing, etc.; *Charya*, which balances outer methods with inner ones; *Yoga*, which emphasizes internal methods; and *Anuttarayoga*, or *Mahanuttarayoga*, which exclusively relies upon internal methods.

FOUR INITIATIONS: Vase, secret, wisdom, and word. The first introduces one to the five Buddha-wisdoms, purifies the negativities of the body, gives permission to practice the development phase of tantra, and provides the seed of the Emanation Body of a Buddha. The second introduces one to the secrets of the tantric interpretation of sexuality, purifies the negativities of speech, gives permission to practice the illusory body yoga, and provides the seeds of the Beatific Body of a Buddha. The third introduces one to the tantric meaning of the "consort," purifies the negativities of mind, gives permission to practice clear light yoga, and plants the seeds of the Truth Body of a Buddha. The fourth initiation introduces one to the combination of the two truths, simultaneously purifies the negativities of body, speech, and mind, gives one permission to practice the yoga of great unification, and plants the seeds of the Essence Body of a Buddha.

The three lower divisions of Tantra involve only the vase initiation. The three higher initiations are exclusive to Highest Tantra.

FOUR NOBLE TRUTHS: The truths that unenlightened existence is permeated by suffering; that the cause of that suffering is delusion operating through compulsive karmic patterns; that there is a spiritual state beyond suffering; and that there is a distinct path leading to that state of cessation of suffering.

FOUR OPPONENT FORCES: Four practices used to counteract the karmic imprints of negative actions.

FOUR SEALS: All phenomena are impermanent; all contaminated things have the nature of suffering; all phenomena are selfless; and nirvana is peace.

GANDEN MONASTERY: The monastic community established by Tsongkhapa and which thereafter served as the head of the Geluk lineage. It has been totally destroyed by the Chinese invaders, but a small replica of it has been re-established by the Tibetan refugees in Mungod, South India, to preserve the tradition.

GARUDA BIRD: A mystic bird symbolizing the energy that destroys negativity within.

GELUK: Lit., "The Wholesome Way." The eclectic order of Buddhism founded by Tsongkhapa as a fusion of the older lineages.

GUHYASAMAJA: Lit., "The Secret Assembly." The main tantric system brought to Tibet by Marpa the Translator. Marpa's lineage of Guhyasamaja now serves as the principal tantric practice within the Geluk, whereas it has been largely substituted within the Kagyu system by the Heruka Tantra.

GURU: See LAMA.

HEARING: Tib., *Thos-pa.* This actually means the study of a text or subject, rather than the passive act of hearing. In Buddhism, however, a text is first read and explained to a student by someone who has similarly received it. This imparts the oral transmission of the text. Hence the word *thos-pa,* or "hearing" is used.

HINAYANA: Lit., the "Smaller Vehicle." A term given to a particular category of practice in which refuge is taken only in the scriptures revealed during Buddha's life, the aim is personal nirvana, and the path consists largely of the trainings of ethics, concentration, and wisdom.

KADAM: The lineage of Tibetan Buddhism established by Atisha, who came to Tibet in 1042. The Kadam acted as a general foundation for all the new orders—Sakya, Kagyu, and Geluk—and provided the springboard for the philosophical sophistication of the Geluk.

KAGYU: The order of Tibetan Buddhism rooted in Marpa the Translator, who spent twelve years studying in India during the mid-eleventh century under various gurus, most significant of whom were Naropa and Maitreya. Marpa passed his lineages to Milarepa, who in turn passed them on to Gampopa, a monk of the Kadam Order. This led to a fusion of these two traditions, as expressed in Gampopa's *Jewel Ornament of Liberation.* After Gampopa's death the Kagyu splintered into four and then twelve subsects. Of these, Tsongkhapa studied with the Drikung Kagyu for five years and from them received the *Guhyasamaja Tantra,* the *Six Yogas of Naropa,* the *Five Treatises on Mahamudra,* etc.

KARMA: Lit., "action" or "deed." Karma is most often used to denote the process of physio-psychic evolution, which is controlled by actions of body, speech, and mind. According to the laws of karma, no experience is causeless; rather, everything that occurs has its seed in a previous action; and every action sows its seed on the mind that will eventually ripen in accordance with its nature. In brief, an evil deed produces the seed of future suffering, and goodness produces the seed of happiness.

Technically, karma is of two main types: contaminated and non-contaminated. The latter refers to a deed done with awareness of emptiness; this produces no effect on the doer. Contaminated karmas are bad, good, or steady, resulting in lower rebirth, good rebirth, and rebirth in the realm of form, respectively.

LAMA: Lit., "Possessing No Ceiling" or "Possessing No Equal." This is the Tibetan equivalent of the Sanskrit term *guru.* In tantric practice, the guru's body is seen as the Sangha, his or her speech as the Dharma, and his or her mind as the Buddha.

LAM RIM: Lit., "Stages on the [spiritual] path." A general name for the form of Buddhism brought to Tibet by Atisha in 1042. This tradition has been integrated into the Kagyu, Sakya and Geluk orders of Tibetan Buddhism, though it is a speciality of the Geluk.

LIBERATION: Tib., *Thar-pa.* Refers to freedom from compulsive karmic patterns and the mental and para-mental obscurations.

MAHAMUDRA: Lit., "The Great Seal." A general name for the approach of completion stage tantra to emptiness. However, it is used in another context by the Kagyu order, where it is applied more generally.

MAHAYANA: Lit., "The Great Vehicle." The vehicle in which refuge is taken in the scriptures revealed after Buddha's death that were propagated by masters such as Nagarjuna and Asanga, as well as in the earlier scriptures accepted by the Hinayana. Also, unlike the Hinayana, whose basis is renunciation, the basis of the Mahayana is great compassion; and its aim, rather than personal nirvana, is fully omniscient buddhahood.

MANDALA: Symbol of the innate harmony and perfection of being.

MANTRA: A collection of mystic sounds that, if recited in connection with correct meditation, produces a magical or magico-spiritual effect. Each tantric system utilizes many mantras.

MANTRAYANA: The vehicle of mantras; a synonym for the Vajrayana.

NIRVANA: Generally refers to the Hinayana attainment of arhantship, or personal liberation from samsara, but can also include full buddhahood. In the former case, delusions and their instincts are destroyed, giving freedom from cyclic compulsions; in the latter, the innate tendency of the mind to grasp at inherent existence is destroyed as well, granting omniscience.

NYINGMA: The "old orders" of Tibetan Buddhism, i.e., the orders that adhere to the scriptural translations made prior to the eleventh century.

OBSCURATION: Skt., *Avarana*. This is of two types: obscurations to liberation from cyclic existence, and obscurations to omniscience. A Mahayana practitioner destroys both; a Hinayana practitioner destroys only the former.

PRAJNAPARAMITAYANA: Lit., "The Perfection of Wisdom Vehicle." The exoteric Mahayana.

PRATYEKABUDDHA: The Hinayana practitioner who attains nirvana by following his personal path and living in solitude. He is contrasted to the sravaka arhant, who attains it largely by listening to teachings and living in groups.

RED HAT SECTS: These are all sects of Tibetan Buddhism other than the Geluk, which is characterized by a yellow hat. The yellow hat had been used in early India, but, at the advice of a dakini, was changed to red. The significance of yellow is earth and the increase of the sublime, whereas red symbolizes fire and the destruction of enemies. The color was changed in India because the Buddhists were consistently being beaten in debate by the Hindus, which was weakening the movement. Tsongkhapa felt that the use of the red hat was obsolete, for debate in Tibet had become used not to defeat other philosophers but as a means of spiritual training and development. Therefore, he changed the hat back to yellow, the color of increase.

REFUGE: See THREE JEWELS.

SAKYA: The order of Tibetan Buddhism founded in the mid-eleventh century under Drogmi the Translator and later propagated by the line of Sakya Panditas.

SAMADHI: Meditative powers of mind. As a mental faculty, samadhi is the ability to concentrate one-pointedly. In meditation, samadhi becomes the ability to totally absorb the mind in an object of concentration.

SHAMATA: A degree of concentration characterized by mental and physical ecstasy. The nine stages leading to shamata are degrees of concentration.

SAMYAKSAMBODHI: Lit., "complete, pure, perfect enlightenment."

SANGHA: Conventionally, the monastic community; however this is sometimes broadened to include the entire community of spiritual aspirants. Ultimately, the Sangha are those with direct experience of ultimate reality, or emptiness. These are the High Ones.

SARMA: The "new sects" of Tibetan Buddhism—Sakya, Kagyu, Kadam, and Geluk—i.e., the sects that adhere to the scriptural translations made after the eleventh century.

SIX PERFECTIONS: The practices of generosity, ethical discipline, patience, perseverance, meditation, and wisdom, based upon the altruistic aspiration to attain buddhahood as a tool to benefit the world.

SIX REALMS: The dimensions of hell-beings, hungry ghosts, animals, humans, asuras, and gods.

SPIRITUAL FRIEND: Skt., *Kalyanamitra.* A synonym for the guru.

SRAVAKA ARHANT: The Hinayana practitioner who has attained nirvana mainly through listening to teachings.

SUTRA: A text containing the exoteric teaching of Buddha. Sutras are of two kinds: Hinayana and Mahayana.

SUTRAYANA: The Vehicle of the Sutras, i.e., the exoteric aspect of the Buddhist path. This includes both the Hinayana and the Prajnaparamitayana, or Bodhisattvayana.

TANTRA: In one sense, the esoteric teachings of Buddha. Tantra literally means "stream" or "thread," the "stream" or "thread" of innate wisdom embracing all experience.

THREE BASKETS: The three categories of scripture—Vinayapitaka, Sutrapitaka, and Abhidharmapitaka.

THREE HIGHER TRAININGS: Ethical discipline, concentration, and wisdom. These are the principal themes of the Three Baskets of Scriptures and are the very substance of the Hinayana path.

THREE JEWELS: The three objects of spiritual support as viewed within a Buddhist framework. In the Tibetan tradition, the guru or lama is also mentioned, but rather than being a fourth object of refuge, he or she is the "three-in-one." See BUDDHA, DHARMA, and SANGHA.

THREE SCOPES OF SPIRITUAL APPLICATION: Application on the basis of the wishes to gain higher rebirth, personal liberation from samsara, and liberation possessed of omniscience as a means to benefit all other beings.

TWO LEVELS OF TRUTH: Conventional and ultimate. The latter is emptiness; all other levels belong to the former category.

TWO STAGES OF TANTRA: In the three lower classes of tantra this term refers to the "yoga with symbols" and the "yoga without symbols." In Highest Tantra it refers to the generation and completion phases. The former is largely concerned with the generation of the vision of the world as mandala, sounds as mantra, and thoughts as the innate wisdom of bliss and voidness. The latter stage mostly deals with completion of this process by the practice of channeling all the vital energies to the heart, producing the illusory body, realizing the two types of clear light, and attaining the state of great union.

VAJRA: Tib., *rDor-je*, or "best stone," that is, the diamond or, more correctly, the diamond sceptre of five points. Just as a diamond is indestructible, so are the body, speech, and mind of an Awakened One. The five points represent the transformation of the five ordinary aggregates—form, feeling, distinguishing awareness, volition, and primary consciousness—into the five wisdoms—mirror-like wisdom, and the wisdoms of equanimity, discrimination, accomplishing, and ultimate reality.

VAJRADHARA: Lit., "The Holder of the Vajra." The primordial Buddha, the primordial state of enlightenment. To attain to the state of Vajradhara is the goal of the Vajrayana.

VAJRAYANA: "The Diamond Vehicle." A synonym for the Tantrayana, the path of secret mantras, the tantric way.

VIPASHYANA: Meditation upon emptiness.

YELLOW HAT SECT: A popular name for the Geluk, who reverted to the use of the yellow pandit's hat of early Indian Buddhism in contradistinction to the red hat later in vogue in neo-classical India and thereafter used by all other sects of Tibetan Buddhism. See RED HAT SECTS.

YOGA: Tib., *rNal-'byor*, or "true spiritual application." This does not refer to physical exercises, as it so often seems to do in the Hindu system, but to spiritual practices. Etymologically, *rnal* means "true" and *'byor* means "path."

YOGI: One who follows yoga, or a true spiritual path.

Notes

Introduction

1. Tib., *Lam-sgron*. This text, together with its autocommentary, is preserved in the Tibetan commentarial canon, the Tengyur. Several English translations of the root text exist. See *Atisha and Tibet*, A. Chattopadhyaya and Lama Chinpa (Calcutta: Indian Studies Publishers, 1967). More recently a translation of Atisha's autocommentary to *A Lamp for the Path to Enlightenment* has appeared in translation, *A Lamp for the Path and Commentary*, by Richard Sherburne (London: Allen & Unwin, 1983).

2. The dates of the early Indian Buddhist masters are very difficult to establish with any degree of precision due to the lack of surviving documentation. Generally, Nagarjuna is placed in the first to second century C.E., and Asanga in the third to fourth.

3. This Dharmakirti should not be confused with Dharmakirti the logician who wrote the *pramana* literature.

4. This is present-day Indonesia. Most scholars accept the theory that Atisha studied somewhere in Sumatra. However, there is evidence in Tibetan tradition that suggests that it was near Borobodur, Java and I feel that this is more likely.

5. See *Atisha and Tibet*.

6. Tib., *Lam-rim-tha-rgyan*. An English translation of this work is available: *The Jewel Ornament of Liberation*, translated by H.V. Guenther (London: Rider and Co., 1959).

7. See *The Opening of the True Dharma* by Jamyang Khyentse, translated by A. Berzin and Sherpa Tulku (Dharamsala, India: Library of Tibetan Works and Archives, 1979).

8. Tib., *bDe-lam-lam-rim*.

9. Tib., *'Jam-dbyangs-zhal-lung*.

10. Tib., *Myur-lam-lam-rim*.

11. Tib., *Lam-rim-snying-gu*.

12. I included this commentary—though not the prayer appended to it—in *Bridging the Sutras and Tantras* (Ithaca, New York: Snow Lion Publications, 1981).

13. Tib., *Lam-rim-bla-brgyud.*

The Path to Enlightenment

1. Shakyamuni, which literally means "the Sage of the Shakya Clan," is simply another name for the historical Buddha. He is known by this epithet because his family was of the Shakya lineage.

2. Five principal scriptures resulted from the visions Asanga had of Maitreya Buddha after the former completed twelve years of retreat. These are known in Tibetan as the *Mi-pam-de-nga* (Tib., *Mi-pham-sde-lnga).* Western scholars attribute these to Asanga, as it was he who wrote them down. Traditional Buddhists, however, credit them to Maitreya, for it was he who inspired them.

3. Tib., *rJe-btsun-bla-ma.* The term simply means "holy guru."

4. This quotation is taken from Maitreya's *Uttaratantra,* another of the *Five Works of Maitreya* mentioned in note 2 above.

5. Tib., *Sangs-rgyas.*

6. The Third Dalai Lama's own rite of this nature is translated in Appendix I of this volume.

7. This and the Shantideva quotations that His Holiness gives in his commentary to each of the subsequent perfections are from *A Guide to the Bodhisattva's Way of Life* (Skt., *Bodhisattvacharyavatara).* Shantideva's *Guide* is considered to be the clearest practical exposition of the bodhisattva perfections to be written in classical India.

Appendix II: *Biography of the Third Dalai Lama*

1. The first month of spring.

2. Panchen Sonam Drakpa had been the Second Dalai Lama's principal student. Later in life he became the guru of the young Third Dalai Lama. His monastic textbooks still dominate the course of studies at Drepung Monastery.

3. That is, Cho-khor-gyal Monastery, which had been built by the Second Dalai Lama at the Lake of Visions.

4. Palden Lhamo, or Shridevi, is the wrathful manifestation of the female Bodhisattva Tara, symbol of the active compassionate energy aspect of enlightenment. The First Dalai Lama had made the Tara tantric system one of his main meditational practices, and the Second Dalai Lama had continued the tradition, in addition making Palden Lhamo his principal protective practice.

5. Tib., *dKa'-gdams-gleng-'bum.*

6. Tib., *sNying-po-don-gsum.*

7. This brief prayer has a vast array of applications, from basic meditations such as love, compassion and insight, to exotica such as making or stopping rain, faith healing, consecrating medicines, etc. See *The Life and Teachings of Lama Tsong Khapa,* edited by Prof. Robert Thurman, (Dharamsala, India: Library of Tibetan Works and Archives, 1982).

8. The extensive biography mentions this place as Kharachin; the short biography gives the name as Kharchin.

9. The month usually beginning with the new moon of April. It is necessary to say "usually," as the Tibetan leap year leaps a month, causing the subsequent year to begin somewhat late.

10. I was naturally pleased to see the emphasis that the biographer Tsechokling places on *Essence of Refined Gold.* He does this partially because *Essence* is an important *Lam Rim* scripture and the biography is part of his history of the *Lam Rim* tradition (*Lives of the Lam Rim Preceptors;* Tib., *Lam-rim-bla-brgyud*); but he obviously holds the text in special regard in order to mention it twice in such warm and glowing terms.

Bibliography of Texts Quoted

I. Texts Herein Translated

Third Dalai Lama. *Essence of Refined Gold*
Byang-chub-lam-gyi-rim-pa'i-khrid-yig-gser-gyi-yang-zhun-ma

Third Dalai Lama. *A Lam Rim Preliminary Rite*
Lam-rim-byor-spyod

Tse-chok-ling. *Biography of the Third Dalai Lama*
Lam-rim-bla-brgyud-las-rgyal-dbang-gsum-pa'i-rnam-thar

II. Discourses of the Buddha

Chapter of the True One Sutra
Satyakaparivartasutra
bDen-pa-po'i-leu'i-mdo

Descent into Lanka Sutra
Lankavatarasutra
Lang-kar-gshegs-pa'i-mdo

Jataka Stories
Jatakanidara
sKyes-pa-rabs-kyi-gleng-gzhi

King of Absorptions Sutra
Samadhirajasutra
Ting-nge-dzin-rgyal-po'i-mdo

Meeting of Father and Son Sutra
Pitaputrasamagamasutra
Yab-dang-sras-mjal-ba'i-mdo

Root Text of the Guhyasamajatantra
Guhyasamajamulatantra
bSang-bdus-rtsa-rgyud

Sutra of Purification with the Thirty-five Buddhas
Triskandhakasutra
Byang-chub-sems-dpa'i-ltung-bar-gshags-pa

Sutras on Discipline
Vinayasutra
'Dul-ba'i-mdo

Sutras on the Perfection of Wisdom
Prajnaparamitasutra
Shes-rab-kyi-pha-rol-tu-phyin-pa'i-mdo

III. Early Indian Works

Aryadeva. *Four Hundred Stanzas*
Chatuhshatakashastrakarika
bsTan-bcos-bzhi-brgya-pa-zhes-bya-ba'i-tshig-leur-byas-pa

Ashvagosha. *Fifty Verses on Guru Yoga*
Gurupancasika
bLa-ma-lnga-bchu-pa

Atisha. A *Lamp for the Path to Enlightenment*
Bodhipathapradipa
Byang-chub-lam-gyi-sgron-ma

Chandrakirti. A *Guide to the Middle View*
Madhyamakavatara
dBu-ma-la-'jug-pa

Maitreya. *The Ornament of Mahayana Sutras*
Mahayanasutralamkarakarika
Theg-pa-chen-po'i-mdo-sde-rgyan-gyi-tshig-leur-byas-pa

Maitreya. *The Ornament of Clear Comprehension*
Abhisamayalamkara
mNgon-par-rtogs-pa'i-rgyan

Nagarjuna. A *Letter to a Friend*
Suhrllekha
bShes-pa'i-spring-yig

Nagarjuna. *Fundamenral Treatise on Wisdom*
Prajnanamamulamadhyamakakarika
dBu-ma-rtsa-ba'i-tshig-leur-byas-pa-shes-rab-ces-bya-ba

Nagarjuna. *The Precious Garland*
Ratnavali
Rin-chen-'phreng-ba

Shantideva. A *Guide to the Bodhisattva's Way of Life*
Bodhisattvacharyavatara
Byang-chub-sems-dpa'i-spyod-pa-la-'jug-pa

IV. Indigenous Tibetan Texts

Gampopa. *The Jewel Ornament of Liberation*
Lam-rim-thar-rgyan

Fifth Dalai Lama. *The Instructions of Manjushri*
'Jam-dbyangs-zhal-lung

Shvamar Rinpochey. *The Red Hat Lam Rim*
Shva-mar-lam-rim

Pabongkha Dechen Nyingpo. *Liberation in the Palm of One's Hand*
Lam-rim-thar-pa'i-lag-skyang

Tsongkhapa. *Great Exposition of the Stages on the Spiritual Path*
Byang-chub-lam-rim-chen-mo

Tsongkhapa. *An Intermediate Exposition of the Stages on the Spiritual Path*
Lam-rim-'bring

Tsongkhapa. *A Concise Exposition of the Stages on the Spiritual Path*
Lam-rim-bdus-don

Tsongkhapa. *The Three Principal Practices of the Path*
Lam-gtso-rnam-gsum

Namgyal Monastery

Namgyal Monastery was originally founded in Tibet by the Third Dalai Lama. From the time of its creation it has served as the private monastery of each of the successive Dalai Lamas. Due to the prestige of the monastery, the fact that it was located in the Potala and was the private monastery of the Dalai Lama, the Chinese have not allowed it to function.

At present, the monastery is re-established in India and has many young monks undergoing the thirteen-year training curriculum devised by H.H. the present Dalai Lama and the former Abbot, Ven. Lobsang Nyima. Namgyal has also established a North American Seat of the monastery in Ithaca, New York in conjunction with a new teaching institute. Namgyal Monastery Institute of Buddhist Studies in Ithaca follows the same curriculum as that in India except the curriculum is presented as a condensed five-year program. The Institute combines its Tibetan monastic faculty with Western resident scholars and a large adjunct faculty of preeminent scholars of Tibetan Buddhism. It is open to qualified men and women students on either a full or part-time basis. Namgyal has been given a beautiful piece of land just outside Ithaca is currently hoping to build a retreat center and guest house in order to be able to handle greater numbers of visitors and students interested in Buddhism and sacred arts.

Anyone interested in furthering the work of the monastery in Dharamsala, India by foster-sponsoring a young monk in his education, or an older monk for the traditional three-year meditation retreat, or making a general contribution may write directly to the Monastery in Dharamsala, India, or if you wish to help sustain and develop Namgyal in America, as a teaching institute and as the American seat of the Dalai Lama's personal monastery, write directly to Namgyal Monastery in Ithaca, New York. All donations to the North American Seat of Namgyal are tax-deductible. Namgyal Monastery Institute of Buddhist Studies is a registered 501(c)(3) tax-exempt non-profit organization.

Namgyal Monastery
Thekchen Choeling
McLeod Ganj
Dharamsala
Distt. Kangra (H.P.) 176219
INDIA

Namgyal Monastery
Institute of Buddhist Studies
P.O. Box 127
Ithaca, NY 14851 USA
Tel: 607-273-0739
FAX: 607-272-5654